DAVID H.

ANGLO-SAXON POTTERY

Second edition

SHIRE ARCHAEOLOGY

Cover Illustration
A fifth-century *Buckelurne* from Sandy, Bedfordshire.
(Photograph by D. H. Kennett.)

British Library Cataloguing in Publication data:
Kennett, David H.
Anglo-Saxon pottery. — 2nd ed — (Shire archaeology)
1. Anglo-Saxon pottery, 400-900
I. Title
738. 3'0942
ISBN 0-7478-0006-5

Published by
SHIRE PUBLICATIONS LTD
Cromwell House, Church Street, Princes Risborough,
Aylesbury, Buckinghamshire, HP17 9AJ, UK.

Series Editor: James Dyer.

Copyright © David H. Kennett, 1978 and 1989.
All rights reserved.
No part of this book may be reproduced or transmitted in any form or by any means,
electronic or mechanical, including photocopy, recording, or any information storage and
retrieval system, without permission in writing from the publishers.

ISBN 0 7478 0006 5

First published 1978. Second edition 1989.

Printed in Great Britain by C. I. Thomas & Sons (Haverfordwest) Ltd,
Press Buildings, Merlins Bridge, Haverfordwest, Dyfed SA61 1XF.

Contents

LIST OF ILLUSTRATIONS 4

PREFACE 5

NOTE ON SECOND EDITION 5

GLOSSARY 6

NOTE ON ILLUSTRATIONS AND TEXT 6

1. THE STUDY OF ANGLO-SAXON POTTERY 7

2. FABRICS AND TECHNOLOGY 10

3. DISTRIBUTION 15

4. DATING 20

5. SHAPE AND DECORATION OF FUNERARY POTTERY 21

6. DOMESTIC POTTERY 28

7. MUSEUMS 59

8. FURTHER READING 62

INDEX 66

List of illustrations

Fig. 1. The surviving urns from Shropham, Norfolk *page 9*
Fig. 2A. The distribution of Anglo-Saxon funerary pottery of the fifth to seventh centuries *page 13*
Fig. 2B. Density of cremation urns and accessory vessels *page 14*
Fig. 3. Anglian urns *page 30*
Fig. 4. Shouldered vessels *page 31*
Fig. 5. Early globular urns *page 32*
Fig. 6. Early globular urns *page 33*
Fig. 7. Three early urns from Heworth, near York *page 34*
Fig. 8. Vessels ornamented with grooves in standing and hanging arched patterns *page 35*
Fig. 9. Fifth-century bowls *page 36*
Fig. 10. Accessory vessels from inhumation graves *page 37*
Fig. 11. Urns with simple chevron designs *page 38*
Fig. 12. Urns with complex chevron designs *page 39*
Fig. 13. Buckelurnen *page 40*
Fig. 14. Buckelurnen *page 41*
Fig. 15. Buckelurnen *page 42*
Fig. 16. Decorated shoulder-boss urns with decoration confined to upper part of pot *page 43*
Fig. 17. Linear designs *page 44*
Fig. 18. Linear ornament with stamps *page 45*
Fig. 19. Vertical lines as a decorative feature *page 46*
Fig. 20. Panel styles as decoration *page 47*
Fig. 21. Triangular panel-style ornament with bosses: the Kettering long-boss potter *page 48*
Fig. 22. Linear decoration with stamps and panel styles: the Kettering I potter *page 49*
Fig. 23. Sixth-century pottery *page 50*
Fig. 24. Sixth-century pottery *page 51*
Fig. 25. Swastika and 'wyrm' designs *page 52*
Fig. 26. Animals as decoration *page 53*
Fig. 27. Lugged and rusticated vessels *page 54*
Fig. 28. Cooking pots and accessory vessels *page 55*
Fig. 29. Jutish and Frankish pottery from Kent and the Isle of Wight *page 56*
Fig. 30. Seventh-century pottery *page 57*
Fig. 31. Middle Saxon pottery *page 58*

Preface

This book is about Anglo-Saxon pottery, a group of material I first began to study in the 1960s. My researches then, as now, are part of the more general study of Anglo-Saxon cemeteries. Since 1966, many people have helped me in that study. To three I feel an especial debt: Professor Leslie Alcock, now of the University of Glasgow; Miss M. D. Cra'ster of the Cambridge University Museum of Archaeology and Anthropology; Mrs L. E. Webster of the British Museum.

For access to the collections in their care, for permission to examine and draw their pottery and to publish my figures I am grateful to the authorities and staff at the following museums: Bedford Museum; Moyse's Hall, Bury St Edmunds; the Cambridge University Museum of Archaeology and Anthropology; the Herbert Art Gallery and Museum, Coventry; Hull Museums; Ipswich Museum; the Westfield Museum, Kettering; the Lynn Museum, King's Lynn; the Jewry Wall Museum, Leicester; Lincoln City and County Museum; the British Museum, London; the Museum of London, London; Luton Museum and Art Gallery; the museum of the Kent Archaeological Society, Maidstone; Newark Museum and Art Gallery; Northampton Central Museum and Art Gallery; the Castle Museum, Norwich; Rutland County Museum, Oakham; the Ashmolean Museum, Oxford; Peterborough City Museum and Art Gallery; New Place Museum, Stratford-upon-Avon; the Winchester City Museum; the Wisbech and Fenland Museum, Wisbech; Worthing Museum; the Yorkshire Museum, York.

For his advice and encouragement, I wish to thank the series editor, James Dyer.

DHK

Note on second edition

The second edition of *Anglo-Saxon Pottery* seeks to integrate developments that have taken place since the publication of the first edition within the original basic text. However, some portions have been recast, especially that on 'Fabrics and technology'; I am grateful to Tony O'Donovan, a professional potter of Mansfield, for assistance here. There are new chapters on 'Distribution' and 'Domestic pottery'; the former has two new maps. The list of sites as a bibliographic exercise has been

6 *Anglo-Saxon Pottery*

dropped in favour of a table facing the site map, and publications formerly listed there have been integrated with the 'Further reading'.

DHK, 1989

Glossary

Burnished: a surface rubbed with either the moistened finger or with a wet object before firing, giving a metallic sheen; also used of a similar surface produced by rubbing after firing.
Carinated: a vessel is carinated if it has a sharp inward angle to the body (for example 37, 42, 43).
Faceted: a carination cut away with small segments to give a many-sided appearance (for example 36, 45, 46).

Note on illustrations and text

There is no agreed way of illustrating Anglo-Saxon pots; several styles are used on the figures. The late T. C. Lethbridge maintained that sections were less valuable than a full view of the decorative scheme, and this I have generally followed for the decorated pots. Plain pots, where the cross-section can be recovered, are shown with one-quarter cut away, as is usual in the illustration of prehistoric and Roman pots. Bases when complex are shown in section, even if the decoration of the pot is shown across the full width of the drawing.

All drawings are by the author, being the inked tracings of originals made in museums between 1966 and 1977. They are reduced to a consistent scale of one-quarter linear, with the stamps being shown at one-half scale.

At various points in the text a number appears in brackets: for example (54). This refers to a pot illustrated; the figure number is omitted as the pots are numbered in a single sequence.

1
The study of Anglo-Saxon pottery

Anglo-Saxon pottery has been illustrated by diligent antiquaries since the seventeenth century but it is only since the 1930s that systematic study has been undertaken. It is still a study with limitations. Much of the evidence for pottery, as for other artefacts of Anglo-Saxon England of the fifth to ninth centuries, the period covered by this book, is derived from graves. This is especially so between AD 400 and 700. Archaeological study until the late 1960s was almost exclusively concerned with the evidence for the dead rather than with an examination of settlement sites. Even with the new directions in Anglo-Saxon archaeology, insufficient work has been done to permit general conclusions concerning the type of pots used on domestic sites. Only for the eighth and ninth centuries is there a wide understanding of pottery not funerary in context, but this is regional in its application, concentrating on eastern England. The pottery discussed and illustrated in this book is from a similarly confined but slightly wider area. Anglo-Saxon pottery of the fifth to seventh centuries is found primarily in England but very little is from west or north of a line drawn between Bournemouth, Birmingham, Bradford and Bridlington (map, figure 2A). In Scotland, Wales and the rest of England native culture was largely aceramic; the pottery which is found there is wheel-made and imported from the eastern Mediterranean and from western France.

Anglo-Saxon pottery, with the exception of a few of the earliest vessels, is insular in production. Technically this hand-made pottery is of the highest standard: the making of Anglo-Saxon pottery is discussed in chapter 2. The good quality is due to the use to which many of the surviving complete pots were put, namely to contain the fragmented bones of cremated individuals. It is probable that some forms of Anglo-Saxon pottery were exclusively made for this use (for example 75, 109, 119), but cremations are also found in cooking pots (135, 142, 143). Some pots are found in inhumation graves as part of the accoutrements of individual burials (36 is from grave 205 at Mitcham, London). These too may have been specially made for burial with the dead.

That pots were made for a specific use enlarges our knowledge of Saxon society. Potters can be distinguished serving a small area. Figures 21 and 22 show two whose work has been discerned

8   *Anglo-Saxon Pottery*

at Northamptonshire sites. Other potters can be suggested from the use of similar fabrics and general decorative features on pots found over 50 miles (80 km) apart, as with the vessels from Souldern, Oxfordshire (85), and Sandy, Bedfordshire (86); a third similar vessel is known from Croydon, London. The separate studies of large cremation cemeteries in East Anglia, Lincolnshire and Humberside by T. C. Lethbridge and J. N. L. Myres have revealed a number of workshops and potters. The work of eleven different potters was identified at Caistor St Edmund, Norfolk.

The bulk of the material for the study of Anglo-Saxon pottery derives from 38 sites each with over forty known pots. These are all listed under 'The major sites' in chapter 3, together with five other sites of recent publication from which rather fewer pots have been recorded.

Many cemeteries discovered in the nineteenth century are now represented by only a few pots. Figure 1 shows all the pots from Shropham, Norfolk (1-5). Plain vessels were not saved; many were given away as 'duplicates'. Even where the pots were kept, few were adequately recorded and fewer still illustrated. An exception is Little Wilbraham, Cambridgeshire, where 121 urns were found in 1851: ten of the forty plates of R. C. Neville's *Saxon Obsequies Illustrated* record the pots. Before this only individual interesting pots from the smaller sites were chosen for illustration, as with three of the thirteen pots from Sandy, Bedfordshire (76, 80, 86).

Usually only the complete pots were retained, as at Castle Acre, Norfolk, from where twelve of over fifty found in 1891 were kept. Many of the pots found here as elsewhere were scattered fragments throughout the area of the cemetery. The fine complete pots seen in museum cases are the rarity of discovery; today they are the product of patient hours of restoration.

Opposite page
Fig. 1. THE SURVIVING URNS FROM SHROPHAM, NORFOLK: A FIFTH-CENTURY GROUP. (Scale ¼; stamps ½).
1. *Buckelurne* of group III.
2 and 3. Anglian urns with decoration combining chevron patterns and standing arched grooves.
4. Anglian urn with chevron pattern within linear grooves.
5. Urn with linear ornament of stamps set between collars.

The study of Anglo-Saxon pottery

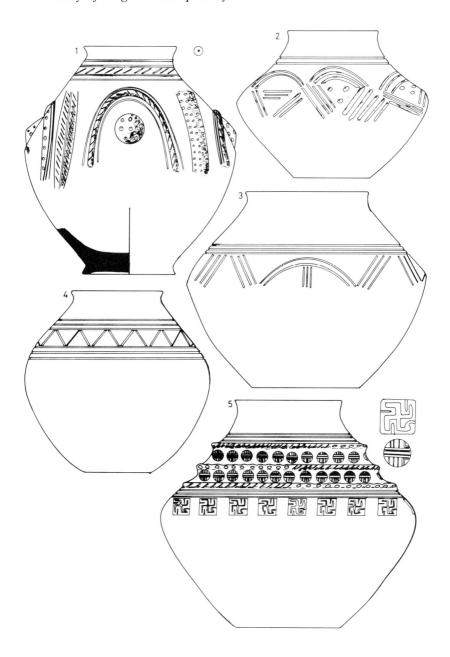

2
Fabrics and technology

Anglo-Saxon pottery has a variety of surface colours. Black is probably the commonest when the total quantity of known urns is considered but various shades of brown, red, pink, grey and, above all, deep red-brown are known in significant proportions. The distinctive Icklingham potter (119) fired his pots to deep red-brown. At any site the range will be considerable even when the number of pots extant is small. The seventeen pots from Croydon, London, include vessels in a deep red-brown slightly corky ware and only lightly smoothed, in a very similar fabric which has been highly burnished (deliberately rubbed before firing and made to shine when baked), in a dark grey gritty ware with roughened surfaces and in a dark grey burnished ware. The variations do not seem to be a consequence of a difference of date. At a site where all the pots are considered to date to within the fifth century, as at Heworth, near York, the range includes light brown unburnished, red-brown burnished, dark grey un-burnished and brown veering to grey unburnished. The last-named pot also has pink among its surface colours.

Surface colour is a product of the firing technique but the range of possible shades is influenced by the choice of clay and inclusions within the clay. With a microscope one can determine the make-up of the grog.

A potter setting out to make his pot, or more probably the day's batch of pots, must first select his clay. The clay chosen for the majority of Anglo-Saxon pots is local to the maker, but it has rarely been used on its own. Examination of the pottery found in the cremation cemetery at St John's College Cricket Field, Cambridge, suggests that the potters whose products are buried there had in their 'workshops' stockpiles of various grits like flint chips, granite, felspar, limestone chips, crushed limestone, chalk, vegetable matter, grass, straw, crushed Roman brick and crushed fragments of broken pots — the failures of earlier firings. The original clay was then worked to the desired consistency by adding those inclusions which the individual potter thought appropriate for the pot he was trying to create in the quantities he felt necessary. Some pots have much more foreign matter than others; some are almost lacking in grits. The presence of grits assists in the drying of the pot when finished and reduces the shrinkage inherent in the drying and firing processes.

Fabrics and technology 11

Having acquired the ball of clay, the potter placed it on a smooth, presumably stone surface: mat-line and wood-grain impressions have not been detected on the bases of Anglo-Saxon pots. Two possible techniques were then available to the potter. The simplest vessels (59, 149, 166) were made by opening a hole in the centre of the clay ball and fashioning the hole to the external shape desired. Very thin pots (165) can be made by this technique. The alternative method of building up a pot is to roll the clay into a long sausage and then to coil it above a solid base. Some bases are themselves coil-built, certainly among the pots from St John's College Cricket Field, Cambridge.

Many pots have protruding bosses. Some bosses are solid. These are made by adding a shaped piece of clay to the existing vessel and luting the clay boss to the outside of the pot. Lugs (140-1) and small round bosses (143) on cooking pots can be made in this fashion. Arched lugs (23) and bar-lips (136-9) are also made of a separate piece of clay which has been luted on to the existing pot. It is rare, but not unknown, for a heavily decorated pot to have the bosses made of separate pieces of clay. One decorative style using this technique is the shoulder-boss urn, with decoration confined to the upper part of the pot (90).

More often the boss is made from clay which is integral to that of the pot. This technique has an adverse effect on the construction of the unfired vessel and makes the drying of the green pot more difficult. It also hinders the firing to a consistent colour. Vertical bosses are used to divide panels of ornament (102, 107) and this can be combined with vertical lines, either beside the boss (104-5) or on the boss itself (111). The use of vertical lines on a boss dividing ornamental panels can be extended into the upper decorative area of the pot so that the panels of ornament are further broken up (109, 112). These sixth-century bossed pots have narrower bosses than the pots with bosses, known as *Buckelurnen*, produced in the fifth century (1, 29, 73-85). On *Buckelurnen* the bosses are often used as the field for decoration, leaving the body of the vessel plain (73-4, 83, 86) or with only minimal enhancement (29). Vessels with elaborate bosses are more difficult to fire; the collection from St John's College Cricket Field, Cambridge, contains several *Buckelurnen* in sherds which have broken round the edges of the bosses, under the pressure of the earth compacting down upon them.

After making the pot, the potter allowed it to dry and to harden. During drying and firing the vessel will lose over one-eighth (12½ per cent or more) of its linear size and this can

12 *Anglo-Saxon Pottery*

reduce the volume of the pot by as much as one-third. Pots dry fairly slowly, with the upper part becoming stiffened more readily than the base. When the rim and upper portion had become sufficiently firm the Anglo-Saxon potter probably followed the modern craft potter's practice of inverting the pot to allow the base to stiffen. As the vessel was inverted, the potter's hand inside the pot could have made the base slightly convex on the exterior (109, 111-15). Pots of the fifth and sixth centuries have a sagging appearance to the base, but this is dissimilar to the later Saxo-Norman wares with true sagging bases and a pronounced angle between the side of the pot and the base.

When the pot had been made to the size and shape required it was dried. After drying, the vessel was fired. Firing was possibly in a kiln, but only two Anglo-Saxon pottery kilns have been found, both at Cassington, Oxfordshire. These were of a simple type with a single stoke-hole, a flue and a firing chamber. The form of the covering is unknown. The general type of kiln is not known. The late Surgeon-Commander F. R. Mann, who single-handed excavated the urns from Caistor St Edmund, conducted a large number of experiments into the making and firing of Anglo-Saxon pots. He concluded that most, if not all, were fired in a substantial garden bonfire, kept alight until all the grass and twigs had been carbonised. Pots fired in this atmosphere came out with surfaces in the darker colours of Anglo-Saxon wares but portions of the urns in contact with the fire were scorched red or buff. Individual position within the fire explains the differing surface colours of Anglo-Saxon pots. Thereafter the pots required finishing.

Bonfire-fired pots and even those baked in a simple kiln are porous; they need smoothing and polishing with a wax to give them the burnished finish. The stamped decoration was most successfully applied within 24 hours of manufacture, and incised lines within two or three days. Further polishing then embellished the pot.

Stamps vary from the simple cross, circle, square and triangular shapes through groups of criss-cross lines within a circle or a rectangle to much more elaborate forms with animals and swastikas. An antler tool with an end impression in the form of a St Andrew's cross is known as a surface find from West Stow Heath, Suffolk. Excavations at the settlement produced the find of another antler tine with a very worn cross-hatched square stamp, three by three squares, cut into it. There was also a trial stamp on a block of clay among the finds here. At Lackford,

Fabrics and technology

Suffolk, one of the pots has its stamps with textile impressions made on a clay die. Wood, which does not survive except in desiccated or waterlogged conditions, could also have been used to make pottery stamps. At various sites pots have been found with stamps made from the terminals of brooches of sixth-century types and also from the side knobs of cruciform brooches. Other jewellery used as pottery stamps includes brooch springs, twisted wire possibly from a spiral type of sleeve clasp, a finger ring, buckles and the curved beaded edge of a circular brooch.

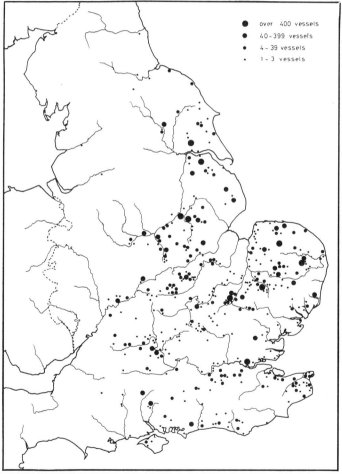

Fig. 2A. THE DISTRIBUTION OF ANGLO-SAXON FUNERARY POTTERY OF THE FIFTH TO SEVENTH CENTURIES.

14   *Anglo-Saxon Pottery*

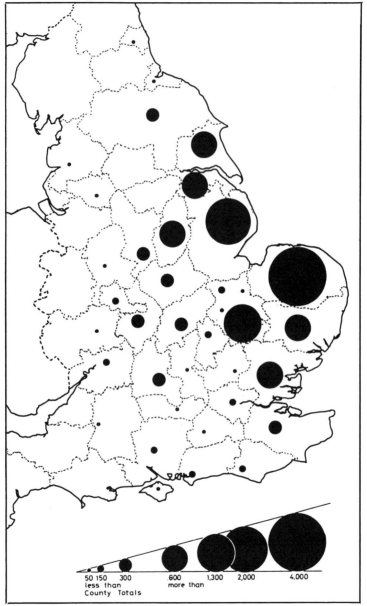

Fig. 2B. THE DENSITY OF CREMATION URNS AND ACCESSORY VESSELS TO INHUMATION GRAVES FOUND IN ANGLO-SAXON CEMETERIES.

3
Distribution

Around 14,000 Anglo-Saxon pots are known from about 350 cemeteries in England. Of these the eight largest cremation cemeteries have yielded two-thirds of the total number of pots. The eight sites, each with more than 600 pots are: Spong Hill, North Elmham, Norfolk, with over 2700 pots; Loveden Hill, Hough-on-the-Hill, Lincolnshire, with around 1800 pots; Caistor St Edmund, Norfolk, where 1000 pots were found; Sancton, North Humberside, which has produced 850 pots; St John's College Cricket Field, Cambridge, and Mucking, Essex, at each of which a minimum number of vessels is over 700; and Elsham, South Humberside, and Lackford, Suffolk, both of which have produced over 600 pots. Probably of an equivalent size is Newark, Nottinghamshire, from which over 400 pots are known, but the early records are incomplete.

These nine sites from seven modern counties can be supplemented by substantial finds elsewhere in each of these counties. In Norfolk substantial numbers of pots survive from Castle Acre, Field Dalling, Illington and Markshall; large numbers were recorded but the vessels are now lost at Brettenham and Great Walsingham. It is unknown how many other vessels were found at a site like Shropham, the five surviving pots from which are illustrated on figure 1. It is usually interpreted that these great cremation cemeteries represent the burial place for a wide tract of surrounding countryside. However, major cemeteries are known from adjacent medieval parishes at Brettenham, Illington and Shropham. The two first-named each produced over two hundred pots and the third may have done. It is more probable that each, in use for over a century and a half, was the burial ground of a small group of farmsteads which were grouped together in the eighth century to form the nucleus of the subsequent medieval parish. At Illington 212 urned cremations were found at a site in use from the early fifth century to the end of the sixth century (say about 180 years). Given a life expectancy of thirty years, these interments represent a population of about 35-40 people. In Domesday Book, in 1086, Illington is recorded as having one tenant and 23 peasants, which represents at four or five per household a population of between 92 and 115. Brettenham had 18 peasants, suggesting an eleventh-century population of between 72 and 90; more populous Shropham had

16   *Anglo-Saxon Pottery*

52 peasants listed, giving a minimum population of around 200. In the eighteenth century, when life expectancy was around sixty years, a village of this size had between seven and eleven burials recorded each year. The lower general age at death in the fifth and sixth centuries, around thirty, would increase the death rate to between fourteen and twenty each year. But what is unknown is what proportion of the population was entitled by local custom to urned burial of their ashes.

Others have seen the cremation cemeteries of Norfolk and elsewhere as representing local crematoria to which bodies were brought for burning and interment.

The finds from the cremation cemeteries of Norfolk represent almost one-third of the total number of known Anglo-Saxon pots. The county has eight of the sites with over 40 pots. Lincolnshire has six such sites, and Cambridgeshire, Humberside and Suffolk each have three.

County totals for known pots reflect the distribution of principal sites. By modern administrative county, as shown on figure 2B, the totals are:

over 4000 pots	Norfolk
over 2000 pots	Lincolnshire
over 1300 pots	Humberside, Cambridgeshire
600-1000 pots	Suffolk, Essex, Nottinghamshire
300-600 pots	none
150-300 pots	Warwickshire, Leicestershire, Northamptonshire, Derbyshire, Oxfordshire, North Yorkshire, Kent
75-150 pots	Hampshire, West Midlands, Bedfordshire
50-75 pots	West Sussex, London, Gloucestershire, East Sussex
under 50 pots	Cleveland, Hertfordshire, Berkshire, Surrey, Staffordshire, Wiltshire, Isle of Wight, Buckinghamshire, Lancashire, Tyne and Wear, Greater Manchester, Scotland
none yet known	Avon, Cornwall, County Durham, Cumbria, Devon, Dorset, Merseyside, Shropshire, South Yorkshire, Wales, West Yorkshire

Within each of the groupings, counties are shown in descending order of magnitude. On figure 2B the categories 75-150 pots and 50-75 pots are combined. Partly this is because new discoveries

Distribution

would instantly revise the position of any county. Hence since the late 1960s Gloucestershire, Hampshire and West Sussex have had their county totals transformed by the finding of single sites, respectively Butler's Field at Lechlade, Portway at Andover and Compton Appledown.

Totals given in the table and on figure 2B are for known pots, which can only be approximate, given the paucity of records for discoveries made in the eighteenth and nineteenth centuries. During tree planting, more than twenty urns were recorded at Drayton Lodge, Norfolk, in 1849, and fragments of others were subsequently reported in years up to 1852. At Kempston, Bedfordshire, Victorian illustrations record six pots not now surviving and the excavators noted much smashing of vessels to get at 'the gold which they had heard was always buried in one' pot by labourers who first found the site. Here also there is no guarantee that all the pots saved in 1863-5 reached a museum. At Sutton Bonnington, Nottinghamshire, there is record of a 'number of urns' found in about 1850, but the actual number is unknown. Outside the east wall of the Roman fort at Burgh Castle, Norfolk, 'a great many fragments of urns' were discovered in 1756; numerous pieces of urns were found but none of the vessels was taken up whole at Haw Hill Piece, Rendlesham, Suffolk, in 1837 and earlier years. If better records existed of these and other sites the totals would be both more accurate and larger. However, the poorness of the contemporary record for some sites does not alter the weight of distribution of Anglo-Saxon pottery in eastern England north of the river Thames.

If *surviving* pots were taken as the criterion for listing, the county total would be less for both Derbyshire and North Yorkshire, reducing the former to under fifty surviving vessels and the latter to between fifty and 75 surviving pots.

To establish totals for the traditional counties of England, both combinations of present-day counties and splits of amalgamated ones would be necessary. To aid this, certain counties have been shown by constituent parts on figure 2B. North Humberside and South Humberside are shown each as counties with between six hundred and one thousand pots. The former corresponds to the number known from the East Riding of Yorkshire, but without the cemeteries around York added to that number. The old county of Lincolnshire had both the modern county and South Humberside within its boundaries; about 2800 pots are known from this area. Historic Warwickshire included most of the area now within the administrative county of the West Midlands; over

18 *Anglo-Saxon Pottery*

three hundred pots are known from the old county. Except for a dozen pots from sites on the Middlesex bank, the total from London should be added to that for the modern county of Surrey. The historic county of Surrey has between fifty and 75 known pots.

Historic Oxfordshire has few sites producing large numbers of Anglo-Saxon pots; the great majority in the modern county were found in the Vale of the White Horse district transferred from Berkshire in 1974. The four constituent parts of the modern county of Cambridgeshire are shown by individual spots on figure 2B. As will be obvious, most of the pots in the county were found at sites near Cambridge; very few pots are known, except as single finds, from either Huntingdonshire or the Isle of Ely. The Soke of Peterborough has produced about seventy pots. Although not shown on the map, sites in Rutland account for eighty of the pots from modern Leicestershire.

ANGLO-SAXON POTTERY: THE MAJOR SITES

The list gives all sites known to have had at least forty vessels found at them, whether the pots are surviving or not. An asterisk (*) denotes that a reference to the site will be found in chapter 8, 'Further reading'. The number of pots found at each site is given, followed by the museum or museums where they are now kept.

Bedfordshire
Kempston: 49+ pots: Bedford Museum; British Museum, London.

Cambridgeshire
Girton College: 250+ pots: Cambridge University Museum of Archaeology and Anthropology; Girton College, Cambridge.
Little Wilbraham: 135 pots: Cambridge University Museum of Archaeology and Anthropology.
St John's College: 700+ pots: Cambridge University Museum of Archaeology and Anthropology.

Derbyshire
King's Newton: 200 pots: Ashmolean Museum, Oxford (6 pots).

Essex
Mucking: 700 pots: Thurrock Local History Museum, Grays.
Springfield: 100 pots: Chelmsford and Essex Museum.

Gloucestershire
Lechlade*: 32 pots: Oxfordshire County Museum, Woodstock.

Hampshire
Portway, Andover*: 65 pots: Andover Museum.
Worthy Park: 46 pots: Winchester City Museum.

Distribution 19

Humberside
Elsham: 630 pots: Scunthorpe Borough Museum and Art Gallery.
Kirton-in-Lindsey*: 50+ pots: Lincoln City and County Museum; British Museum, London; Manchester Museum.
Sancton*: 850 pots: Hull Transport and Archaeology Museum; Ashmolean Museum, Oxford.

Leicestershire
Thurmaston*: 119 pots: Jewry Wall Museum of Archaeology, Leicester.

Lincolnshire
Ancaster: 40+ pots: Grantham Museum.
Baston*: 44 pots: Lincoln City and County Museum.
Fonaby*: 28 pots: Scunthorpe Borough Museum and Art Gallery.
Loveden Hill: 1800 pots: Lincoln City and County Museum; Grantham Museum.
South Elkington*: 204 pots: Lincoln City and County Museum; Louth Museum.
West Keal*: 29+ pots: Lincoln City and County Museum.

Norfolk
Brettenham: 200+ pots: Cambridge University Museum of Archaeology and Anthropology (1 pot); Maidstone Museum and Art Gallery (manuscript).
Caistor St Edmund*: 1000+ pots: Castle Museum, Norwich.
Castle Acre: 100+ pots: Castle Museum, Norwich; Lynn Museum, King's Lynn.
Field Dalling: 47 pots: Castle Museum, Norwich.
Great Walsingham: 40+ pots: Ashmolean Museum, Oxford (2 pots).
Illington: 212 pots: Castle Museum, Norwich.
Markshall*: 100+ pots: Castle Museum, Norwich.
Spong Hill*: 2700+ pots: Castle Museum, Norwich.

Northamptonshire
Kettering: 106+ pots: Northampton Central Museum and Art Gallery; Kettering.

North Yorkshire
Heworth*: 90+ pots: Yorkshire Museum, York.

Nottinghamshire
Kingston-on-Soar: 200+ pots: Nottingham University Museum (6 pots).
Newark: 400+ pots: Newark Museum and Art Gallery.

Oxfordshire
Abingdon: 89 pots: Ashmolean Museum, Oxford.
Long Wittenham: 46 pots: British Museum, London.

Suffolk
Eye: 150 pots: Moyse's Hall, Bury St Edmunds (2 pots).
Lackford*: 600+ pots: Cambridge University Museum of Archaeology and Anthropology; Moyse's Hall, Bury St Edmunds.
Snape: 58+ pots: British Museum, London; Moot Hall, Aldeburgh; Ipswich Museum.

Warwickshire
Alveston: 32+ pots: New Place Museum, Stratford-upon-Avon.
Bidford-on-Avon: 150+ pots: New Place Museum, Stratford-upon-Avon.

West Midlands
Baginton: 84 pots: Herbert Art Gallery and Museum, Coventry.

West Sussex
Compton Appledown: 40+ pots: Chichester District Museum.

4
Dating

Anglo-Saxon pottery is notoriously difficult to date with any great precision. Much cannot be placed closer than a relevant century. Of itself it is undatable. It can be dated only by what is found with it, but the majority of Anglo-Saxon pottery comes from cremation cemeteries in which few other objects have been found in a sufficient state of preservation to permit a chronological attribution to be made: a bronze brooch will become a piece of fused metal when it is subjected to cremation heat. It is the brooches which date the pots, not the pots which date the brooches.

A relative sequence based on the development of types and their decoration can be advanced. It is secured at the beginning and to a lesser extent at the end. The earliest Anglo-Saxon pots are those of types found also in the continental homelands of the ancestral English. Types found only in the Netherlands, Germany and Scandinavia are presumed to be of fourth-century date or earlier; types found there and in England are assigned to the fifth century, when contemporary chroniclers and later historians such as Bede record a large-scale movement of people from the north European littoral to England. Pottery types found only in England are assigned to the sixth century or later. Some of the latest cremation urns (for example 134 from Lackford) have cable decoration and animal stamps which may be compared with the manuscript art of the seventh century.

For the seventh century, a few pots can be dated by their association in inhumation graves with coins, and others, less reliably, by their association with objects whose parallels have been found in graves with coins.

For eastern England in the eighth and ninth centuries the dating relies on the discovery of pots used to conceal coin hoards in and for some sites only, such as Whitby Abbey, on the pottery being later than the known foundation date of the site.

5
Shape and decoration of funerary pottery

Anglo-Saxon pottery of the fifth, sixth and early seventh centuries, as found in cremation cemeteries, has three basic shapes: (i) rounded profile; (ii) carinated profile; (iii) shouldered profile. Bases are usually rounded: very few Anglo-Saxon pots have completely flat exterior surfaces within the base angle; on the majority the base is slightly sagging. A small but significant group of pots have either a solid pedestal base (for example 80) or a foot-ring giving a pedestal base (for example 1, 23, 77 and 142). In general the most distinctive profiles are the earliest.

Decoration on Anglo-Saxon pots is varied. A general progression can be seen from designs using straight grooves in horizontal and chevron patterns and those with arched grooves to vessels where bosses are the most prominent feature of the decorative scheme. These give way gradually to designs based on stamped ornament, which at first retain the use of bosses. The latest cremation urns are those with stamped ornament, but in the seventh century accessory vessels from inhumation graves are either plain or ornamented with simple designs.

The notes which follow and the accompanying illustrations are in an approximate chronological order. Figures 1, 3-9, 11 and 13-15 are of fifth-century vessels; the pots shown on figure 12 and 16-24 are broadly of sixth-century date; varying dates may be placed on those illustrated on figures 10 and 25-9, while seventh-century pottery is drawn on figure 30.

Plain urns can be of any date; the most distinctive shapes are fifth-century, especially those with a carinated profile. The *Anglian urns,* named after their concentration in the Frisian-Angle areas of eastern England, have the carination about midway between the base and the rim (6, 7, 8); an alternative name is *biconical urn.* More specialised is the form with the neck distinctively concave, known as *hollow-necked urns* (10, 131, also found rarely without decoration). Among pots with rounded profiles, the earliest, also of Frisian-Angle derivation and with continental analogies, are *globular urns,* which can have either a short upright rim (21, 26) or an everted flaring rim (18). Early decorative schemes, such as complex linear grooving with

22 *Anglo-Saxon Pottery*

chevron patterns (19), chevron and standing arched grooves (22) and standing arched grooves and stamps (24, 27), are represented among the large globular urns from St John's College Cricket Field, Cambridge. The earliest *Buckelurnen* include those of perfect globular shape (29). Later plain urns have less geometrically exact profiles (146-7), with the exception of *shouldered urns*. Some of these are fifth-century (11, 14) and shoulder bosses begin then (12-13; also 25 on a globular urn). A less sharp profile is found on sixth-century examples (17).

Pots decorated with arched grooves can use either standing arches (30, 33-4) or less often hanging arches (35). The German terms of *stehende Bogen* and *hangende Bogen* are often used to designate these urns. Standing arches can be combined with a zone of linear ornament (30), with rows of stamps (31) or with shoulder bosses (32).

Fifth-century bowls exhibit a wide range of forms (figure 9). Bowls are vessels with a rim diameter equal to or greater than the height. Many are carinated; these may be plain (47), decorated with horizontal grooves (42), ornamented with horizontal grooves and chevrons (43) or decorated with a zone of chevron-and-dot ornament (37). Rounded profiles are also known (41, 48).

Vessels with a faceted carination can have either a pedestal foot (36), a round base (38) or a small flat base (45, 46). As with bowls, they are usually accessory vessels to inhumation graves, usually of the fifth century. Akin to these are vessels with bosses on the carination, either with a pedestal foot (39) or a flat base (40); the feature is also known on bowls with rounded profiles (48).

Accessory vessels tend to be small pots and have simple linear schemes of ornament (49-50, 53, 148). The majority are plain, often of crude designs (52, 54-62 are the range from St John's College Cricket Field; 149).

Pots decorated with grooves at the simplest are those with plain horizontal grooves (10, 91). More complex is a combination with vertical grooves (99, 101), leading to vessels decorated with panels of ornament (100) and combined with bosses (102). Another simple decorative form is the plain chevron design

Shape and decoration of funerary pottery

(63-4), found also delineated by linear grooves (4) and as a combination of the zone of chevrons and the free chevrons (65). It can be combined with fingertip impression to give chevron-and-dot designs (66). Chevron ornament can also be used in combination with standing arched grooves (3) and in more complex patterns placing the arches above the chevrons to form face-like patterns (2). An unusual decoration includes a series of swastikas and swastika-like lines within a chevron-ornamented pot (129). Still within the fifth century are combinations of chevrons and a row of stamps with the decoration confined above the carination (67). The same restriction of ornament is found on vessels where stamps are used as an integral part of the chevron pattern (68-9). Sixth-century developments show the stamps as more prominent both within the chevron designs (70) and on vessels whose ornament combines horizontal lines with chevrons (71). A multiplication of the number of lines used in each chevron (72) is also found.

Pots with bosses at their most simple are plain urns decorated purely with bosses (12-13, 25) or with arched handles (23); but early bossed urns are usually more complex. For the majority the German word *Buckelurne* (plural *Buckelurnen*) is used: it has the literal meaning of 'bossed pot'. They are found in north Germany in fifth-century contexts. Five groups, broadly contemporary, have been distinguished in England:

Group I, with feet, decorated with linear or line-and-dot ornament, possibly with finger-tipping, but without stamps (73-4, 76, 79-80, 83). About 25 are known.

Group II, without feet, but decorated as group I, again without stamps (81, 85). About fifty are known.

Group III, with feet, and with restrained use of stamps (1, 29, 82, 84). About twelve are known.

Group IV, without feet, and with restrained use of stamps (75). About fifteen are known.

Group V, with or without feet, with considerable use of stamps (77-8, 86). About forty of these individual urns are known.

In these pots some of the earliest individual potters have been distinguished. One is known from two small pots at East Shefford, Berkshire (82, 84); two vessels from St John's College Cricket Field, Cambridge (73-4), may be from a single workshop. Others are more widely scattered, including a potter suggested by a group V *Buckelurne* at Thurmaston, Leicestershire, and another at Lackford, Suffolk, which have three stamps in

24 *Anglo-Saxon Pottery*

common. Similarity of fabric combined with bosses in the form of standing arches links a group II *Buckelurne* from Souldern, Oxfordshire (85), with one of group V from Sandy, Bedfordshire (86). Visually akin in fabric and design is a group IV *Buckelurne* from Croydon, London. The links back to standing arched grooves will be clear in a number of *Buckelurnen* (1, 74, 78, 85-6). The boss develops into a continuous swag (75-6, 82, 84), a link also with chevron designs (80). Bosses with no supporting ornament (83) or with sparse use of other features (73) are known. At their most elaborate some *Buckelurnen* have incipient panels of ornament (77). The use of the pedestal foot is found also on some much less elaborately conceived pots where the bosses are much less prominent in the decorative scheme (39). Shoulder-boss urns are known with simple chevron patterns (87, 88), and using chevrons with swastika-like lines (128); one further development is the use of shoulder bosses to demarcate panels of vertical lines (89). More complex is the incorporation in sixth-century vessels of horizontal ornament with stamps (90). A later development of Anglo-Saxon pottery with bosses is the long-boss style, where pots have bosses on the lower half with linear grooving or stamps, or both, above (121-2). On a few pots there are vertical depressions instead of bosses; these are termed *melon-ribbed* (124). Bosses also feature on sixth-century pots with panels of linear ornament (102) or stamps (104-5, 107-12, 116, 118, 123).

Pots with stamps begin with those where the stamps are subordinate to the linear grooves within which they are placed (92, 113); this is a development from the use of linear grooving (91). Stamps can be arranged as roughly horizontal lines (114). Here the linear grooving is absent, but other vessels (93, 95) have stamps and grooves in approximate equilibrium. The grooves may be replaced by raised collars (5). By the end of the sixth century urns are found with the stamps as the dominant feature of linear arrangements (94, 96, 117). Linear ornament with stamps can be combined with the use of chevrons (97) and with bosses (98, 115).

Panel styles of ornament at their most simple are vertical lines divided either by stamps (100) or by horizontal and diagonal lines (101); shoulder bosses can be used (89, 99). These fifth-century types are succeeded by vessels with panels of vertical grooves delineated by prominent bosses (102) and by rectangular panels

Shape and decoration of funerary pottery 25

of ornament using stamps set within bosses (104-5, 123). Another sixth-century style is based on stamped swags, either set below a zone of linear ornament with stamps (106) or placed within horizontal grooves (126). Triangular panel styles of ornament are found mostly with bosses. On the majority the stamps are demarcated by grooves (107-12) but some do not have the accompanying feature (116, 118). Occasionally melon-ribs replace the bosses (125). A particularly elaborate form of triangular panel style is that of the Kettering long-boss potter, named after the long vertical grooves beside and extending above the bosses. Each of the two complete urns (109, 112) has seven bosses with four verticals. His other traits include the use of stepped stamps found on one Kettering urn (109) and on a vessel with a pedestal foot from Thorpe Malsor, Northamptonshire (110), and the arrangement of double dots which together with a fabric analogy suggests that an urn from Newton-in-the-Willows, Northamptonshire (111), is his work. Another potter using panel style is the Icklingham potter (also known as the Illington/Lackford potter), whose products are found on many sites in East Anglia. They include simple linear designs as well as panel-style decoration and at their most elaborate a pot with linear designs and panels delineated by bosses; the prominent feature of each of the ten panels is a swastika-shaped boss with stamps in the interspaces (119). Panel style with delineated triangular panels of ornament was used by a potter working in or near sixth-century Cambridge, six of whose products, recognised from sherds, are known from St John's College Cricket Field (107 is the only complete example). However, late sixth-century potters more frequently had a repertoire of designs which was wide. One can be distinguished at cemeteries in central Northamptonshire. At Kettering Stamford Road his products used linear designs with stamps (113-14); on one (115) bosses form a subsidiary element. Individual stamps link his products to a vessel with linear ornament at Holdenby (117) and one with triangular panels at Islip (116, a sherd); the latter shares a common stamp with a similar vessel from Burton Latimer (118). While panel styles are often combined with bosses, some pots are known with rectangular panels of ornament separated only by vertical grooves (120, an elaborate example with seven different designs in nine panels using eight different stamps).

Swastika and 'wyrm' designs have been noted as elements in other decorative schemes. The swastika was among the symbols

26   *Anglo-Saxon Pottery*

of the god Thor, the deity of thunder, also known as Thunor to the Anglo-Saxons. The symbol can be drawn well and used like a stamp (127) or incorporated in other decorative schemes (129), sometimes only partially sketched (128). The dragon in mythology watched over the dead: the great poem *Beowulf* speaks of his role. On pottery the idea was transferred to a legless beast, the 'wyrm', used both singly and as a frieze (130). An alphabet was developed in northern Europe in the fifth century. These symbols, known as runes, were sometimes transferred to pots, most significantly with the 'T' rune associated with the god Tiw or Tig. Signs on pots are usually rune-like (159). The protection of the god of war could be replaced by a desire to let the spirit of the dead person escape. Small drilled holes are found; other pots have a small piece of glass inserted in the base (79). Window urns can take many forms.

Animals have a special place in Anglo-Saxon mythology. Metalwork ornament is based on animals. Pots can be decorated with a frieze of animals (131) or with stylised beasts incorporated in a decorative scheme (132). Animal stamps are found both on fifth-century vessels (133) and on those of the seventh century whose other ornament relates to manuscript art (134).

Lids were used with cremation urns. None is figured here; their recognition as common dates to the 1970s and 1980s, with the full excavation of the cemetery at Spong Hill, North Elmham, Norfolk. Most are circular with a central hold above the generally flat surface. One from Spong Hill has an elaborate figure sculptured on it.

Domestic pottery of the fifth to seventh centuries is used for cremation containers, as evidenced by sooted vessels from Kempston, Bedfordshire (143-4, 146). Shapes and decoration are discussed in chapter 6.

Kent in the Anglo-Saxon period is different. Its jewellery has extensive, but not exclusive, contacts with the Rhineland, Belgium and northern France. Its pottery includes vessels with comparisons in eastern England, such as the vessel with multiple chevrons from Howletts (72). The majority of the pots are more akin at the earliest stages of the ceramic sequence to the pottery in Jutland; as the historian Bede remarked, the inhabitants of Kent were Jutes. Most of these pots in a hard leathery black ware

Shape and decoration of funerary pottery 27

are open bowls (151-2). Much of the pottery of Kent is possibly imported, often in red or pink wares, and decorated with a repeated stamp or combing in linear bands. The range includes jars (158), also known in a dark grey ware (153, 156), and bottles (154), including one from Wingham (155) found in a rich seventh-century grave. The Isle of Wight was part of the Jutish area; its pottery includes imports (157) and jars (159).

Seventh-century pottery is almost exclusively found accompanying inhumation burials: the great cremation cemeteries which provide so much of the evidence for earlier centuries cease to be used *c*.600/625. Exceptions are found (134, 162). Seventh-century pots have low bodies and tall necks. Most are undecorated (160-1, 163-4), but the use of bosses (169) and comb-point decoration (167-8) is known. The shape is used for cremation urns, decorated with rouletted swags (162). One inhumation cemetery has also produced a jar (165) and a crucible (166).

6
Domestic pottery

Until the end of the 1970s the domestic pottery of early Anglo-Saxon England had been little studied. The assumption had been made that cremation urns were merely cooking pots and storage vessels re-used, and the major excavations on sites like Walton, Buckinghamshire, and West Stow, Suffolk, have largely confirmed that impression. At West Stow the sherds found in the fill of the huts of the village excavated between 1965 and 1972 are similar to complete vessels from the ill recorded mixed-rite cemetery discovered in 1849. This accords with evidence from sites like Kempston, Bedfordshire, where at least one cremation vessel (144) has extensive sooting on the base.

Plain cooking pots of the fifth and sixth centuries are generally unburnished and of a variety of shapes (144-7, 150). They may have bosses (143) or vestigial lugs (145). Rarely are these forms found complete on domestic sites; vessels from the mixed-rite cemetery at Kempston, Bedfordshire (143-50), and from the predominantly cremation cemeteries of Lackford, Suffolk (135, 142), and St John's College, Cambridge (140), are used to illustrate the shape and decoration of the commoner types of domestic wares.

Lugged pots with the lugs on the side of the pot usually have three lugs; the vessel may have a rounded base (140) or a pedestal foot (141). Other lugged vessels have two lugs drawn out of the rim (135). The lug on the rim is developed into a protected lug, the bar-lip, designed to keep the fire from scorching the cord on which the pot has been suspended from a tripod. The bar-lip developed from a simple ridge of clay below an unprotected hole (136) through a simple ridge of clay below the hole (137) to a simple and then an enlarged lug (138-9).

Rusticated surfaces are found on some lugged pots (135). Here the whole surface is alternately pushed in and then pushed up. Many of the features at West Stow village include at least one sherd of rusticated ware among their pottery assemblages. This surface treatment is not confined to lugged vessels (135) but is also found on bucket-shaped cooking pots (142), which except for

Domestic pottery 29

size resemble bucket-shaped accessory vessels from inhumation graves (149).

Middle Saxon pottery shows a dramatic change from earlier centuries. The evidence is mainly from domestic sites, often in towns, which begin to be a feature of the landscape in the late seventh and early eighth centuries. Hand-made pots continued as with those found at the eighth-century village at Maxey, Cambridgeshire (formerly Northamptonshire). Much of the known pottery, however, was wheel-made with more regular thickness to the walls of the pot. Forms changed. Cooking pots were more prominent (171) but a few pitchers were made retaining stamped ornament (170). Most of this pottery is known under the general term *Ipswich-type ware* after the site where it was first recognised, but monasteries in north-east England produced their own fabrics. This sandy, micaceous ware, now known as *Whitby-type ware*, is found both in hand-made cooking pots (172) and in wheel-made cooking pots (173). These and contemporary fabrics foreshadow the introduction of a better, and faster-turning, potter's wheel in the ninth century; thereafter medieval pottery may be said to begin.

Anglo-Saxon Pottery

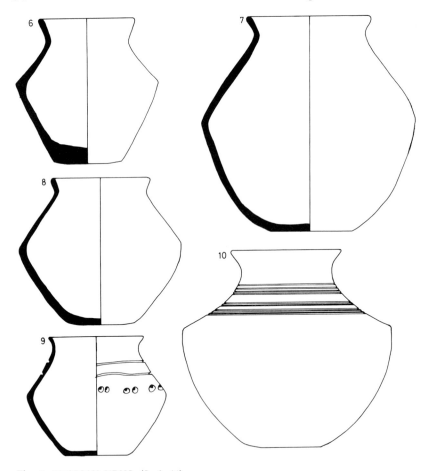

Fig. 3. ANGLIAN URNS. (Scale ¼)
  6. Plain biconical urn from Heworth, near York.
  7. Plain biconical urn from Kettering Stamford Road, Northamptonshire.
  8. Plain biconical urn from Brixworth, Northamptonshire.
  9. Biconical urn with grooves and 'twin eye' decoration, from Kempston, Bedfordshire.
  10. Urn with hollow neck and linear grooves, from Castle Acre, Norfolk.

Opposite page
Fig. 4. SHOULDERED VESSELS. (Scale ¼)
  11 and 14. Plain shouldered urns from Heworth, near York.
  12. Shouldered urn with shoulder bosses, from Heworth, near York.
  13. Shouldered urn with shoulder bosses, from St John's College Cricket Field, Cambridge.
  15. Shouldered bowl from Brixworth, Northamptonshire.
  16. Shouldered accessory vessel from Burton Latimer, Northamptonshire.
  17. Shouldered urn with shoulder grooves, from Brixworth, Northamptonshire.

Shouldered vessels

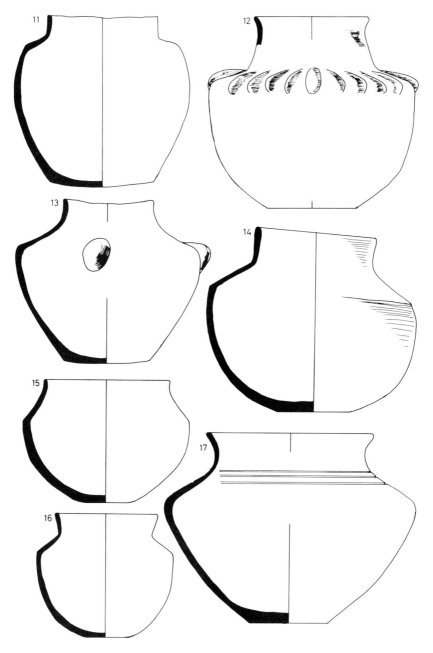

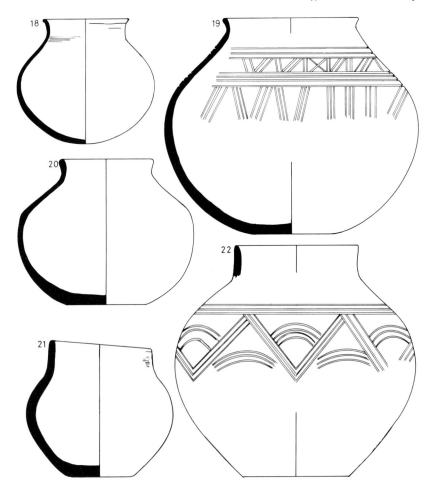

Fig. 5. EARLY GLOBULAR URNS. (Scale ¼)
18. Plain globular urn, probably an accessory vessel, from East Shefford, Berkshire.
19. Globular urn with linear grooves and chevrons, from St John's College Cricket Field, Cambridge.
20. Plain globular urn from St John's College Cricket Field, Cambridge.
21. Plain globular urn from Heworth, near York.
22. Globular urn with chevron and standing arched grooves, from St John's College Cricket Field, Cambridge.

Early globular urns

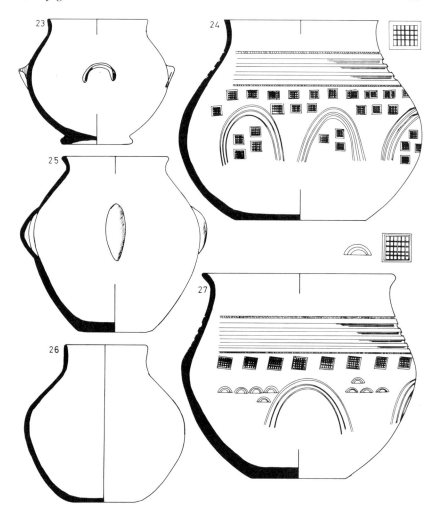

Fig. 6. EARLY GLOBULAR URNS. (Scale ¼; stamps ½)
23. Footed globular urn with four arched lugs, from Brixworth, Northamptonshire.
24. Globular urn with linear grooves, standing arched grooves and stamps, from St John's College Cricket Field, Cambridge.
25. Globular urn with bosses, from St John's College Cricket Field, Cambridge.
26. Plain globular with upright rim, from Market Overton, Leicestershire.
27. Globular urn with linear grooves, standing arched grooves and stamps, from St John's College Cricket Field, Cambridge; probably from the same workshop as 24.

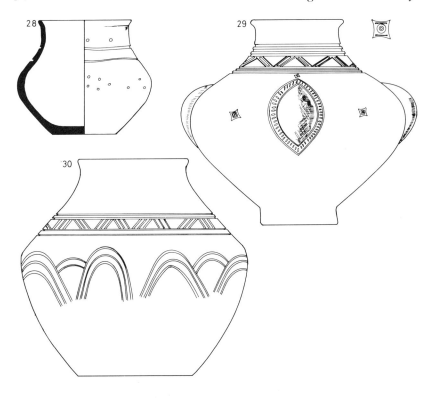

Fig. 7. THREE EARLY URNS FROM HEWORTH, NEAR YORK. (Scale ¼; stamps ½)
28. Globular urn with irregular linear grooves and impressed dimples; compare with urn from Kempston (9).
29. Globular *Buckelurne* of group III.
30. Urn with zone of linear ornament above standing arched grooves.

Opposite page
Fig. 8. VESSELS ORNAMENTED WITH GROOVES IN STANDING AND HANGING ARCHED PATTERNS. (Scale ¼)
31. Anglian urn, of biconical shape, with linear grooves and stamps above standing arched grooves, from St John's College Cricket Field, Cambridge.   32. Urn with linear grooves and wide standing arched grooves with small bosses on the shoulder, from Kirton-in-Lindsey, Humberside.   33. Urn with standing arched grooves and linear grooves, from Heworth, near York.   34. Anglian urn from St John's College Cricket Field, Cambridge, with standing arched grooves in a field of dimples.   35. Wide-mouthed urn with multiple hanging arched grooves, from St John's College Cricket Field, Cambridge.

Vessels ornamented with grooves

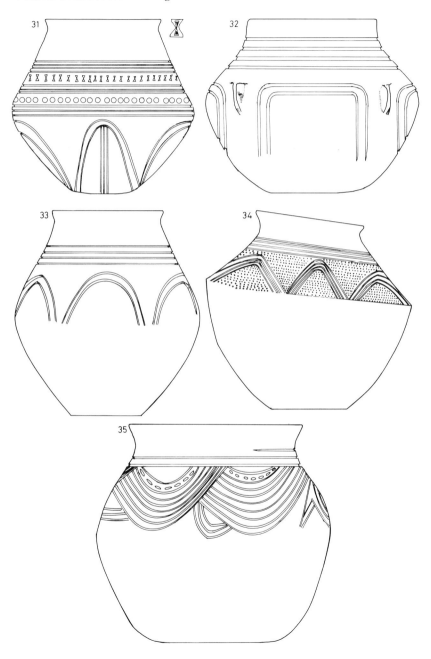

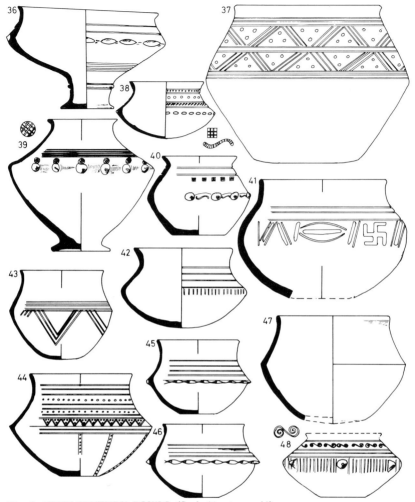

Fig. 9. FIFTH-CENTURY BOWLS. (Scale ¼; stamps ½)
36. Bowl with faceted carination and pedestal foot, from Mitcham, London, an accessory vessel in grave 205.   37. Carinated bowl with chevron-and-dot ornament, from St John's College Cricket Field, Cambridge.   38. Bowl with faceted carination, from Sandy, Bedfordshire.   39. Carinated bowl with bosses on the carination and a pedestal foot, from Duston, Northamptonshire.   40. Bowl with bosses on the carination, from Barrington B, Cambridgeshire.   41. Bowl with rounded profile and grooved decoration, from St John's College Cricket Field, Cambridge; the base is not extant.   42. Carinated bowl from Snettisham, Norfolk.   43. Carinated bowl with chevron ornament, from grave 20 at Luton, Bedfordshire.   44. Carinated bowl with line-and-dot ornament, from Barrington B, Cambridgeshire.   45 and 46. Bowls with faceted carination and linear ornament, from Barrington B, Cambridgeshire.   47. Plain carinated bowl from St John's College Cricket Field, Cambridge.   48. Rounded bowl with bosses, grooves and stamps, from Heworth, near York; the rim is restored.

Accessory vessels

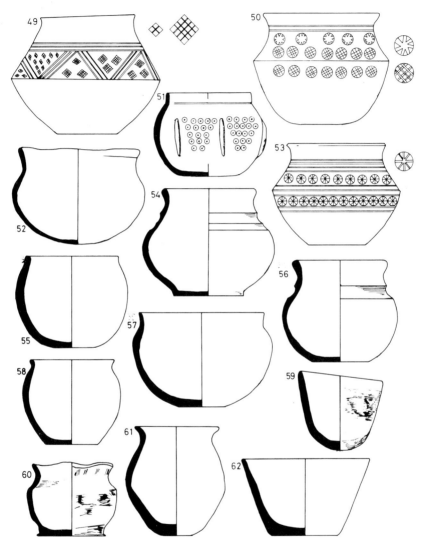

Fig. 10. ACCESSORY VESSELS FROM INHUMATION GRAVES. (Scale ¼; stamps ½) 49-62. Decorated and plain accessory vessels from inhumation graves at St John's College Cricket Field, Cambridge.

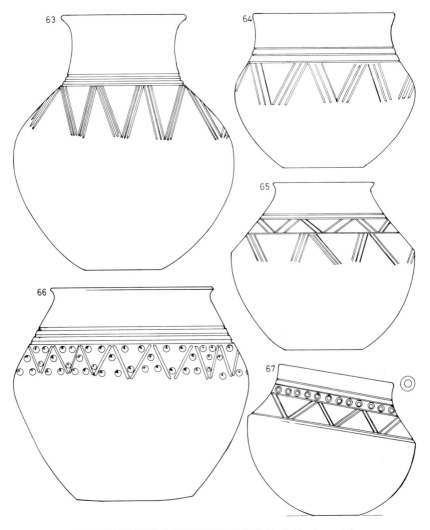

Fig. 11. URNS WITH SIMPLE CHEVRON DESIGNS. (Scale ¼; stamps ½)
63. Globular urn with three-line chevrons, from Heworth, near York.
64. Bowl with three-line chevrons, from St John's College Cricket Field, Cambridge.
65. Anglian urn, of biconical shape, with zone of two-line chevrons above three-line chevrons, from Kettering Stamford Road, Northamptonshire.
66. Urn with chevron-and-dot ornament, from Sandy, Bedfordshire.
67. Anglian urn, misshapen of biconical form, with row of stamps above two-line chevrons, found at Dersingham, Norfolk.

Urns with complex chevron designs

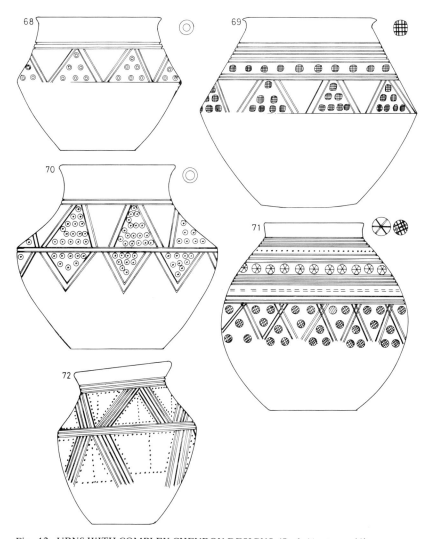

Fig. 12. URNS WITH COMPLEX CHEVRON DESIGNS. (Scale ¼; stamps ½)
  68. Chevrons and stamps on carinated bowl from Castle Acre, Norfolk.
  69. Multiple linear grooves with a row of stamps and chevrons with stamps on carinated bowl from Kettering Stamford Road, Northamptonshire.
  70. Double row of chevrons and stamps on urn from Castle Acre, Norfolk.
  71. Multiple grooves and stamps above chevrons with stamps on globular urn from St John's College Cricket Field, Cambridge.
  72. Complex multiple-line chevrons with stabbing on urn from Howletts, Kent.

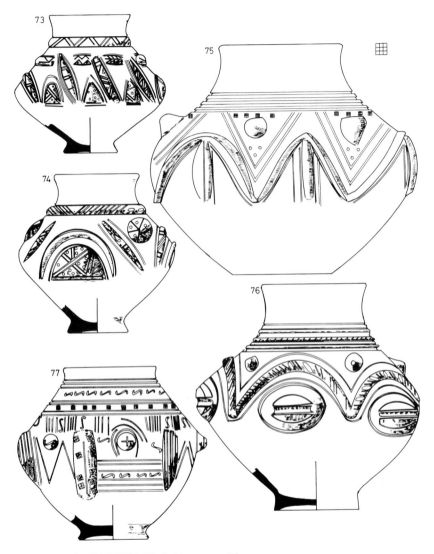

Fig. 13. BUCKELURNEN. (Scale ¼; stamps ½)
 73 and 74. *Buckelurnen* of group I, from St John's College Cricket Field, Cambridge; the two urns are possibly by the same potter.
 75. *Buckelurne* of group IV, from Heworth, near York, with continuous swag.
 76. *Buckelurne* of group I, from Sandy, Bedfordshire, with continuous swag.
 77. *Buckelurne* of group V, from Linton Heath, Cambridgeshire.

Buckelurnen

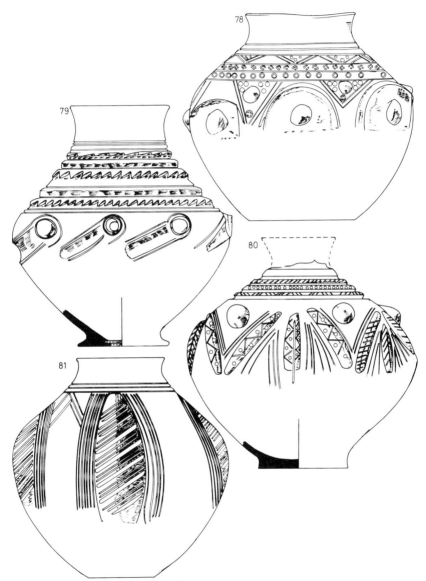

Fig. 14. BUCKELURNEN. (Scale ¼)
78. *Buckelurne* of group V, from Kempston, Bedfordshire, with standing arched bosses.
79. *Buckelurne* of group I, from Castle Acre, Norfolk, with piece of glass in the base.
80. *Buckelurne* of group I, from Sandy, Bedfordshire, with chevron-and-dot ornament.
81. *Buckelurne* of group II, from St John's College Cricket Field, Cambridge.

Anglo-Saxon Pottery

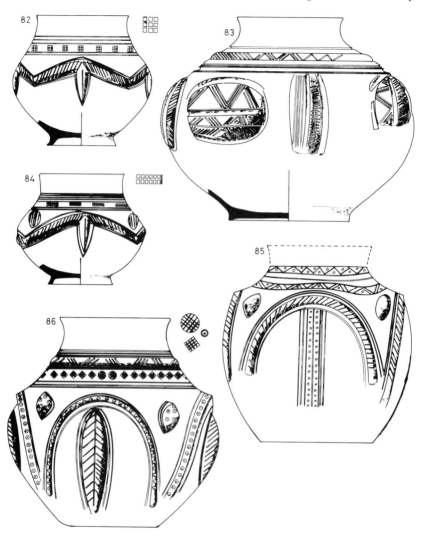

Fig. 15. BUCKELURNEN. (Scale ¼; stamps ½)
82 and 84. *Buckelurnen* of group III, from East Shefford, Berkshire, probably by the same potter.
83. *Buckelurne* of group I, from Luton, Bedfordshire.
85. *Buckelurne* of group II, from Souldern, Oxfordshire.
86. *Buckelurne* of group V, from Sandy, Bedfordshire. Both 85 and 86 are in a similar fabric, as is an urn of similar style from Croydon, London.

Decorated shoulder-boss urns

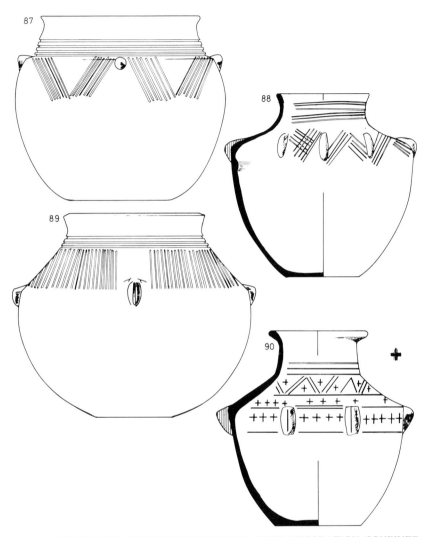

Fig. 16. DECORATED SHOULDER-BOSS URNS WITH DECORATION CONFINED TO UPPER PART OF POT. (Scale ¼; stamp ½)
87. Shoulder-boss urn with seven-line reverse chevrons, from The Mount, York.
88. Shoulder-boss urn with four-line chevrons, from Burton Latimer, Northamptonshire.
89. Shoulder-boss urn with panels of vertical lines, from The Mount, York.
90. Shoulder-boss urn with linear decoration including a cross stamp, from Burton Latimer, Northamptonshire.

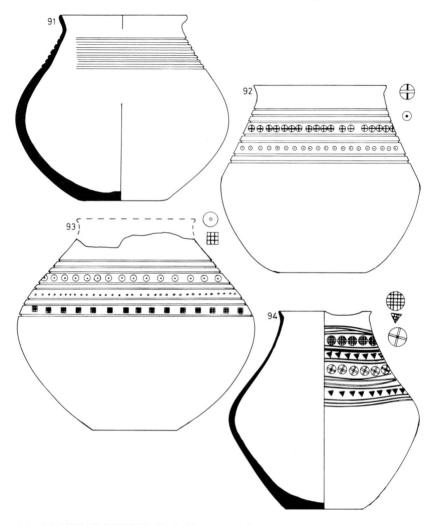

Fig. 17. LINEAR DESIGNS. (Scale ¼; stamps ½)
91. Urn with straight linear grooves, from Downham Market, Norfolk.
92. Urn with linear grooves and stamps, from Castle Acre, Norfolk.
93. Urn with linear grooves and stamps, from Newnham, Cambridge; the rim is restored.
94. Urn with linear grooves and stamps, from Kempston, Bedfordshire.

Linear ornament with stamps

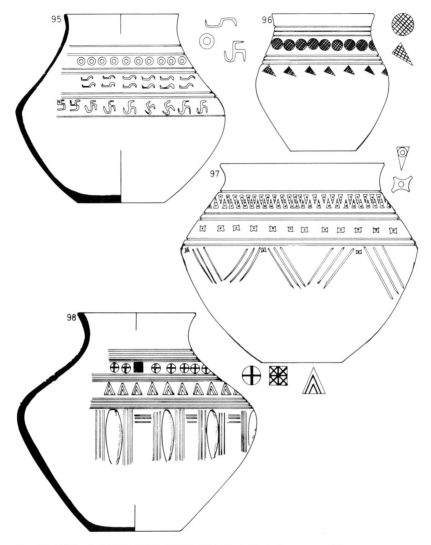

Fig. 18. LINEAR ORNAMENT WITH STAMPS. (Scale ¼; stamps ½)
95. Urn from Lackford, Suffolk, with three rows of stamps set between grooves.
96. Accessory vessel from Newnham, Cambridge, with grooves and two rows of stamps.
97. Urn from Newnham, Cambridge, with two rows of stamps and three-line chevrons.
98. Urn from Pitsford, Northamptonshire, with two rows of stamps within linear grooves above close-set bosses delineated by vertical grooves.

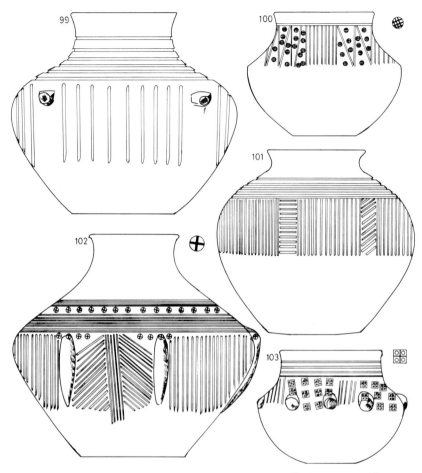

Fig. 19. VERTICAL LINES AS A DECORATIVE FEATURE. (Scale ¼; stamps ½)
99. Shoulder-boss urn from Kirton-in-Lindsey, Humberside, with deep-cut and wide-spaced vertical lines.
100. Hollow-necked urn from Heworth, near York, with vertical lines alternating with panels of stamps.
101. Globular urn from Lackford, Suffolk, with panels of vertical lines divided by horizontal and diagonal lines.
102. Urn from Sedgeford, Norfolk, with panels of vertical lines and feathered lines divided by bosses.
103. Accessory vessel from Tottenhill, Norfolk, with vertical lines, stamps and small shoulder bosses.

Panel styles as decoration

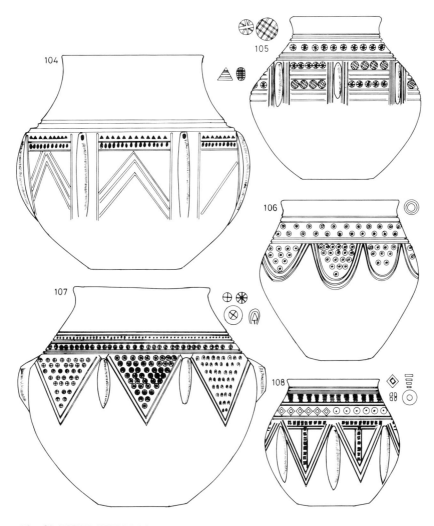

Fig. 20. PANEL STYLES AS DECORATION. (Scale ¼; stamps ½)
104. Urn with rectangular panel style with bosses, from Broughton, near Malton, North Yorkshire.
105. Urn with horizontal lines and stamps as panels between bosses, from Kettering Stamford Road, Northamptonshire.
106. Urn with stamped swags, from St John's College Cricket Field, Cambridge.
107. Urn with triangular panels of stamped ornament, from St John's College Cricket Field, Cambridge; there are five similarly decorated urns from this site.
108. Urn with triangular panels of ornament between bosses, from St John's College Cricket Field, Cambridge.

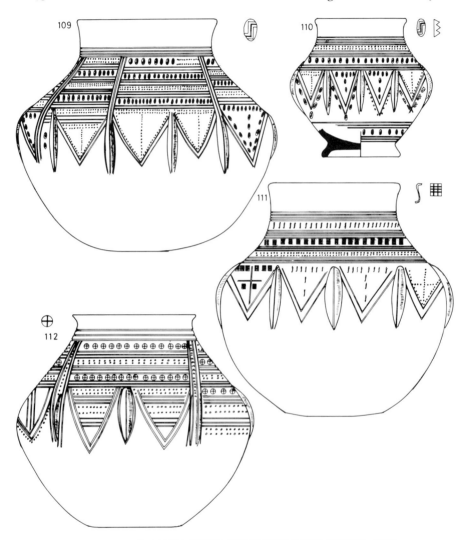

Fig. 21. TRIANGULAR PANEL-STYLE ORNAMENT WITH BOSSES: THE KETTERING LONG-BOSS POTTER AND HIS PRODUCTS. (Scale ¼; stamps ½)

109 and 112. Urns from Kettering Stamford Road, Northamptonshire, with long bosses dividing linear ornament with stamps and a series of triangular panels of ornament. Fragments of a third urn are extant.

110. Small-footed urn from Thorpe Malsor, Northamptonshire, with double dots and a stamp similar to that on 109.

111. Urn from Newton-in-the-Willows, Northamptonshire, with double dots as a feature of the ornament.

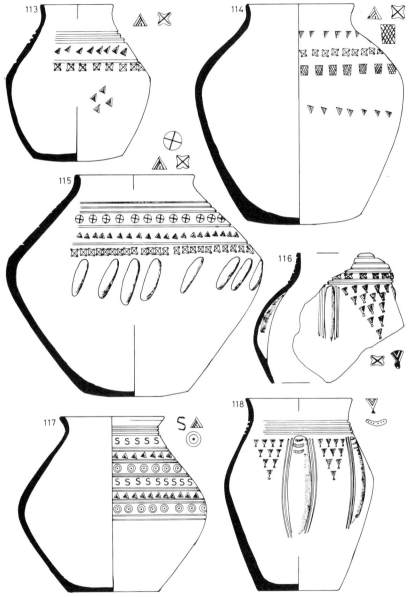

Fig. 22. LINEAR DECORATION WITH STAMPS AND PANEL STYLES: THE KETTERING I POTTER. (Scale ¼; stamps ½)
113, 114 and 115. Urns from Kettering Stamford Road, Northamptonshire.
116. Sherd of large urn from Islip, Northamptonshire.
117. Urn from Holdenby, Northamptonshire.
118. Urn from Burton Latimer, Northamptonshire.
Urns 113, 114, 115 and 117 share a triangular stamp; urns 113, 114, 115 and 116 share a cross stamp; urns 116 and 118 share a wine-glass stamp.

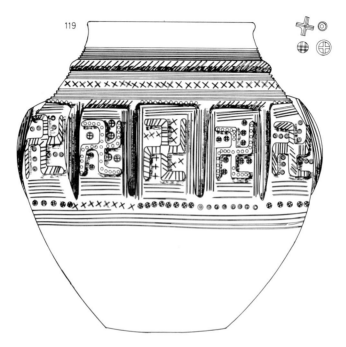

Fig. 23. SIXTH-CENTURY POTTERY. (Scale ¼; stamp ½)
119. Large vessel by the Icklingham potter, from Lackford, Suffolk.

Opposite page

Fig. 24. SIXTH-CENTURY POTTERY. (Scale ¼; stamps ½)
120. Vessel with panels of ornament placed in spaces defined by vertical lines; nine panels are present using seven stamps in eight designs. Urn found at St John's College Cricket Field, Cambridge. 121. The long-boss style with bosses alternating with vertical grooves on pot from Linton Heath, Cambridgeshire. 122. The long-boss style with vertical lines on accessory vessel from East Shefford, Berkshire. 123. Panels of ornament between bosses; the panels alternate on this pot from St John's College Cricket Field, Cambridge. 124. Melon-ribbing, a form of reverse bosses, on vessel from Sandy, Bedfordshire. 125. Triangular panel style of ornament set between single melon ribs on urn from Kettering Stamford Road, Northamptonshire. 126. Linear ornament of zone of stamped swags on urn with girth bosses, from St John's College Cricket Field, Cambridge.

Sixth-century pottery

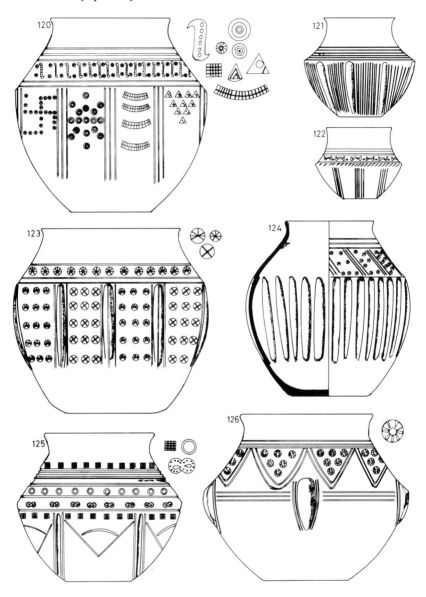

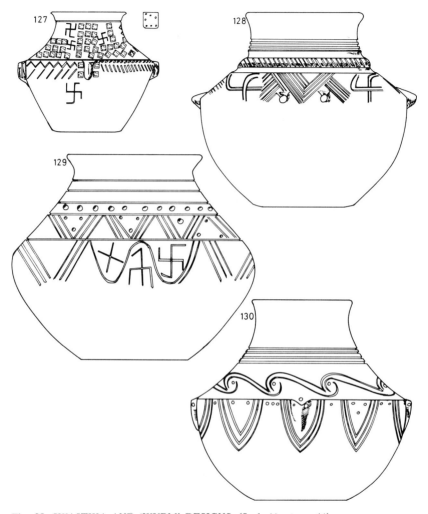

Fig. 25. SWASTIKA AND 'WYRM' DESIGNS. (Scale ¼; stamp ½)
127. Urn with a swastika used like a stamp, from Lackford, Suffolk.
128. Urn with drawn imitation double-line swastika, from The Mount, York.
129. Urn with swastika and swastika-derived designs included in a chevron pattern, from Great Casterton, Leicestershire.
130. Urn with 'wyrm' design from Kettering Stamford Road, Northamptonshire; sherds of a second urn of this design are known from the site.

Animals as decoration

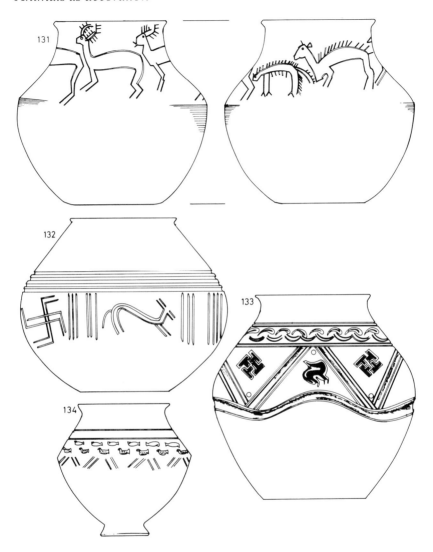

Fig. 26. ANIMALS AS DECORATION. (Scale ¼)
131. Drawn frieze of animals on Anglian urn from Linton Heath, Cambridgeshire (two views are shown).
132. Drawn animals, stylised on globular urn from Lackford, Suffolk.
133. Animal stamp as feature of seventh-century urn from Lackford, Suffolk.
134. Vessel with stamps shaped like fishes and ducks, from Lackford, Suffolk.

Anglo-Saxon Pottery

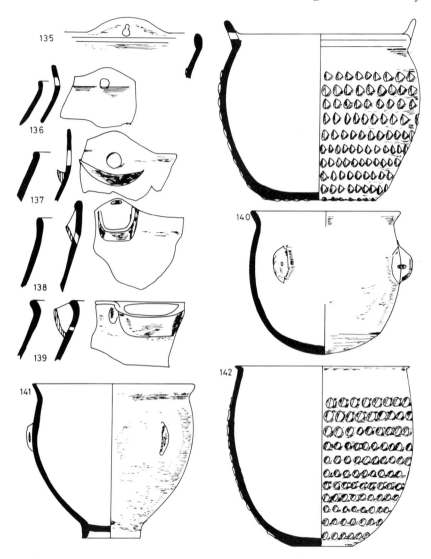

Fig. 27. LUGGED AND RUSTICATED VESSELS. (Scale ¼)
135. Cooking pot with rusticated outer surfaces and base and lug handles, from Lackford, Suffolk.
136-139. Four sherds showing the development of the bar-lip.
140. Round-based pot with side lugs, from St John's College Cricket Field, Cambridge.
141. Lugged pot with pedestal foot, from Newnham, Cambridge.
142. Rusticated vessel with plain base, from Lackford, Suffolk.

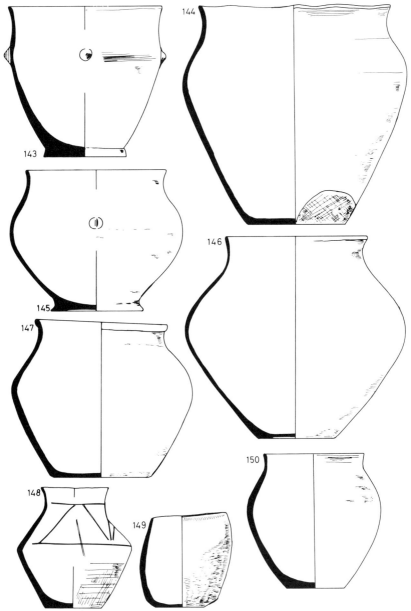

Fig. 28. COOKING POTS AND ACCESSORY VESSELS. (Scale ¼)
143-147 and 150. Cooking pots from Kempston, Bedfordshire, reused as cremation urns; 143 has four bosses, 145 has three pinched non-functional lugs.
148 and 149. Accessory vessels from Kempston, Bedfordshire.

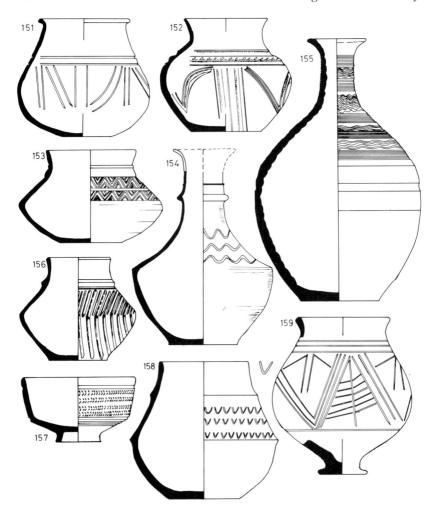

Fig. 29. JUTISH AND FRANKISH POTTERY FROM KENT AND THE ISLE OF WIGHT. (Scale ¼; stamp ½)
151. Jutish bowl from Howletts, Kent.
152. Jutish bowl from Faversham, Kent.
153. Wheel-made bowl from Faversham, Kent.
154. Wheel-made bottle from Strood, Kent; the rim is restored.
155. Wheel-made bottle from rich seventh-century grave at Wingham, Kent.
156. Wheel-made jar with ribbed surface, from Breach Down, Kent.
157. Imported bowl, wheel-made with rouletted decoration, from Chessel Down, Isle of Wight.
158. Wheel-made jar from Bourne, Kent, with V-shaped stamp.
159. Wheel-made jar from Chessel Down, Isle of Wight. The design may be a T rune.

Seventh-century pottery

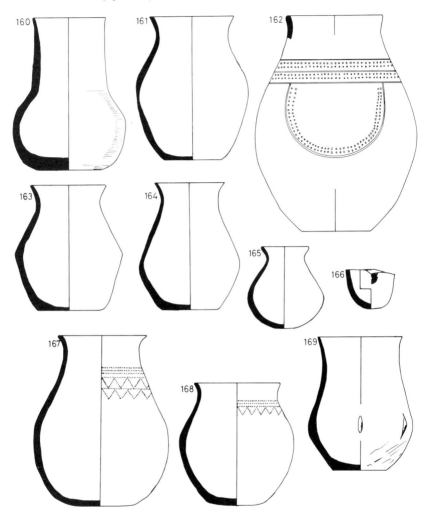

Fig. 30. SEVENTH-CENTURY POTTERY. (Scale ¼)
160. Plain accessory vessel from Chamberlains Barn, Leighton Buzzard, Bedfordshire.
161, 163 and 164. Plain accessory vessels from Kempston, Bedfordshire.
162. Cremation urn with rouletted swag, from St John's College Cricket Field, Cambridge.
165. Plain accessory jar from Chamberlains Barn, Leighton Buzzard, Bedfordshire.
166. Crucible from Chamberlains Barn, Leighton Buzzard, Bedfordshire.
167. Jar with comb-point decoration, from Chamberlains Barn, Leighton Buzzard, Bedfordshire.
168. Jar with comb-point decoration, from Marina Drive, Totternhoe, Bedfordshire.
169. Jar with small pinched-out bosses, from Cransley, Northamptonshire.

Anglo-Saxon Pottery

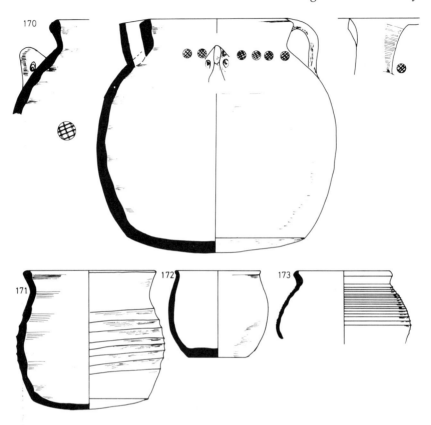

Fig. 31. MIDDLE SAXON POTTERY. (Scale ¼; stamps ½)
170. Ipswich ware pitcher from Richborough Castle, Kent, seventh to eighth century.
171. Ipswich ware cooking pot from Framlingham Castle, Suffolk, eighth to ninth century.
172. Hand-made cooking pot from Whitby, North Yorkshire, eighth to ninth century.
173. Whitby ware pot (lacks base) from Whitby, North Yorkshire, eighth to ninth century.

7
Museums

The museums listed have extensive collections of Anglo-Saxon pottery; their exhibitions are good and informative. The best way to become familiar with Anglo-Saxon pottery is to handle the pots in museum storerooms and basements. Most museums will readily grant facilities to do this provided that a prior appointment is made and confirmed in writing. The list notes the total number of pots and the most important constituent elements of the collection.

Ashmolean Museum of Art and Archaeology, Beaumont Street, Oxford OX1 2PH. Telephone: 0865 278000. 250 pots, include pieces from Abingdon (Oxfordshire), Fairford (Gloucestershire), Haslingfield and both cemeteries at Barrington (Cambridgeshire), Sancton (Humberside). Also pottery from domestic site at Sutton Courtenay (Oxfordshire).

Bedford Museum, Castle Lane, Bedford MK40 3XD. Telephone: 0234 53323 or 54954. 40 pots from cemetery at Kempston, settlement site at Harrold.

British Museum, Great Russell Street, London WC1B 3DG. Telephone: 01-636 1555. 250 pots, no one geographical emphasis: cemetery material includes pots from Burton Latimer (Northamptonshire), Croydon (London), Faversham and Howletts (both Kent), Kempston (Bedfordshire), Kirton-in-Lindsey (Humberside), Loveden Hill and Sleaford (both Lincolnshire).

Cambridge University Museum of Archaeology and Anthropology, Downing Street, Cambridge CB2 3DZ. Telephone: 0223 333516 or 337733. 1800 pots, including all of the finds made at Lackford in 1947, finds made at St John's College Cricket Field, Cambridge, in 1888, and those made in 1881 and 1886 at Girton College. Also the 100 surviving pots from Little Wilbraham, and pots found in inhumation graves in various Suffolk cemeteries.

Castle Museum, Norwich, Norfolk NR1 3JU. Telephone: 0603 611277 extension 24. 3700 pots, including cemeteries found at

60   *Anglo-Saxon Pottery*

Caistor St Edmund, Castle Acre, Field Dalling, Illington, Markshall, Spong Hill (North Elmham); more recent finds from last-named are with Norfolk Archaeological Unit at Union House, Gressenhall, East Dereham.

Herbert Art Gallery and Museum, Jordan Well, Coventry, West Midlands CV1 5RW. Telephone: 0203 833333. 84 pots from ill recorded site at Baginton, West Midlands.

Hull Transport and Archaeology Museum, 36 High Street, Hull, North Humberside HU1 1NQ. Telephone: 0482 222737. The Mortimer Archaeological Collection includes 800 pots, mostly from Sancton, including unpublished material of excavations by N. Reynolds between 1976 and 1980.

Lincoln City and County Museum, Broadgate, Lincoln LN2 1HQ. Telephone: 0522 30401. 2000 pots, from Ancaster, Baston, Loveden Hill, South Elkington, West Keal.

Maidstone Museum and Art Gallery, St Faith's Street, Maidstone, Kent ME14 1LH. Telephone: 0622 54497. 60 pots from Sarre, Bifrons and other sites excavated in the nineteenth century.

Moyse's Hall, Cornhill, Bury St Edmunds, Suffolk IP33 1DX. Telephone: 0284 63233 extensions 2112 and 2113. 200 pots from cemetery and settlement at West Stow; some of the 1874 and 1914 discoveries at Lackford.

Museum of London, London Wall, London EC2Y 5HN. Telephone: 01-600 3699. Collection includes cemetery material from Mitcham (London), and growing number of Saxon pots found in domestic contexts in the City of London.

Newark Museum and Art Gallery, Appletongate, Newark, Nottinghamshire NG24 1JY. Telephone: 0636 702358. 400 pots from cemetery at Newark.

Northampton Central Museum and Art Gallery, Guildhall Road, Northampton NN1 1DP. Telephone: 0604 37413. 150 pots, including part of the finds from Kettering Stamford Road, most of those from other sites in the county, for example, Brixworth, Holdenby, Islip.

Museums 61

Peterborough City Museum and Art Gallery, Priestgate, Peterborough, Cambridgeshire PE1 1LF. Telephone: 0733 43329. 50
pots from cemeteries at Longthorpe, Nassington and Woodstone; also material from settlement site of seventh and eighth
centuries at Maxey.

Rutland County Museum, Catmos Street, Oakham, Rutland,
Leicestershire LE15 6HW. Telephone: 0572 3654. 80 pots from
Great Casterton, Empingham, Market Overton, North Luf-
fenham.

Yorkshire Museum, Museum Gardens, York, North Yorkshire
YO1 2DR. Telephone: 0904 29745. 80 pots; Heworth, The
Mount, Broughton near Malton.

8
Further reading

There are few books about Anglo-Saxon pottery. Much work is published as reports on cemeteries and domestic sites; the more recent of these are listed below, together with the few general books and some articles in periodicals which should be accessible in larger libraries. The latter deal with more specialist aspects of the subject.

Arnold, C. J. *An Archaeology of the Early Anglo-Saxon Kingdoms*. 1988. Especially pages 75-80 and 110-18. Recent introduction to context, emphasises the social aspect of archaeological research.

Briscoe, T. 'Anglo-Saxon Pot Stamps', *Anglo-Saxon Studies in Archaeology and History*, 2 (1981), 1-36. Analysis and classification based on 3677 individual pot stamps.

Briscoe, T. 'The Use of Brooches and Other Jewellery as Dies on Pagan Anglo-Saxon Pottery', *Medieval Archaeology*, 29 (1985), 136-42.

Cook, A. M. *The Anglo-Saxon Cemetery at Fonaby, Lincolnshire*. Society for Lincolnshire Archaeology, 1981. Report on mixed-rite cemetery discovered in 1956; 28 pots including 12 cremation urns. Material in Scunthorpe Borough Museum.

Cook, A. M., and Dacre, M. W. *Excavations at Portway, Andover 1973-1975*. Oxford University Committee for Archaeology, 1985. 65 pots from cemetery with 87 cremations including un-urned. Andover Museum.

Drury, P. J., and Wickenden, N. P. 'An Early Saxon Settlement within the Romano-British Small Town at Heybridge, Essex', *Medieval Archaeology*, 26 (1982), 1-40.

Eagles, B. N. *The Anglo-Saxon Settlement of Humberside*. 1979. Two-volume work with many illustrations. Good with comparative items for cemeteries at Heworth, near York, Kirton-in-Lindsey, South Elkington, West Keal.

Evison, V. I. (editor). *Angles, Saxons and Jutes: Essays Presented to J. N. L. Myres*. 1981. Contains essays by P. Schmid on bowls from the continental domestic site at Feddersen Wierde, near Bremerhaven; by B. Green, W. F. Milligan and S. E. West on 'The Illington/Lackford Workshop', a pottery style found in East Anglia; and by D. Brown on 'Swastika Patterns,' linking metalwork to pottery styles.

Evison, V. I. (editor). *Medieval Pottery from Excavations:*

Further reading 63

Studies Presented to Gerald Clough Dunning. 1974. Contains essays by V. I. Evison on 'The Asthall Type of Bottle', a wheel-thrown pot, and by P. Rahtz on 'Pottery in Somerset, AD 400-1066', a contrasting type to that prevalent in eastern England.

Evison, V. I. *Wheel-Thrown Pottery in Anglo-Saxon Graves.* Royal Archaeological Institute, 1979. A full corpus of pots akin to vessels 153-9 of the present book.

Farley, M. 'Saxon and Medieval Walton, Aylesbury, Excavations 1973-4', *Records of Buckinghamshire*, 20 part 2 (1976). Well reported domestic site.

Hills, C. *The Anglo-Saxon Cemetery at Spong Hill, North Elmham Part I*. Norfolk Archaeological Unit, 1977. Beginning of publication of large cemetery known since 1711 and from which 2322 pots were excavated in 1968 and between 1972 and 1982. Further reports: *Part II* (1981), *Part III* (1984), *Part IV* (1987); additional reports in preparation.

Hurst, J. G. 'The Pottery' in D. M. Wilson (editor), *The Archaeology of Anglo-Saxon England*, 283-349. 1976. Valuable for Middle Saxon pottery; weaker on earlier period.

Kennett, D. H. 'Pottery and Other Finds from the Anglo-Saxon Cemetery at Sandy, Bedfordshire', *Medieval Archaeology*, 14 (1970), 17-33. Seeks out the scattered finds from one cemetery. 14 pots found at various dates, 1740 to 1866, now in four museums: Bedford Museum; Cambridge University Museum of Archaeology and Anthropology; British Museum, London; and Ashmolean Museum, Oxford.

Kinsley, G. *The Anglo-Saxon Cemetery at Millgate, Newark-on-Trent, Nottinghamshire*. Archaeology Section, University of Nottingham, 1989. Report on excavations between 1958 and 1978 on a site known since before 1742 and explored intermittently since then.

Lethbridge, T. C. *A Cemetery at Lackford*. Cambridge Antiquarian Society, 1951. Old-style report, illustrates only 150 of the 500 pots excavated in 1947. Drawings generally very good.

Mayes, P., and Dean, M. J. *An Anglo-Saxon Cemetery at Baston, Lincolnshire*. Society for Lincolnshire History and Archaeology, 1976. 44 pots from cemetery excavated 1966; material in Lincoln City and County Museum.

Miles, D., and Palmer, S. *Invested in Mother Earth*. Oxford Archaeological Unit, 1985. Interim report on mainly inhumation cemetery at Lechlade, Gloucestershire, which produced also 32 cremation urns.

Myres, J. N. L. *Anglo-Saxon Pottery and the Settlement of England*. 1969. A good introduction with correlation to documentary background but weak on cross-dating and other considerations of metalwork and inhumation graves. Drawings usually less stylised than those of the same author's *A Corpus of Anglo-Saxon Pottery of the Pagan Period*.

Myres, J. N. L. 'The Anglo-Saxon Pottery of Lincolnshire', *Archaeological Journal*, 108 (1951), 65-89. Published in the same issue as the report on the major cemetery from South Elkington. Together these form the only full county survey but necessarily omit the finds of the last forty years.

Myres, J. N. L. 'The Anglo-Saxon Pottery of Norfolk', *Norfolk Archaeology*, 27 (1939), 185-212. Preliminary survey, illustrated mainly by photographs.

Myres, J. N. L. *A Corpus of Anglo-Saxon Pottery of the Pagan Period*. 1977. Vast, two-volume work which tries to figure all complete pots known before about 1974 which were then surviving. Omits pots known only from manuscript illustrations. On that basis reasonably complete for most counties, but not for Northamptonshire or Cambridgeshire. Most of the 750 pages are catalogue and drawings of over 4000 pots. Drawings intelligible but need to be used with care.

Myres, J. N. L., and Green, B. *The Anglo-Saxon Cemeteries of Caistor-by-Norwich and Markshall*. 1973. Full report on 502 cremation urns and 57 inhumation burials from the first excavated by Surgeon-Commander F. R. Mann between 1932 and 1938; over 100 vessels from the second recorded by G. P. Larwood in 1948. Dating offered has been considered exceptionally early. Material in Castle Museum, Norwich.

Myres, J. N. L., and Southern, W. H. *The Anglo-Saxon Cemetery at Sancton, East Yorkshire*. Hull Museums, 1973. Catalogue and good drawings of 144 pots recorded at various dates from 1854 to 1909 and 200 pots excavated between 1954 and 1958. Material in Hull Museums and the Ashmolean Museum, Oxford.

Neville, R. C. *Saxon Obsequies Illustrated*. 1852. Magnificent aquatint illustrations of complete urns found at mixed-rite cemetery in 1851 at Little Wilbraham, Cambridgeshire.

Richards, J. D. *The Significance and Form of Anglo-Saxon Cremation Urns*. 1987. Reviews cremation pottery from a symbolic standpoint and uses a computer to evaluate the importance of vessel shape. The opening seventy pages are abstruse anthropological writing; the rest offers a new per-

Further reading 65

spective on the importance of shape and associations.

West, S. E. *West Stow Anglo-Saxon Village*. Suffolk County Planning Department, 1985. Report on the village and its finds excavated 1957 to 1961 and 1965 to 1972. Much pottery. Includes report on mixed-rite cemetery found in 1849 and 1852.

Williams, P. W. *An Anglo-Saxon Cemetery at Thurmaston, Leicestershire*. Leicestershire Museum, 1983. Account of cemetery of 119 urns excavated in 1954; material in Leicester Museum.

Various editors. 'Medieval Britain in 19xx'. Annual review of past year's work in each issue of the periodical *Medieval Archaeology*. As yet the source for new finds at Compton Appledown, Elsham, Field Dalling, Springfield near Chelmsford and Worthy Park; also for recent excavations at Newark, Sancton and Snape.

Periodicals

Three periodicals regularly carry articles about Anglo-Saxon pottery: these are *Anglo-Saxon Studies in Archaeology and History* (an occasional serial publication of the Oxford University Committee for Archaeology), *Antiquaries Journal* (two issues per year, Society of Antiquaries of London) and *Medieval Archaeology* (annual publication of the Society for Medieval Archaeology). Some county periodicals also have papers on the subject, particularly since about 1969: *Bedfordshire Archaeological Journal* (now *Bedfordshire Archaeology*), *Proceedings of the Cambridge Antiquarian Society* and *Lincolnshire History and Archaeology*.

Index

Abingdon, Oxfordshire 19, 59
Accessory vessels 22
Alveston, Warwickshire 19
Ancaster, Lincolnshire 19, 60
Andover, Hampshire 17, 18, 62
Anglian urns 21
Animals as decoration 26
Arched grooves 22
Arnold, C. J. 62
Asthall-type bottle 27, 56, 63
Baginton, Coventry 19, 60
Bar-lip pottery 11, 28, 54
Barrington, Cambridgeshire 36, 59
Bases 11-12, 21
Baston, Lincolnshire 19, 60, 63
Beowulf 26
Bidford-on-Avon, Warwickshire 19
Bifrons, Kent 60
Bosses 11, 23-5, 31
Bottles 27, 56, 63
Bourne, Kent 56
Bowls 22, 36
Breach Down, Kent 56
Brettenham, Norfolk 15, 19
Briscoe, T. 62
Brixworth, Northamptonshire 30, 31, 33, 60
Broughton, North Yorkshire 47, 61
Buckelurnen 11, 22, 23, 24
Burgh Castle, Norfolk 17
Burton Latimer, Northamptonshire 25, 31, 43, 49, 59
Caistor St Edmund, Norfolk 8, 12, 15, 19, 60, 64
Cassington, Oxfordshire 12
Castle Acre, Norfolk 8, 15, 19, 30, 39, 41, 44, 60
Chamberlain's Barn, Leighton Buzzard, Bedfordshire 57
Chessel Down, Isle of Wight 56
Chevron designs 22-3
Compton Appledown, West Sussex 17, 19, 65
Cook, A. M. 62
Cransley, Northamptonshire 57
Croydon, London 8, 10, 24, 59
Dating 20
Dersingham, Norfolk 38
Distribution 15-19
Domestic pottery 26, 28-9
Downham Market, Norfolk 44
Drayton Lodge, Norfolk 17
Drury, P. J. 62
Duston, Northamptonshire 36
Eagles, B. J. 62
East Shefford, Berkshire 23, 32, 40, 42, 51
Elsham, Humberside 15, 19, 65
Empingham, Leicestershire 61
Evison, V. I. 62, 63
Eye, Suffolk 19
Fairford, Gloucestershire 59
Farley, M. 63

Index

67

Faversham, Kent 56, 59
Field Dalling, Norfolk 15, 19, 60
Fonaby, Lincolnshire 19, 62
Framlingham Castle, Suffolk 58
Frisian-Angle urns 21
Girton College, Cambridge 18, 59
Globular urns 21, 22
Great Casterton, Leicestershire 52, 61
Great Walsingham, Norfolk 15, 19
Green, B. 64
Haslingfield, Cambridgeshire 59
Heworth, North Yorkshire 10, 19, 30, 31, 32, 34, 35, 36, 38, 40, 61, 62
Heybridge, Essex 62
Hills, C. 63
Holdenby, Northamptonshire 25, 49, 60
Howletts, Kent 26, 39, 56, 59
Hurst, J. G. 63
'Icklingham potter' 10, 25, 62
Illington, Norfolk 15, 19, 25, 60, 62
Imported pottery 7, 26
Ipswich, Suffolk 28
Ipswich-type wares 29, 58
Isle of Wight 26
Islip, Northamptonshire 25, 49, 60
Jutes 26
Kempston, Bedfordshire 17, 18, 26, 28, 30, 41, 44, 55, 57, 59
Kennett, D. H. 63
Kent 26, 56
Kettering, Northamptonshire 19, 25, 30, 38, 39, 47, 48, 49, 51, 52, 60
Kettering long-boss potter 25, 48
King's Newton, Derbyshire 18
Kingston-on-Soar, Nottinghamshire 19
Kinsley, G. 63
Kirton-in-Lindsey, Humberside 19, 35, 46, 59, 62
Lackford, Suffolk 12-13, 19, 20, 23, 25, 28, 45, 46, 50, 52, 53, 54, 59, 60, 62, 63
Lechlade, Gloucestershire 17, 18, 63
Lethbridge, T. C. 6, 8, 63
Lids 26
Lincoln 60
Linear ornament 22-3, 24, 32, 34, 35, 36, 37, 38, 39, 44, 45, 49
Linton Heath, Cambridgeshire 40, 51, 53
Little Wilbraham, Cambridgeshire 8, 18, 59, 64
London, City of 60
Longthorpe, Peterborough, Cambridgeshire 61
Long Wittenham, Oxfordshire 19
Loveden Hill, Lincolnshire 15, 59, 60
Luton, Bedfordshire 36, 42
Mann, F. R. 12, 64
Marina Drive, Totternhoe, Bedfordshire 57
Market Overton, Leicestershire 33, 61
Markshall, Norfolk 15, 19, 60, 64
Maxey, Cambridgeshire 29, 61
Mayes, P. 63
Middle Saxon pottery 29, 58
Mitcham, London 7, 36, 60
Mucking, Essex 15, 18
Myres, J. N. L. 8, 63-4
Nassington, Northamptonshire 61
Neville, R. C. 64

68 — *Anglo-Saxon Pottery*

Newark, Nottinghamshire 15, 19, 60, 63
Newnham, Cambridgeshire 44, 45, 54
Newton-in-the-Willows, Northamptonshire 25, 48
Northamptonshire potters 7, 25, 48, 49
North Luffenham, Leicestershire 61
Panel styles 24-5, 47-51
Pitsford, Northamptonshire 45
Rendlesham, Suffolk 17
Reynolds, N. 60
Richards, J. D. 64
Richborough Castle, Kent 58
Rusticated urns 28-9, 54
St John's College, Cambridge 10, 11, 15, 18, 22, 23, 28, 31, 32, 33, 35, 36, 37, 38, 39, 40, 41, 47, 51, 54, 57, 59
Sancton, Humberside 15, 19, 59, 60, 64, 65
Sandy, Bedfordshire 8, 24, 36, 38, 40, 41, 42, 51, 63
Sarre, Kent 60
Sedgeford, Norfolk 46
Shouldered urns 22
Shropham, Norfolk 8, 9, 15
Sleaford, Lincolnshire 59
Snape, Suffolk 19, 65
Snettisham, Norfolk 36
Souldern, Oxfordshire 8, 24, 42
South Elkington, Humberside 19, 60, 62, 64
Spong Hill, North Elmham, Norfolk 15, 19, 26, 60, 63
Springfield, Essex 18, 65
Stamps 12, 13, 24, 25, 33, 36, 37, 39, 45, 46-51
Strood, Kent 56
Sutton Bonnington, Nottinghamshire 17
Sutton Courtenay, Oxfordshire 8, 59
Swastika ornament 25, 52
Thor (Thunor) 26
Thorpe Malsor, Northamptonshire 25, 48
Thurmaston, Leicestershire 19, 23, 65
Tottenhill, Norfolk 46
Walton, Buckinghamshire 28, 63
West, S. E. 65
West Keal, Lincolnshire 19, 60, 62
West Stow Heath, Suffolk 12, 28, 60, 65
Whitby, North Yorkshire 20, 58
Whitby-type ware 29, 58
Williams, P. W. 65
Wingham, Kent 27, 56
Woodstone, Cambridgeshire 61
Worthy Park, Hampshire 18, 65
York 43, 52, 61

Cambridge

Gary and Christy Bonn

First published in the UK in 2014.
Copyright © 2014 Gary and Christian (Christy) Bonn
The rights of Gary and (Christy) Christian Bonn to be
identified as the authors of this work have been asserted in
accordance with sections 77 and 78 of the Copyright Designs
and Patents Act 1988.
Cover design copyright © 2014 Gary and Christian
(Christy) Bonn.
All rights reserved.
This book is sold subject to the condition that it shall not,
by way of trade or commence, be lent, resold, hired out or
otherwise circulated. No part of this publication may be
reproduced, stored in a retrieval system or transmitted, in any
form or by any means, without the prior permission in writing
of the author, nor be otherwise circulated in any form of
binding or cover other than that in which it is published and
without similar condition including this condition being
imposed on the subsequent purchaser.

ISBN-13: 978-1503252882
ISBN-10: 1503252884

Chapter 1

Look down over Cambridgeshire, down between the puffy white clouds caught in an easterly breeze and totally failing to drop any rain on the parched lawns and fields. The clouds are saving it for Wales. Once there, they'll swell, turn dark, consider hailstorms, and pick on sheep.

There are the pinnacles, spires, ancient colleges, and parks of Cambridge; a place that thinks it has the best university in the world. It holds this opinion as do many cities but with Cambridge it's almost a religion. You can imagine the city tapping the shoulders of passers-by and saying, "Ahem, we have the best university in the world, you know." This would probably not be regarded as assault unless the person came from Oxford.

Today Cambridge fills with tension and adrenaline. It's also filling with cars, buses, trains, the barely controlled hysteria and panic of those about to attend college interviews, and one bursting bladder.

Take the train clanking into the station right now. It carries several bundles of panic. One of them, Cheryl, in a daze of torment, tries not to think about her interviews. She might just as easily try to blow out the sun. She clutches her hands tight, unclasps them, smooths her skirt, checks her collar's

1

straight...

Juliet sits opposite, bare arms resting on the table between them. Indeed, she's opposite in many ways: for instance, Cheryl is a picture of spotless, middle-class conformity; Juliet, with spiky hair, facial studs, and torn jeans stuffed into calf-length para-boots, is not.

Juliet's not panicking; she's exhausted, trying to nurse her best friend through the train journey and get her to the interviews in a mental state that will enable Cheryl to answer questions without hiding under a chair. Right now Juliet's wondering why Cheryl is so ridiculously intelligent but unsure of herself at the same time. On one hand Cheryl has an IQ of 160 +, on the other, she becomes tongue-tied over questions like, 'What's up?', although, if you think about it, that's a really complicated question for someone who understands the theory of relativity.

Juliet and Cheryl have been friends from toddler group, all the way through school, and share clothes, makeup, free time —and Cheryl steals Juliet's boyfriends when Juliet starts to scare them.

Cheryl has also been out with both of Juliet's brothers. The brothers had a lifetime of growing up with a younger sister they considered a second-class person—even species. Juliet's quick wits, sharp tongue, and bullet-like knuckles made it clear she was not. She grew up hard; they grew up bruised and attracted to their next-door neighbour, Cheryl, whom they considered relatively feminine and demure. Cheryl was a delight to them—until they realised her brain could beat both of theirs put together, without her twitching an intellectual eyelash.

Another difference between Juliet and Cheryl is that Cheryl left school with enough A-grades for a small village of pupils—Juliet left school as early as she could, determined to be the world's first passionate plumber.

Juliet loves the way Cheryl asked her to go to Cambridge on this critical day. She thinks it's just about the biggest compliment she's ever had and is seriously considering forgiving Cheryl at least one boyfriend snatch. Maybe one during primary school.

"Cheryl, stop bloody fidgeting. Your hands are like spiders on caffeine."

Cheryl jerks from her pre-interview hell back into reality. "Oh ... what? I'm not really nervous..." She smooths her skirt again and clutches her handbag tight. "What's there to be nervous about?" She chews a fingernail.

Juliet can't help chuckling. "Um ... not getting a place at Cambridge?" She thinks, Oops, wrong thing to say. Cheryl needs an argument not more panic. "Of course you'll get in." She thinks Cheryl's bound to argue with that. Again.

Cheryl widens her eyes. "But the interviews are awful."

"Oddly enough, I do remember you telling me about them. Roughly at twenty-minute intervals for the last month."

"They're going to put something I've never seen in my hands and ask me what it is."

"Never seen? Then at least it won't be a penis. Tell them it's a deep-sea or freshwater thingummy."

"What if it's a cryptovolans vertebra?"

"Didn't they come out of the sea?"

"No. They were..."

Juliet interrupts just in time to avoid another of Cheryl's

attempts to educate her. "I know for a fact that crypto … wot you said, liked swimming and sunbathing. They invented the bikini; everyone knows that."

Cheryl's tension melts a bit and she's giggling, if a little hysterically.

Juliet relaxes, thinking she's at last making progress with Cheryl's nerves.

Cheryl says, "You're fidgeting too."

"Too right. I need a piss but I refuse to use train toilets. Men use them and I don't want to stick to the seat."

The train squeals, screeches, and rattles itself to a halt. Cheryl leans forward and clutches Juliet's fingers. "Oh God, we're here. Thanks so much for coming. I couldn't face this without you."

Her big grateful eyes break Juliet's heart. Juliet says, "I came to look after Cambridge while you're here, not the other way around."

Cheryl's happy smile is formed of three crescents, eyes and mouth. The mouth curving low at the middle, the eyelids curving up—a smile that makes men flex muscles and walk into lampposts. Juliet thinks, Yay! she's smiled at last. I've done it.

As they get up, Cheryl opens her handbag and squeaks. "I've lost my map of Cambridge!"

"Nobody can lose a map they were given less than an hour ago when they haven't moved since."

"No, really; it's gone."

"OK, apart from you. Take mine."

"Where would I be without you?"

"Right now? Probably in Antarctica and asking where

King's College is."

~

At the last moment, when interviewees are split from parents and friends, Cheryl clutches Juliet's T-shirt, and says, "It's going to be alright, isn't it?"

Juliet's heart breaks again. Cheryl is pale and close to tears.

Juliet hugs her, pulls back, pretends to tidy Cheryl's hair, and says, "It'll be fine if you don't scare them with your mighty intellect." Juliet plays her trump card. She looks down. "Actually, it's me that's scared."

"Why?" says Cheryl.

"You'll get in, I know it. You'll be moving up in the world. We'll still be friends, right? You won't forget me?" She almost hates herself for manipulating like this but it rescues Cheryl from panic.

Cheryl relaxes. Her face fills with confidence. "Of course ... oh, Juliet ... how could you even think...?" She's pulled away in the tide of movement and gives a parting wave.

A weight lifts from Juliet's soul. Cheryl, pale, lip-biting and fidgeting, is safely in the hands of people who will probably not lose her.

Juliet takes a deep breath, clears her mind, and thinks, Cambridge! city of old buildings, books, and student-priced clothes. You're mine, all mine—after I've had a piss.

The Ladies' toilets in the college are crammed with middle-aged mums elbowing each other out of the way. Juliet believes her elbows are harder, more experienced, and her spiky hair and facial studs mark her out as a scary person, so getting a cubicle shouldn't be difficult.

A freezing jet of water erupts from a bursting pipe and blasts her makeup off, at, she guesses, over a thousand kilopascals.

"Bloody wot!" Under pressure, Juliet's normal eloquence can slip into secondary-school snash.

The janitor's screams harmonise perfectly with those of the other women, most of whom have stopped milling around in earnest silence and started running around screaming instead.

The snapped plastic pipe jerks and thrashes like a conductor's baton. Arcs of water scythe through the panic. The terrified janitor's no help. She's got the maintenance door open, and is dithering as if already at the limit of her technical expertise.

Juliet pulls her away, shouting, "I'll sort it." She reaches in, closes the mains stopcock, and notes the plumbing controls are a mixture of brand-new-shiny and antediluvian-cobwebbed.

The water stops hurtling across the room and calms to a dribble.

"Thank you," whimpers the janitor.

"No worries. I'll just put my knickers and socks under the hand dryer for an hour or two and all will be well."

The room's nearly empty of people now; the tiled walls, running with water, considerably cleaner than when Juliet came in. The only people remaining are herself, the janitor, and a twinset-and-pearls middle-aged woman sitting on the sink unit and keeping her feet above the diminishing flood.

Juliet says to the janitor, "Right, whoever put this lot in was a total git. There's your problem. That's only a single-stage pressure-regulator and it's not up to the job and ... holy what? who ran the in-pipe next to the hot water? Amateurs! You'll need a thermal expansion chamber." She leans in further and thinks, They haven't removed any of the old plumbing. Blimey, there's enough copper and lead here to buy half the city. She says, "If I load the old cistern, you'll be back in business 'til all this can be sorted." She reaches in and the spiky yellow teeth of a rat go for her fingers.

The janitor screams even louder and, arms flapping around her head, runs out of the Ladies'.

Juliet says to the rat, "Bite me, kiddo, and I'll turn you into a furry scrotum warmer and give you to my granddad for Christmas. Think hard; there are several stages involved and none of them are likely to be fun for you." She leans on her elbows and stares into the shiny black eyes. "For instance, think about the first. It involves you, me, a basin wrench, and a sad little squeak."

The rat blinks, retreats, scurries into the gloom, and nervously gnaws something.

Juliet says, "If that's you chewing an electrical cable, stop this instant. At least wait until I'm out of the room."

Blissful silence.

Juliet pulls an ancient lever, spins two valves and opens the mains, filling the place with the music of a tank gurgling. Nothing explodes, collapses, or goes wrong. Juliet thinks, They don't make plumbers like they used to.

She jumps and bangs her head on a pipe when twinset-woman's voice, coming from right beside her, says, "Do animals ever talk back to you?"

Juliet notes the woman's heavy German accent. "No! do you often ask strangers that?" She drags her top half out of the maintenance unit and wonders how she's going to remove seventy years' worth of cobwebs from her hair, face, arms and T-shirt. A glance at herself in a mirror makes her think, I look like a grey-haired gorilla, albeit a rather scrawny one.

The woman looks her up and down. "You come to my department, ja? You can wash and have your clothes cleaned. You're a liability looking like that. If you pass any anthropologists they'll freak and start writing papers."

Great, Juliet thinks, is she some sort of kinky person that wants to watch me undress? Ho hum, interesting: do I put myself into the hands of a weirdo or go around all day looking like a weirdo? She looks pretty odd with all that wild grey hair and the way she stares at me like I'm food or something.

Juliet replies, "Sounds great," and follows her out of the Ladies'.

The crowded mums outside look at Juliet with a variety of expressions, most of which she interprets as either, 'Oh, poor thing' or, 'I'm glad it's her and not me'.

The janitor, knuckles pressed to her pale cheeks, says to Juliet, "Is it still there? The rat ... did you kill it?"

"Yes, it's still there and alive in an electrical Schrődinger sort of way. If it gives you any hassle, just say, 'Sweaty old testicles' to it. Never fails."

Juliet and the woman walk down the oak-panelled corridor. Short and squat, the pearls swinging across her tweed jacket, the woman studies Juliet. "How come a teenager knows so much about plumbing?"

"I'm a plumber—well my mum is. I'm her apprentice. I replaced my first washer at the age of five."

"You sound too intelligent to be a plumber. More like an academic, ja?"

"Nobody can be too intelligent to be a plumber. In fact, I'm way too intelligent to be an academic."

That has the woman stumped. She looks at Juliet, blank expression and no words.

Juliet goes on, "My uncle is an academic, a senior lecturer. Politics, pressure, schemes, egos, and papers, endless papers, endless rivalry and sucking up to industry for funding. Mum is a plumber, works when and where she wants. No hassle and you get to practise contortions that would have the writers of the Kama Sutra looking like amateurs. Of the two choices, what would you go for?"

They turn corner after corner, trot across a windy quadrangle, and enter a building that, Juliet thinks, if it isn't already a museum, should at least be in one.

Old has a smell. Ancient is the concentrate. This building is filled with the distillation. Sunlight, coming through high arched windows, angles down in bright shafts making patches of carpet shine like jewels.

Juliet thinks, Oh boy! I could work in a place like this. There must be enough lead in the plumbing to make me twitch with joy. I bet you could replace everything here for free and still come away a scrap-metal millionaire.

She says to the woman, "Um ... what's your name?"

"How impolite of me. Call me Hildegarde. And yours?"

"Juliet. Uh ... with all the fun in the toilets, I never got to use one. Are there any around here?"

Hildegarde narrows her eyes and tips her head to one side. "Ja." She points between stone pillars to a door of inlaid wood. "There."

Hmm, Juliet thinks, why the narrowed eyes? She suspects my other intention? The door opens silently as she pushes it and enters a heaven designed just for her. She gasps, giddy with excitement, "The taps alone must be nearly a hundred years old. The sinks ... are ... OMG!" She darts round touching things, running her fingers over patterned ceramic basins, and totally forgets that someone is waiting for her. She dives into a cubicle. "Yes! Victorian toilets ... and the pipe running from the cistern has a..."

She leaps onto the quartered oak seat, caresses a join, and thinks, Someone stood up here maybe over a hundred years ago and...

Hildegarde, wondering what the delay is, pushes the door open, clomps across the tiled floor, and barks at Juliet, "Are you alright? If you need to use the toilet standing up, I'd suggest opening the seat first." The strident voice fails to make Juliet jump again—she's in a world of bliss.

She murmurs, "A man stood here. He had molten lead. He wiped it with a moleskin glove ... look, it's perfect. A perfect lead olive seal made by a real craftsman..." Juliet's overcome.

The world shimmers, her imagination takes over, or does it? She's not sure, but sees a man with long, greasy blond hair, sapphire blue eyes, intense concentration, and he works so quickly.

She thinks, Bugger me! He seals the join with running lead

faster than I could with end-fed and solder. He must have died a long time ago but I want to have his babies.

Hildegarde says, "Are you alright, young lady?"

"Yes ... no ... who cares?" The vision goes. She slumps to the seat, leans her head back against the pipe, and thinks, Oh, to have my personal olive touched so professionally, so perfectly, with such attention to detail. She gasps out, "The toilet ... an octagonal oval with a blue pattern glazed in ... it's all too much."

"Are you actually needing to use it?"

"Yes. Give me a moment ... possibly the greatest in my life."

"In your own time." Hildegarde shakes her head and closes the door.

Juliet thinks, Oh wot? The toilet paper is modern tissue. They could at least have supplied that hard, crackly cellulose type used only a couple of generations ago. OK, it would have made my eyes water but that's all part of the experience. I feel cheated.

She goes to wash her hands. Hildegarde waits as Juliet curses the person who ordered a soap dispenser to be fixed to ancient tiles.

Hildegarde says, "Are you ready?"

"Ready? Oh boy, yes. Ready for anything!"

"Follow me." Hildegarde opens the door and bumbles along more corridors.

Juliet follows her into an oak-panelled room, and basks in the wonderful smell of books that haven't had a bath in centuries.

Hildegarde sits on a desk. Picking up a book that threatens

to drop to the floor, she says, "Put that somewhere, young lady."

Juliet takes it, looks at the spine, sees the title has worn away, and opens it. "Grief, it's handwritten! But in the weirdest letters." She reads aloud, "Malleus Malleficarum, The Witches' Hammer. What's that all about?"

"A work of fiction. A tragic comedy. A treatise on the stupidity of man. Well, men."

"Does it have a happy ending?"

"That's up to you."

Juliet wonders, What sort of an answer is that? This woman is getting stranger every time she opens her mouth. She promised me the opportunity to go back into the world in clean clothes and not looking like something from a low-budget zombie film. I'll give her one last chance.

"Hildegarde, do tell me how I'm going to wash all this crud out of my hair and clothes."

"That involves going down some stairs to my department. You'll need a blindfold."

"Actually I won't. I think stairs and blindfolds may be a health and safety issue."

"Alright, let us try a different tack. I'm a professor. What department do you think I run? And don't even think about arts or sciences."

Juliet wasn't expecting that. From all she's learned through her uncle, universities wantonly lump everything into one or other pigeon hole, even if a subject is not remotely pigeon-shaped. She says, "Computers?"

"Damn fine try, young lady, but a million miles off."

Juliet's bored of this game already and decides to end it.

12

"Training goldfish to sing? Necromancy? Building wishing-wells that actually work? Where's the washing machine?"

Hildegarde stares, mouth hanging open. Juliet wonders if her reply overstepped some sort of mark.

Pulling herself together, Hildegarde says, "Spectacular!"

Juliet wonders if 'spectacular' refers to her or what just happened to the room. She thinks, What the hell? When holes appear in the ground, they don't do it silently. I mean you'd expect screaming and the sound of falling masonry.

She stares at a staircase, mahogany bannisters and all, beside her. She's certain that it wasn't there a moment ago. The stairs seem to go down for ever, tapering to a tiny, mind-wrenching point of perspective. The book drops from her fingers and bounces off her boot.

Hildegarde slips from the desk. "Blunt, arrogant, rude, you talk down to people and left that poor janitor humiliated, confused and speechless. Are you sure you don't want to be an academic?"

Juliet croaks, "I want to be a plumber." She can't take her eyes off the stairs. Her brain is a mess of confusion. She thinks, Was that staircase there when I came into the room and I just didn't see it? Am I cracking up? In my world I want staircases to act more responsibly.

She's reminded of a childhood incident in which she went to pick up a pretty stone in the garden. The stone uncoiled, hissed, and slithered away. She learned not only about grass-snakes and wet knickers but also that expectation and reality don't always match up. A piece of wisdom she applied in later life when it came to choosing between buying a lottery ticket and a bar of chocolate.

Hildegarde takes a deep breath and continues her assessment of Juliet, "That rat understood you when you talked to it. You solve problems when all are panicking around you. You are full of passion—for plumbing, which is a bit odd I have to say. You can see into the past: ja? That plumber was real. You translated an almost unreadable ancient text into English; you probably didn't even think it was ancient text. Only one in a million people can do all of those things. That hilarious answer involving goldfish, wishing wells and necromancy shows a degree of lightning-fast, lateral thinking quite amazing in one so young. Finally, from the way you're staring, you're clearly able to see the staircase I summoned, which is invisible to all but the truly gifted. You were right: no blindfold for you. Now, come down to my department and we'll kit you out with a first-year gown and sort your hair. You've passed your interview with flying colours. Welcome to Morgan Le Fey, or Muffy, College, Cambridge. Your course begins today."

Juliet wonders if her brain is about to explode and leave via her nostrils. "What? I didn't come here for an interview."

"Eventually you will come to learn that that statement is utterly incorrect."

"And I need to get back to Cheryl this afternoon. She'll only have room in her head for worrying if she's going to be accepted or not. Someone's got to get her home."

"Alright, get her home and then..."

"But I don't want..."

"Precisely. Anyone that wants to get into Muffy is the wrong material. Nobody chooses Muffy: Muffy chooses them."

"Our deal was clean clothes and then I'm out of here."

"You can leave if you want to but that won't change anything. You are a student whether you like it or not. Your course won't stop now wherever you are. It's better to stay here as there's a supportive team in case anything life-threatening happens. Anyway, it's a wonderful challenge."

"Life-threatening? What on Earth do you teach down there?"

"That's almost impossible to answer because what you learn is more or less your choice. Essentially it's exactly the opposite of anything taught anywhere else on Earth. I expect you'll make it up as you go, just like the rest of us." She takes Juliet's arm. "Your adventure just started. Let's go and see what amazing things the next three years will bring you."

Chapter 2

Juliet walks down a few stairs with Hildegarde who pushes open a door-sized panel on the left-hand side and leads her into fresh air, warm sunlight, gentle breezes, and a verdant area about the size of a tennis court. They're surrounded by the emerald greens of grass and fern, the browns and silver of lofty trees. Vividly-coloured apples, plums and oranges hang in abundance. An ultramarine sky not only arches overhead but appears to plunge underneath everything too.

Juliet gasps. Hildegarde turns to her. "Yes, you are underground and above it at the same time. The first thing you learn in Muffy is that you know nothing and must start again from scratch. This is the original garden of Eden as it was at the beginning of creation. This is where it all started."

Juliet looks round. "A bit cramped."

A sparrow flutters and settles on a twig beside her. The head and shoulders of a woman rise from a pool nearby. She looks round, says, "Oh ... wrong turn," and slips under the water again.

Hildegarde goes on, "The garden was sufficient for Adam and Eve."

A tree rustles and a low mellifluous voice says, "And me." The head of a serpent, iridescent viridian scales and dark

16

green eyes, lowers itself into view. Satan yawns and tips his head to one side. "Ooh, what have we here? An Eve-thing with bits of metal in its face. Want some fruit?"

Juliet shakes her head. "No thanks. I'm more of a fast food person."

"You want me to throw it?"

Hildegarde slaps him aside. "Quiet, I'm inducting a student."

Satan retreats; foliage muffling his reply, "I can do Cornish pasties..."

Hildegarde ignores him. "God made the Garden of Eden and Adam and Eve. One of the first things he said was, 'Name all the animals'."

"Like that sparrow?"

The sparrow, rearranging feathers with its beak, chirrups, "I'm not sparrow, I'm Arthur."

Hildegarde nods. "You have to understand that God, Adam, and Eve were beginners and God is often rather vague in his commands. He also said, 'Go forth and multiply'. His idea being to extend Eden as the population grew. He wasn't ready for the vast enthusiasm humans have for copulation. Half a dozen humans would have been enough company for him." She plucks an apple. "Try one, they taste delicious."

Juliet shrugs. "God really made this place? He's real?"

"Ja. You'd expect him to drop in from time to time but he's a bit busy these days."

A snigger comes from Satan.

Juliet says, "Isn't eating the apples bad?"

Hildegarde replies between crunches, "Maybe from the point of view of the apple. But no, the original sin was actually done by a man and had little or nothing to do with fruit." She jerks her head towards the tree. "You see Satan twisted the word, 'Multiply' and screwed everything up."

Juliet puffs a yellow butterfly from her nose. "Perv, I think it was trying to have sex with one of my studs."

Hildegarde continues, "He taught Mankind mathematics. Mankind went on to multiply, and divide, and subtract, and add. Everyone ended up doing it and the inevitable happened."

"They committed suicide from boredom?"

"No, some man applied the maths to creation and said, 'Hang on, the world can't possibly be flat'. God said, 'Oh shit.' and had to make a new one."

Juliet says, "Does this induction go on much longer? Maybe I'll have a pasty after all. Any chance of a coffee?"

"Come to my office." Hildegarde marches back to the stair door. "The big problem is that everything was created by God, and maths doesn't take that into account. Sooner or later some gifted mathematical genius will prove that the universe can't possibly exist. What's going to happen then? And don't say, 'God knows', because he doesn't and he's shitting himself."

She crosses the stairs, goes up a few, and opens a panel on the other side. "Come in and take your clothes off. There's a shower over there. You can wash yourself and your clothes. Sorry about the lack of pipes and taps. I'll get your gown."

Juliet gawps at the vast room. About a hundred and fifty metres away there's a shower, and a rainbow, and a cloud. The office floor is a swathe of chamomile. The huge wooden desk looks alive. Branches growing from its corners cast dappled shade from rustling silver-green leaves. The walls of the room are a spectacular mosaic of amber panes lit from behind. The ceiling, domed and around two hundred metres high, is an astragal pattern of blue and green stained-glass.

Juliet says, "Posh. What's the rent on this place?" She catches the black gown Hildegarde tosses to her.

"Blood, toil, tears and stomach ulcers. Now get washed and dressed while I order some coffee and fast food, ja? Run your finger across the rainbow to adjust the shower temperature. The plants around the pool are soapwort."

Juliet walks to the pool, strips, steps into blissfully warm water, and lets steaming rain wash her cobwebs away. She mentally straitjackets herself, "Keep sane, girl. Magical staircases, talking snakes—I'm cracking up. I can't take much more of this."

A beautiful woman, the same she saw in the Garden of Eden, rises beside her. Juliet screams, falls backwards and chokes in the water. The mermaid catches and lifts her. "Drowned people—a meal that prepares itself. But don't be scared. I don't eat while on duty."

Juliet sees skin of fine scales, seaweed hair, and a fish tail. The woman waves a sponge. "Do you want me to do your back?"

Juliet gags and splutters. "Piss off! You're lucky I didn't punch the shit out of you. Never jump out at me like that."

"Calm down. You're worse than your mother was."

"You wot?"

"When I washed her." The mermaid's webbed fingers comb cobwebs from Juliet's hair.

Juliet's speech centre temporarily shorts out. "Gwaa?"

19

"Only she made better conversation."

"What? My mum? She was here?"

"Yes." The mermaid frowns and studies Juliet's face. "Do I wash those metal objects stuck in your eyebrows and nose? Oh, there's one in your lip too. What are they?"

"My studs? They're a fashion thing."

The mermaid frowns. "Do they hold your face on?"

"My mum was a student here?"

"And your grandmother and so on. Divine perspicacity only runs in the female side of your family, it seems. Don't move, I need to get this spider out of your ear." She pauses and flicks a doubtful glance at Juliet. "Or is it a fashion thing?"

~

Juliet's washed, dried, fed, and dressed in her gown. She doesn't do gowns, let alone dresses—except this one. It responds to mental instructions and can be worn in any number of ways; long sleeved, short sleeved, ankle length, floor length, with a train, and not at all. Black as a black cat on a moonless night, it enhances the pupils of her eyes and makes them scary as hell. She looked at her reflection in the pool until she was strong enough not to flinch. The gown can be turned inside out for formal occasions. Then it's black with a swirling filigree of gold. She reckons it's the most striking thing since meteorites.

The mermaid, carried away with her own enthusiasm, turned Juliet's spiky blond hair to a shimmering gold. Over one shoulder, Juliet's threadbare knapsack, crammed with her clothes, slightly ruins her overall look.

Hildegarde looks her up and down. "Impressive, frightening and more than a tiny bit tarty. You're about to meet your fellow students. First impressions count. Are you sure you...?"

"Oh boy, yes."

"I'm going to point you at a door but not come with you. I'm probably in the room already."

"Of course you are." Juliet rolls her eyes. "Now what are you on about?"

"Today I've inducted three hundred students simultaneously. If I escort all of them in, there'll be three hundred of me in one room. That's a recipe for one hell of a bloodbath. Three hundred of me wanting to have the last word."

Juliet feels punch-drunk. She considers taking the word 'Punch' from that sentence, and brightens a little. Tonight, if she survives that long, she'll take Cheryl out for an evening they won't remember.

She goes through the door and into a seething crowd of students, only a handful of whom look human. Most of the rest are humanoid, but... She tries not to look at the others. What's more, the various species of students all seem to be in a state of shock and looking at anything but each other. Someone's apparently anticipated this, and the oak panelling, beams, and thatched roof absorb much of the scant light coming from fat candles in wall brackets.

Things move in shadows, shadows that Juliet decides to keep well away from. She tears her gaze from lumbering hairy forms, teeth, claws, and a gown moving without

21

anything visible in it.

Hildegarde stands on a dais. "Freshers of all shapes and species. Welcome to Muffy College." She laughs and adds, "Try not to interbreed too much, ja?" She pauses, perhaps waiting for laughter but receives a horrified silence instead.

She goes on, "Your gowns are your tickets to the college. Wherever you are, put yours on and, if the gown considers everything is safe, for example you're not in a crowded place with cameras on you, you'll be transported here, the college entrance hall."

She points at the floor. "At my feet are student manuals. Take one. Ordinary people, those we call 'sleepers', reading it will see only a copy of Hamlet. But you, all having been in a pool of awakening today, will see maps of the college, lists of professors and lecturers, and the options for self-directed learning. Ja! self-directed. No one gets spoon-fed here. You'll manage your own study. Those who don't work hard enough won't be ready to face reality by the end. The results are usually a sticky mess that only maggots will clear up. You have three years to learn the truth about everything and attempt to stay sane—and alive. Most people manage one or the other."

She waves a copy. "Once you take a manual, it'll record your personal progress, suggest avenues of exploration and, most importantly, the map will tell you what parts of the college not to enter. Your manual knows your skill level and will mark in red areas it deems too dangerous for you. Note that these can change from moment to moment and that the labyrinth is always red. Most corridors have a selection of weapons at the entrance: swords, cudgels, and the like. Make use of them; they are there for a reason. To leave the college, go through the arch behind me and you'll return to the place where you put the gown on. For today, you can use my staircase."

Hildegarde scans the students. "You're on your own now. Best of luck." She turns, summons her stairs and walks out of sight.

The students, still silent, look at each other more closely. An aura of flickering light, like flame round a Christmas pudding, surrounds an orange-skinned woman. Apart from his gown, one figure seems semi-transparent, as if he's made of water. Juliet heads for the dais to grab a manual in the hope she'll learn which types of student are safe to approach and won't eat her.

Something touches her shoulder. She shrieks for the second time today. Whirling round, fists ready to cause serious grief and crunching noises, she sees a lanky ginger-haired man.

He says, "Hi! I'm Errol. Sorry to ask this but are you human?"

Until now that question would have generated a broken nose and rearranged teeth. Juliet groans. "That's how I started off this morning." She relaxes a little, shoulders slumping. "I'm Juliet. I was Juliet the plumber's apprentice. Now I'm Juliet the fuck knows what."

Errol nods, frizzy ginger sideburns and goatee glowing in candlelight. "I was supposed to be going for an interview in the hope of eventually studying astrophysics, now apparently, I'm going to learn about the truth instead. That's an apparent contradiction that I find intriguing." He looks into her eyes,

23

and flinches. "Look, you're not a vampire or something? You know, your eyes are … um."

"I know. It's the gown that does it. Let's grab our books, change into normal clothes, and get out of here. I've got a friend to rescue shortly."

~

Sitting in Market Square and eating Thai noodles with lashings of chilli sauce, Errol and Juliet study their manuals. Errol looks at Juliet and cocks his head. "What's the matter?"

"I want to know why my mum never told me about this."

Errol flicks back a few pages. "Page fourteen, 'Sleepers will always misunderstand or ignore anything you say regarding truth'. It's some sort of divine defence mechanism. You know, you knock on someone's door and say, 'How are you feeling about God today?' You may as well not knock at all and just talk to the door."

"Oh, poor mum, she must have been bursting to tell me." She looks at a random page. "Divine Administration, deaths, reallocation of souls, angel duty—so many jobs after we get a degree. No stacking supermarket shelves for Muffy graduates. Nothing about plumbing. How crap is that? Though there was something about hunting demons and abominations, can't remember the page." She flicks open another and sees:

Go and get Cheryl!

Juliet yelps. "Yikes! Gotta go. See you around." The foam

24

container drops from her hand, chilli sauce splashing down her jeans as she hurtles out of the seat.

Leaving the market, she realises she has no idea how to get to King's. A shrewd guess makes her open the manual again.

Left and through the ... left! you idiot! Stop reading or you'll trip over that...

"Oh right, left..." Juliet interrupts herself by shrieking for the third time as she somersaults over a poodle.

The dog's owner, a tall middle-aged man dressed in a grey flannel suit, helps her up, retrieves the manual, flips through the pages, and passes it to her. "I've never seen someone running while reading Hamlet. I'm not sure it's advisable and will almost certainly lead to a tragic conclusion one way or another."

"Uh, thanks, where's King's?"

Juliet makes it just in time. Interviewees spill from the entrance doors and into the arms of parents and friends.

Cheryl, looking this way and that, squeaks, "Juliet!" breaks into a run, crashes into her, and they fall onto the ancient paving.

Too excited to untangle herself, let alone get up before pouring out her news, Cheryl says, "It was wonderful. I think I'm in!"

"Of course you are."

"Only I got lost for the third interview." Cheryl pants with excitement.

"What?"

"I went to the wrong one. There was another girl called Cheryl Black. We all got confused. Then we worked out the probability of that happening..." she catches her breath, "Then I helped a professor out."

"Of his trousers? You tart."

"No. He had a problem with field theory. You know what that is?"

Juliet rises to kneeling, pulls Cheryl with her, and says, "Probably nothing to do with cows and grass and stuff?"

"No, it's..."

"Stop there."

"Juliet! Guess what I'm going to do?"

"Not biological and natural sciences then?"

Cheryl claps her hands and performs a perfect three-crescent smile of absolute bliss. "He said I may be the most gifted mathematical genius he's ever met. I'm going to do maths! Pure maths."

"Oh … shit."

Chapter 3

The purple van has, 'Victoria's Plumbing Services' emblazoned on the sides in gold lettering. This is after locals complained about the original, 'Victoria's Plumb', growled over the subsequent, 'Victoria's Plumbing' and raged over, 'Victoria's Plumbum' despite the latter being appropriate in at least two respects.

Cheryl, bubbling and bouncing with excitement, and pouring out words as if someone's pressed her fast-forward button, sits in the van beside Juliet who in turn sits next to her mother, whose name, shapeliness and general attitude to middle-class propriety you've probably gleaned already.

Victoria picked them up from the station and has hardly had time to say hello to Juliet due to Cheryl's relentless torrent of excited chatter.

From the back of the van come hollow metallic noises every time Victoria steers on the winding rural roads leading to Brightwell-cum-Sotwell, or as Victoria and Juliet call it, 'Great Soddingwell'.

"Mum," Juliet shouts over Cheryl, "What on earth have you got in the back?"

"Three stainless steel toilets."

"Stainless steel? That's outrageous. Can you imagine someone farting in one? You'd hear it for miles."

"We have to go with the times." The pair of them dissolve into giggles.

Cheryl frowns and looks at them. "What's funny?"

Juliet starts to talk, splutters and gasps out, "Maybe you should call them boom-boxes."

Cheryl says, "What? What are you laughing about?"

Victoria snorts. "You could play musical chairs," and shrieks with laughter.

Cheryl resorts to hitting Juliet's shoulder. "Stop it. Tell me what's funny."

Instead of answering, Juliet wraps her in a fierce hug. She knows, from long years of trying, there's no way anyone's ever going to get Cheryl to understand a joke. "Grab your bag, we're nearly there."

Dropping Cheryl off and pulling into their drive next door, Juliet watches her best friend fumble with the gate, drop her handbag and trip over it. "Mum, that's what I love so much about her. She's either terrified and vulnerable or fizzing with excitement. I have the least boring friend in the world."

Victoria pulls the handbrake on, closes her eyes, and leans her head against the headrest. "Well, how did it go? Your day, not hers." She takes Juliet's hand and squeezes it.

"Mum, it went bang. I finally understand some things about you and your general weirdness. The first thing I need to know is..."

"Rules one to infinity, no questions. I can't answer them in case I influence you in any way. Everything you do must be self-directed. Normal people go to uni to learn but they stay people—except maybe historians. Think of yourself as a seed. Not the seed of any particular plant but something that

28

could grow into any plant or any combination of plants. You have to be of your own making." She opens her eyes and slaps the steering wheel. "However, I can give you some things to make college easier." She flashes Juliet a smile, eyes full of mischief. "I love the gold hair. Great look. You ready for a weird time?"

Juliet opens the passenger door. "Anything to relieve the mindless boredom today has been so far. I..." She freezes, gasps, and points to a cat perched on the apex of their roof. "Is that...? It is! Sheba! But she died..."

"Oh grief, look at her." Victoria blushes, hands over eyes. "Tart."

Juliet slumps back into the seat. "OK, mum. Tell me why our cat, that died years ago, is preening herself in the centre of a circle of toms and driving them into a state of barely controlled sexual frenzy?"

"No questions. Follow me. We don't want to watch what comes next." Victoria's voice is a tremulous squeak. She scrambles out of the van and hurries to the porch.

Juliet follows her into the house but is pulled up sharp when the Toby jug, which has sat on a shelf by the front door for as long as she can remember, says, "Hello, sweetie."

What has always appeared a rigid ceramic face creases into a ruddy and wrinkled smile. Juliet realises he's probably been watching her every day of her life. Memories of stripping off wet clothes after thunderstorms, and steamy, whispered conversations with boyfriends at the front door flash through her mind. "You total bastard."

He winks. "Hey, it wasn't my fault. It's been fun though, and I'm quite incapable of uploading anything anywhere, so relax."

Victoria, halfway up the stairs, calls down, "Don't mind Toby. He's our doorkeeper and has watched our backs..."

Toby interrupts, "And fronts, he-he."

"...since before you were born. Now, get your gown on quick and grab your manual. We're going out together. Wheehoo!"

Juliet heads for her bedroom and wonders what surprises she'll find there. Maybe her childhood fluffy rabbit will be dancing naked on the bed. Through the thatching comes the sound of Sheba mewling seductively. Juliet can just imagine her rolling on her back, arching her spine, and daring any of the toms to move.

However, her bedroom holds no new shocks, though she looks at a photo of her extended family hanging on the wall. A photo that includes spotty male cousins. She dares any of them to move or speak. "That way lies madness," she says to herself, and thinks, Actually, is there ever going to be a sane direction for me from now on? At least I've got Cheryl to keep me in touch with reality... Shit, if Cheryl's the closest thing to normality in my life, I'm bloody doomed.

A gentle tap on the bedroom door is followed by Victoria saying, "Are you decent?"

"Yes, are you?"

"Of course." The door opens and her mother sashays in.

Juliet's jaw drops. She's rarely seen her mother in anything but overalls, jeans, or dressed as a karate instructor. Victoria is wearing what must be her graduation gown. "Mum, I'm not going to the King's Head with you dressed like that!" Juliet collapses on the bed. "You look like a human

30

version of Sheba." A neckline plunging to the navel, everything skin-tight, and fishnet sleeves leading to long, black satin gloves, form an ensemble of nightmare black and eye-spangling golds.

"We're not going to the King's Head, indeed anywhere, unless you put your gown on. Get a move on, we've the second-best evening of our lives ahead of us."

"When's the first-best?"

"When you graduate. This'll be a rehearsal. I'm going to take photos. Neither of us are going to remember much otherwise." She tosses a black velvet bag to Juliet. "For your manual. In college it's always good to have two hands free."

Juliet shrugs, mentally collapses, and loosens the straps on her knapsack. Victoria waltzes around the room, and says, "Now you know why I dragged you out of school to learn plumbing, how to keep a practical head when you enter a house full of panic as the owners watch water pouring through collapsing ceilings, dealing with customers who want to rip you off, problem solving. You're going to need all those skills." She pirouettes, satin perfectly moulding around buttocks that would have ballet dancers hissing with envy.

Juliet averts her eyes and concentrates on getting out of her clothes.

Victoria goes on, "And teaching you martial arts, weapons in particular."

Juliet pulls the gown over her head. Straightening the fabric, she looks up as her mother gasps.

Victoria, hands either side of her face, whimpers. "Oh my little girl … you look..." She surges forward and hugs Juliet. "I'm so proud."

31

"Get off me or you'll be proud of a blue suffocated thing in a moment. Is that perfume or toxic gas?"

"A bit of both, my darling. You want some?"

"I'll need to know what species of gorilla, or whatever, you're trying to attract."

"Stand back, hands out, and close your eyes. I want to look at you and give you a present." Victoria reaches round the bedroom door. A moment later, Juliet feels something cold and hard placed on her palms.

She opens her eyes and looks at one and a half metres of black rod. At one end is a wavy spearhead and cross-piece, at the other, a ridged counterbalance. Despite the surprise and shock at such an unexpected gift, she realises that, A) this has been given for a good reason, and B) it explains why she hasn't been allowed into Victoria's workshop for the last few months. "You made this, didn't you?" she says in awe.

"Oh yes. Tubular carbon shaft, ribbed for grip, flamberge, hollow carbon-steel head with edges tempered to the deepest blue, counterbalance lumpy enough to break bones. It floats just, so you can't lose it in water but you can still swim with it."

"What...?"

"No questions." Victoria flips the blades of two lethal-looking black sai into invisible pockets behind her shoulders. "Now, grab your manual and we're off."

"To do what?"

"Have a nice quiet meal."

"You mean it'll be nice and quiet after we've stabbed it to death?" She pauses, "I love my spear, mum..." She doesn't know how to finish.

32

Victoria rescues her by playing a game they've developed during hours of bending pipes and fitting connections. "But you prefer swords, I know. Name five things you can do with a spear that you can't use a sword for, now!"

"Yikes. Uh ... get stuck in doorways, clear a blocked downpipe, skewer some cute animal and roast it over a fire, push loft-insulation into difficult corners, scratch graffiti on low-flying aircraft, castrate a giraffe ... six already, OK, you win." Juliet runs her hands up and down the oval-sectioned shaft. "Mum, it's beautiful, so beautiful. I haven't a clue what it's for but I know you've put your heart and soul into it. I don't know what to say. Every other Cambridge fresher will be getting a new laptop, or whatever, but I've got something I can stab Sheba with through the thatch to shut her up."

"Talking of which, you've just reminded me. Give me the spear a sec. I've one more thing to give you before you're ready for college. You need a moderator." From her bag she draws a gold chain, tiny links sparkling and hissing as they unravel. A single sapphire in the shape of a tear-drop hangs from it. "Blue, to match your eyes. Put it on and think yourself into it."

Juliet, dazed by so many revelations, stares into the crystal and tips her cupped palms from side to side rolling the treasure so it catches the light. The gem is full of life, full of energy that explodes into the room and tumbles to the floor in the form of a spaniel that races around in a blur of scampering legs and whirling tail. Juliet yelps as it jumps into her arms, splatters a hot slimy tongue over her face, and leaps down again. The dog dives under the bed and scrambles around sniffing and sneezing dust.

"What..." she stares at her mother, "the fuck...?"

"Some students need a moderator to store excess personality, aspects of them that could get in the way of keeping a level head." She sniggers. "Bursts of wild enthusiasm, unquestioning devotion, and loyalty are yours. Sheba never died. I just kept her in my own crystal to avoid any awkward questions about a cat that never grew old. Today I could let her out—and she has some catching up to do, as you saw."

Connections click in Juliet's head as the dog bursts from under the bed, cannons into her legs, thrusts a wet nose into her bottom, scurries from the room, and thunders down the stairs. "Mum … Sheba, the tart of all tarts, is your moderator?"

Victoria blushes. "Look, nobody's perfect. When a child is born you love it unconditionally; it can't help what it is. When the child becomes an adult the process is reversed. The new adult learns just how human parents are and that they can't help how they were made either. Cope or go mad. Shall we go out?"

Chapter 4

Juliet's sitting in an undulating landscape of purple flowers. Reading her manual is a little tricky because the ground rises and falls as hills move beneath it like passing waves and do nothing to settle her churning stomach.

Looking up at the sky gives her vertigo. Clouds travel in different directions, even have head-on collisions.

A pale sun has risen and warmed up the flowers, filling the air with a heavy musk. Victoria, ashen and waxy, hair sticking in lank locks to her face, snores on the ground.

Juliet's concentrating on reading, trying to blot out memories of last night, particularly those involving her mother dancing, singing, falling over, and getting into fights.

Pixies, nixies and brownies. Introductory module for first-year students.

A gentle introduction to mythical creatures – without excessive terror and physical injury.

The aim is to learn what role pixies play in our everyday...

Victoria opens bloodshot eyes, groans, and closes them again. "Juliet … if you love me, get me a new mouth."

Juliet lowers the book. "If you ever behave like that again, in public, in my presence, you'll need a new daughter."

Victoria groans again, sits up, and runs fingers through her hair. "I wasn't that bad."

"What do you remember?"

"Nothing to be ashamed about."

"What do you actually remember?"

"Like I said, nothing."

"Thought you wouldn't. I took videos on my phone."

"Videos of?"

"You snogging a naked demon."

Victoria snorts. "I did?"

"You lost a bet."

"And the point is?"

"You kept betting `til you lost. You wanted to snog a demon. And I have shots of you dancing."

"What's wrong with dancing?"

"Pole dancing. You were outrageous. You're lucky your knickers didn't fly off."

"Bugger, I knew those ones were too tight."

"Mum!"

"It's all part of your education. Yes, I can be your mum back home but here I can also be like me at eighteen."

"You were like that at eighteen?"

"Maybe seventeen … it's all a bit hazy." Victoria points a limp index finger at a cloud. "You, yes, you. Over here and make a pool of awakening." Turning to Juliet, she says, "Help me out of this gown, darling, I need to freshen up,

36

throw up, or both. Either way I don't want my clothes involved."

"What? No way. I'm still furious with you. Sort yourself out."

"Bugger. Why did no one warn me that sex leads to teenagers?" Victoria rises, staggers, and tugs at her gown. "Get your clothes off. You look as if you need a pool of awakening too." The cloud pours steaming rain into a hollow.

Juliet says, "Where are we?"

"Here somewhere." Victoria flops into the growing pool, and moans with the pure delight of having a hangover instantly washed away.

Juliet watches her mother turn from looking like a haggard zombie to something more like a laughing child, splashing water in glittering arcs and singing. Abandoning the manual, she throws off her clothes and races into the pool before the shrinking cloud is used up.

A passing hillock throws them into the air in a tumult of crashing water and glittering rainbows. They flop, howling with laughter, among sodden flowers.

"That was incredible," Juliet says, lying on her back and staring at the sky. The clouds look like faces, dragons, even a flying sheep. In fact none of them look much like clouds. "I feel brilliant." She relaxes, eyes closed, while Victoria moves around sniggering. Juliet asks, "What are you doing?"

"Watching your videos. Whoa! Look at me go. Not bad gymnastics for a forty year old. I'm amazing."

Juliet considers this, Mum ... amazing ... well, yes. Just not in a way I want my friends to know about. What's she up to? It's some sort of lesson, maybe about living life 101%, or something. Why did everyone at the party treat her with such respect, even outright fear in some cases? How come everyone knows her? What is my mother?

But her reflections are cut short by shrieks and gasping laughter. She asks, "Now what?"

Victoria howls again. "I must have taken this one."

Juliet opens her eyes, then narrows them in suspicion. There's something in her mother's tone. "What?"

"Video of you—pole dancing."

"No way!" Juliet leaps to her feet, snatches the phone, and stares. "Oh my God."

~

Dressed, refreshed, and ready for anything, Juliet says, "Right, I have a million questions that you're not going to answer. Tell me what you can."

"I need breakfast."

"Try a little harder, mum. I have my spear handy."

"The party was held in a bolt-hole and hosted by the people, in this case the demons, that made it. This is my bolt-hole," Victoria looks around, "made by me and a few friends that owe me. You can see we're not exactly experts. It's a place I can go when I need some peace, sleep, or a hangover cure. Everyone should have a place like this. The interesting thing will be seeing how you get us back to the college."

"You want me to find a way from a place that I don't know where it is...? did that make any sense? To a place I also don't … oh wot."

Victoria rescues her. "The location of which you don't

38

know."

"I was getting there." Juliet growls and goes on, "Easy, I'll use the manual." She frowns, scans the contents, shakes her head, checks the college map and frowns harder. Remembering her previous technique she flicks to a random page in the notes section.

Your mother is a raving maniac. Making these home-made bubble worlds is totally insane. I'm not getting involved. I don't even want people to know I know about it.

Please remove this page and eat it.

She tears the leaf out and offers it to Victoria who says, "A message for me?"

"The breakfast you asked for." Juliet's frown clears but only because the muscles are exhausted. "OK, maybe the manual's no use here." She wonders if her moderator could help. She clutches the sapphire. The gem twitches and something whirls inside. "Out you come."

The minute figure of a dog chasing its tail and tripping over its ears, fails to emerge.

"Come on, even the most brainless spaniel can't get lost in there. Come out here." She's not sure if the dog knows it's being called. "Right, dog, I'm giving you a name. Mitch. Get your arse out here." She wonders if that's the correct instruction. "And the rest of you."

39

The newly named Mitch erupts from the stone, leaps to the ground in a flurry of yelps, bad breath and flying saliva, grabs the manual in his mouth and tries to shake it to death. He also wags his tail so enthusiastically it destabilises his back end and the paws trip over each other. Juliet abandons any hope that he can help, lifts her spear and taps the pommel against her forehead.

Hmm, 'bubble worlds'. Can I pop my way to the college? She jabs the point into the ground and their surroundings are replaced by the dim musty college entrance hall and a mass of students jostling and heading for lectures. Juliet's less scared to look at passing people and doesn't scream at the sight of students with writhing snakes instead of hair or a person with three chicken heads, all of which wear dark glasses.

Victoria says, "Well done. That's seven ways to use a spear. You could have just called on your gown but that was cool; lateral thinking with style. Style is important in college, very important. What are you going to do now?"

"Pixies, nixies, and brownies." Juliet reaches down and snatches the manual from Mitch, who looks at it in frank astonishment, like he'd forgotten it was in his mouth.

Victoria says, "Brilliant party. I'm off to work. One word of advice. Trust nothing here and no one except yourself."

"Mum, you're something special here. Why are you installing toilets back home?"

"If you hadn't noticed, I'm pretty special at home too. I'm installing toilets because my clients will make an awful mess if I don't. You got time for breakfast?"

"Oh yes, about three days." They make their way through the throng, Victoria imperiously calling for people to get out

40

of the way, and heading for an archway blocked by black and yellow tape, a sign saying, 'Danger! Corridor Closed', and four armed guards wielding weapons that gleam in the poor light.

They tense as Victoria approaches. "Sorry, ma'am, we're to stop anyone..."

Victoria stops in front of them. "What's more dangerous, the entrance hall or whatever's in that corridor?"

The guard says, "no one told us what it was, so we don't know but I'd guess whatever's in the corridor is the most dangerous.'

"Then why are you facing me and not it?"

"I..."

Victoria hisses. "Out of my way."

"But..."

"Look at it this way. If a thing is more dangerous than a dangerous thing, however dangerous it is, there can't be any danger, can there?"

"What? I..."

She draws her sai with a flourish that convinces the guards that they'd like to stand a little further to the sides and accidentally make enough room for her to pass. She says, "Come on, Juliet," and slashes though the tape.

Juliet, on Victoria's left, holds her spear point-down, with both hands grasping the shaft the same way, as if gripping the handlebars of a bike. Anything attacking from above, left, or the front will be scythed but anything from behind will wonder what skewered it and then smashed its brains out with a pommel.

Victoria juggles her sai. "This is the main way to the

canteen—and it's blocked off, so the place should be pretty empty. No queues, yay! They do evil black pudding and mushrooms. Never use the counters on the right. Most of the food's still alive."

They pass side entrances but nothing attacks. Juliet wonders if this is mainly down to Victoria's arrogant and fearless attitude. She thinks, right, style.

Mitch runs ahead and through the arch from which come cooking smells. Juliet relaxes a little until he rockets back yelping in terror. Leaping up, he disappears into the pendant.

Juliet asks, "Does the black pudding ever cause trouble?"

Shouts, grinding noises, and the sound of falling rocks come from ahead.

Victoria frowns at the noises. "That sort of trouble? Not until the day after you've eaten it."

They enter a huge domed room lined with carved stone. Dimly lit counters ring the edge. Tables of varying sizes support candles, plates, elbows and other appendages. Waiters weave through the room and carry drinks on silver trays. To Juliet's right a ring of people gaze up at growing cracks in the ceiling.

To her surprise, Juliet sees three enormous figures, she guesses trolls, one sitting on another's shoulders, while a third passes massive handfuls of clay to it, to fill the holes and cracks.

A golden-gowned man sees Victoria, leaves the group and walks to her. Victoria says, "Morning, Prof, what's coming down?"

The man grunts and shrugs. "Could be foundations being drilled but it's unusually deep. There is legitimate building

42

work on the surface but this may be some sort of probing. You going to hang around, just in case?" He nods at Juliet. "Nice to meet you, young lady. Come and see me when you get a moment."

Victoria says, "I'm staying long enough for breakfast. Then I have toilets to install."

The man's lips twitch a smile. "Yes, you do."

Victoria links arms with Juliet and leads her towards counters piled with steaming food. "You want to know what he's on about? Page three hundred and three of your manual, 'The Knights of Kramer', a secret order determined to destroy witches."

"There are witches down here?"

"Not a chance but there are witches up in the real world. White witches, black witches, maybe even Dashwood-style Hellfire Club warlocks, but they're all harmless—unless you're a wax doll.

The knights have known from the beginning that Muffy exists, but they've never found it. They believe we train witches, and just believing is enough to make it seem real to them. Back in the fifteenth century people made a good living out of hunting witches and the like. Some idiots never give up but pass their delusions to the next generation like heirlooms and syphilis." She stares at the food. "So much black pudding and only one stomach. Life can be so cruel."

"Who's the prof and why do I have to see him?"

"Mike? He's OK, specialises in non-human languages. If he appears to be choking to death, don't bash him on the back; he's probably talking to colleagues. Ooh, what's in the vegetarian broth do you think?"

"Vegetarians?" Juliet loads a plate with deep-fried haggis and chips.

Victoria heads for a table and shouts to a waiter, "Coffee, please." She pulls a chair out, wood rasping over ancient stone. "This is it, my love. Savour the moment; your first day in college. I wonder how many days you'll be here? Days in college are very different; read page 223." She takes a slice of black pudding and crams it whole into her mouth.

"Mum, mind your manners."

Victoria grunts, mouth overfull, until she's able to say, "I'm in a bit of a rush. Work of fundamental importance to do." She grabs a mug from the waiter's tray and lifts another slice of black pudding. "Gotta shift. See you later. Ooh, one last thing. If you need answers, always ask the right questions. Bye." She frowns. "Now that's odd. My gown won't let me go straight to the garden. Hmm, I wonder why someone's watching it? I'll try the house." She disappears.

Chapter 5

The rhythmical thudding and juddering of the building work above causes dust and stones to patter from the ceiling. Juliet doesn't notice what's happening to her food until the haggis becomes intolerably crunchy.

She's deep in thought: Mum always encouraged me to stand up for myself, never compromise, never back down, fight for my rights and those of others. It was a sodding nightmare all the way through school—on the rare occasions they let me in. Am I to go through another three years of constant battles? I'm going to miss plumbing. OK, mum, I believe in you, well the part that doesn't wiggle in front of demons. Here goes...

She pushes the plate away and opens the notes section of her manual. "OK, book, what are you?"

A book, dummy.

Right … ask the right questions. "What makes you different to, say, a book that doesn't write and update itself?"

You're getting warmer.

"Something alive and capable of thinking and writing?"

Well done. I'm a brownie. Not the book, me. I live in this book.

"Hop out. Let me see you. We have at least three years together. Let's get to know one another."

Nope.

"A shy brownie?"

No. I don't like my other shape and I don't go out. I like to stay a tome.

"I'm doing brownies today."

Doing anything in particular to them?

"Learning about them. There's a lecture probably."

In seventeen minutes. Lecture room eighty-three is two minutes' walk. Refer to map. Can we get out of here fast? I think the ceiling's going to collapse and I like books with happy endings.

Juliet dodges hissing dust and rattling stones, and enters the corridor. Gripping the spear in her favourite way, she marches into the deepening gloom.

The far end of the tunnel is darker than before and it takes her a moment to realise the entrance is almost totally covered in tape. Silhouetted figures on the other side appear to be adding further strips. Juliet thinks, Eight uses of a spear.

She slashes two diagonals and kicks her way through.

"Stop right there." "Freeze." "You're under arrest." "Don't hurt me!" Several voices mingle, tinged with varying degrees of panic.

Juliet stops at the sight of four figures in black. The person that appears least afraid is a female figure with four arms and wielding two spears. The figure says, "You are totally outclassed. Drop your weapon and or return to the demonic plane from which you descended."

Juliet groans. "Do I look like a parachutist?"

"What?"

"It's trying to confuse us," says a lanky humanoid, with reptilian skin and alligator heads rising on serpentine necks from each of its shoulders. "Drive it back!"

Juliet, spear pommel on the ground and the shaft held loosely across her body, relaxes and raises a hand. "Much as I'm enjoying our little get-together, four-eyes, I have a lecture to attend. Let's meet up and kill each other later."

The four-armed woman points her two spearheads straight at Juliet's chest. Juliet's right hand drops to just below the head of her spear, while her left sweeps the pommel in a lightning-fast arc and knocks the spears away. She drives the pommel into the forehead of the guard and, using the momentum, swings the flat side of the blade against one of four-eyes's temples. His heads bang together. He and four-arms fall back, screaming and dropping weapons. The third guard runs away, while the fourth empties a sack on the floor before fleeing.

In an explosion of movement, the sack's contents splits into a tumbling horde of tiny figures that leap and cling to Juliet. Winding threads round her and scurrying faster than blurring mice. She's quickly cocooned and helpless. The little humanoids giggle, poke her, and some start playing tig in her hair.

A guard shouts, "General alarm! Monster in the entrance hall."

Any students not already moving away from the scene, flee towards the other end of the room. About a third of them stop and run back, howling in terror, as a night-black demon, too tall to stand upright under the low ceiling and doorway, squeezes through the entrance.

The demon's bony exoskeleton grinds and screeches over the flagstones, elbows and knees bending in all the wrong directions as if someone put him together before reading the assembly instructions.

Juliet, still struggling, but ever observant, notices that about two-thirds of the students are quite unfazed by the demon. Some even wave.

She wants her arms free so she can slap him.

The demon spots her and lets out a low growl. The

threatening and obscene notes in his tone rattle the thatch and vibrate people's sternums. Students drop whatever they're carrying and clutch their chests in an attempt to keep lungs and hearts in place. The demon says, "Hello, Juliet. We meet again. How delicious. Ready for a little kiss? I wonder if you taste as sweet as your mother."

"Piss off and tell these irritating pillocks to untie me and let me get to my lecture."

"You are having your lecture, my little sweetness. I hear you've already identified a brownie and, from what you say, can clearly see the nixies that have tied you up so very intimately. Nice, skin-tight bonds. Very skin-tight." The demon looks her up and down several times and extends scimitar-like claws. "Would you like me to help you out of everything?"

Juliet looks at the nixies cowering at the sight of the demon. "Hello, little nixies. You know what you just did to me? See if you can locate his testicles and do the same, only a lot tighter. Think soprano demon."

The demon laughs. "Sounds fun. Do as she says."

The nixies squeak, drop to the floor, and scramble over and under other each other in a race to get back into their sack. Juliet takes a deep breath as her bonds fall away. She says to the demon, "I have you on my list of things I despise, but am not quite ready to disembowel yet. Don't piss me off any more or you rise to the next list." She marches past him. The gaggle of spellbound onlookers falls back to let her through.

~

She enters a crowded lecture theatre. To her it looks more like a Roman arena, bloodstains and all. Circles of stone seats gleam under the bright blue sky. She still wonders how it is possible to have sky underground but decides not to pursue that. Today has been weird enough and she is only a few minutes in.

Squeezing between students, she heads for the nearest spare seat and sits next to a female humanoid covered in what looks like chitinous skin. The student shuffles to one side and says, in a sing-song girly voice, "Hello, I'm Agatha of Atro City."

"Hi, I'm Juliet of Great Soddingwell." Juliet tucks her spear between her knees and sits on the hard sun-warmed stone.

Agatha says, "I'm sorry, Juliet, but it's that time of the month. Can you help me out?"

"What I'm good at is sitting quietly, listening to lectures, and not getting into any weirdness. Can we settle for that?"

"Can you pull my arm for me?"

"What? No."

"But it's beginning to hurt already. Please. Put your foot against my side and pull as hard as you can." Agatha yelps in pain. "Please, now!"

Juliet, immune to virtually anything except genuine pain and distress, says, "You really...?" but doesn't get to finish as Agatha grabs Juliet's right foot, puts it against her side, and places a wrist between Juliet's hands.

She cries, "Now, now, pull, pull, harder, harder."

Juliet quickly works out that anyone sitting anywhere in a

50

circular arena and causing a disturbance can be seen by everyone else. She tries to ignore the several hundred eyes turned in her direction.

Agatha shouts, "Harder!"

Juliet thinks, Fine, you asked for it.

With the power of embarrassment times two to the several hundred, she pulls.

Agatha cries, "Harder, harder!"

Juliet screams as, after a tearing and snapping noise, the arm seems to come away in her hands. She looks in total horror at the thing she's holding, less horror at Agatha, who still seems to be in one piece, and it dawns on Juliet that Agatha only needs someone to help shed old skin that she's outgrown.

Agatha says, "Now my other arm, now my legs, now split my head..."

By the time it's all over, Juliet's broken into a serious sweat with all the effort and collapses back into her seat.

Agatha collects the discarded skin and begins eating it, crunching with enthusiasm and dribbling. She holds some out to Juliet. "Thank you for that. You want some?"

"No—you're fine." Juliet wrestles with nausea and a squeaky voice.

"You're a human, aren't you? I've never met one but I was swotting up on them this morning."

Juliet answers but only to check if her voice is coming under control, "Really? What were you reading?"

"Recipes."

"When you're quite ready..." A voice booms from below. The familiar squat figure of Hildegarde stands in the arena,

51

glowers and points to Juliet. "That student. Weapons are not allowed in lectures. Put it in the common weapons pool by the entrance."

Juliet, slightly short of patience, barks back, "It's not a common weapon. It's mine."

"Students are not allowed to possess personal weapons."

"This one is."

"Remove it or remove yourself."

"No. Do carry on with the lecture."

"There will be no lecture until you obey my command."

"Fine, I'll just sit here and relax in the sun. Don't mind me."

Hildegarde stands fuming, arms rigid and fists clenched. After a moment she barks, "If that's the way you want to play it. I will leave and return after you have left."

Juliet stays put. Hildegarde waits, stares at her lectern, and the piles of books she's brought in, appears to decide she's not going to carry them out only to have to bring them in again, spins on a heel, and marches out, stamping puffs of dust from the arena floor as she heads for the tunnel.

All eyes turn to Juliet. Agatha says, "You've spoiled our lecture!"

"No I haven't," Juliet snarls, grabs her spear, and works her way past knees and tentacles. Reaching the aisles, a collective sigh of relief at her apparently leaving is replaced by a collective groan of dismay as she heads down to the arena.

She reaches the lectern and snatches up a sheaf of what appears to be blank paper. Flicking through it reveals nothing until a message says:

Don't mess me up. Each leaf is in order. The daft old bat will get confused and screw the lecture up.

"Show me the writing. I'll give the lecture."

Not a chance. You're not a nice person.

"And she is?"

Um ... that's not the point. Leave and let her get on with it. Who do you think you are?

"Juliet. You don't want these notes mixed because you want the knowledge to go out. Professor hoity-toity-stamp-my-little-foot is not here to give it but I am. That means we're on the same side. I'm your friend. Let's get on with it."

Don't do all that logic at me. I get confused.

"I want to give the lecture. I want to hear it too. That makes me twice your friend because you want both as well."

53

I did like the 'Hoity-toity' bit...

"Tell you what. Why don't you show yourself and give the lecture."

I'm a bit shy and almost no one will be able to see me anyway.

"Out you come now. She can't stop you; she has far too big an ego to come back in while I'm here. I'll shake dust from the arena floor all over you. People will be able to see that."

"Yahooooo!" A child-sized human figure pops from the notes and stands on the lectern. Coughing and gasping in a cloud of dust Juliet pours from her hand, he bows to the students. "Allow me to introduce myself. I am a brownie. Henry Bollinger-Bejebus, at your service." He waves Juliet to a spare seat in the front row. "When everyone is settled, we will commence the lecture, while Professor hoity-toity stands fuming in the tunnel and plans how miserable Juliet's life is going to be over the next three years."

Chapter 6

Juliet arrives in her bedroom, scans for anything unusual, swaps her gown for jeans and a T-shirt, screams at the top of her voice, and collapses on the bed.

She responds to a faint tap on the door. "Come in if you don't have fangs, bat wings, a happy smile, or anything else I'll thrust a spear through and stamp on."

The door creaks open. Victoria leans against the architrave. "Hello, my love. How was your first day?"

"The only thing that would make me feel good right now, would be to beat you black and blue and forbid you to be my mother ever again." Juliet opens an eye and sees Victoria is wearing her gown. "No way. No parties. I'm spending the evening working out how much psychotherapy I can afford." She sits up, frowns and narrows her eyes. "I bet you've just come back from the college. Have you been spying on me?"

Victoria grins. "I was merely speaking to my colleagues."

"About me?"

"I didn't talk about you much. They did. At length. Very length." She enters the room, takes Juliet's hand, and sits on the bed. "I have never been so proud in all my life." Her voice catches.

Confused, Juliet realises her mother is close to tears. "Mum, what? You alright?"

"You sussed how a manual works, you beat up a couple of the Vigilante Guild, threatened a demon and made a serious enemy of Hildegarde," she sniffs, "and that was all before lunch. It takes most people months to get that far. Today you impressed the whole college. No one could frighten you, give you orders, or bend you to their will in any way. Don't you see? You've laid your rules on the college, not the other way round. Frankly..." her voice catches again, "that's incredible."

"College... We don't get any choice but to go, do we? Did I really do well?" She squeezes Victoria's hand. "It's all falling into place. Surely that should feel good? Actually it feels like a couple of mountains are falling and I'm the place. You prepared me for college from the very beginning. Everything you ever told me about—made me into. Just tell me it's going to get easier."

"Only if you won't hate me for lying to you. You've set them a challenge beyond anyone's expectations. They're going to do everything they can to break you. You'll grow resourceful, strong, and maybe go further than anyone else."

"I want to be a plumber."

"You are. In my opinion you're the second-best plumber in the world. Now, come with me. I need your help to see what the cat brought in."

~

As they enter the living room, Sheba, hidden under the sofa, lets out a long low yowl. It may not contain words as such but the message about coming any closer and having your entrails removed couldn't be clearer.

Victoria says, "Any ideas?"

"Oh yes." Juliet clutches her sapphire through the T-shirt. "But how important is this and how much can we afford in the way of redecoration and new furniture?"

"I'll open doors and windows. You tip the sofa. And, Juliet..."

"Yes?"

"Pull the pendant outside your T-shirt first."

"Oops, good idea."

On Juliet's command, Mitch appears, lands head-first on the sofa, rolls to the floor and onto Sheba's tail. Juliet freezes, not daring to breathe. She feels like she's lit a fuse and there's nothing she can do. Mitch and Sheba spend an eternal nanosecond meeting each other for the first time. One makes the mistake of thinking he's found a new friend, the other is torn between staying with her quarry and ridding the world of a drooling obscenity with a wiggling wet nose which will be the first thing to be torn off.

Juliet tips the sofa back. Sheba clamps her jaws over a spiky black object and prepares to rocket from the room. Mitch grabs the other end and gets stuck into a tug of war.

The object disintegrates and the two animals leave the room too fast for Juliet to work out who's chasing who.

Victoria races across the room and slams the door. "Right, let's see what we've got."

Juliet scans the shrapnel, some of which still spins on the floorboards. "We have a three-dimensional jigsaw. What the hell is it?" They kneel among the shards.

Victoria picks up one of four windmill-like objects. "We have a drone. If it's a spy drone, there will be a camera and or a microphone."

"This will be them." Juliet lifts a tiny object trailing snapped wires. "Is someone trying to spy on us? Who would want to?" She gets up, heads to the toilet, and flushes the camera away. "Hope you're still watching."

~

Elbows on the kitchen table, Juliet peels an olive from her breakfast pizza and raises it to the tip of her tongue.

Victoria, spooning porridge, says between mouthfuls, "A man in grey, about fifty years old, saw you reading out directions from a book he identified as Hamlet." She pauses. "It's a bit thin but all we have to go on. I'm going to the college to warn people. I think you should... What are you going to do?"

"This bit of olive looks like a slug but I'm still going to eat it. Then I'm going to take a copy of any book but Hamlet and go for a walk round the village, read it, and fall over things."

"Clever. See you later." Victoria rises, pauses, and says, "What's up?"

"I dreamt about him, the man with the poodle. He was chasing me and waving a big book like it was a weapon. I woke up in a sweat. How is it dreams can seem so real?"

"I ... um..." Victoria stumbles over her words. "Good question. Find the answer. See you later." She leaves as Juliet rises and wanders into the living room. Their chaotic method of arranging books, squeezing them into the first available space, means, 'Use of bamboo for emergency water supplies

58

in disaster zones' is sandwiched between, 'William Blake' and a childhood, 'Princess Schrödinger and the Quantum Kitten' story book.

Juliet fancies herself as a heroic disaster-relief plumber, though she's the first to admit this is a fairly uncommon ambition. She takes the book and shouts, "Mitch, walkies!"

Mitch shrugs off the cat curled up and sleeping on him, and crosses the living room, over the coffee table and easy chair, in one enormous bound. Though dynamic and dramatic in execution, the bound lacked effort in the planning stage and ends tangled in a lampshade and among lumps of tumbling pottery.

Juliet limits this particular disaster-relief to unplugging the lamp, freeing Mitch from a spectacular combination of clove-hitch and bowline knots he's made in the cable, and making a note to sort the mess later.

The sun is out, the northerly wind free of clouds; they didn't make it past sheep in Scotland. A gentle breeze flutters the pages of Juliet's book as she wanders away from the thatched cottage and vaguely in the direction of Wittenham Clumps.

Deep in a chapter on the use of manganese oxides to remove arsenic from contaminated water, she's able to convincingly trip over an exposed root and fall screaming into a holly bush.

"Bollocks. Mitch, that was probably your fault." She extricates herself, pulls thorns from skin and clothing, and freezes at the sight of a tiny figure moving at an impossible speed while dodging between shrubs.

Noting the creature's direction, she uses the pretence of

searching for her book to scan for anyone, or any drone, lurking nearby.

She walks very slowly, still reading and turning pages, and silently creeps up on the strange creature.

Sitting among the petals of a wood-anemone is a tiny man giggling to himself. He peeps between petals, jumps down, and races towards a garden. Fascinated, Juliet follows as he darts along the garden path, places something on it, and dives into a flowerbed.

Juliet squats down and clicks her fingers. Mitch tears through a stand of nettles and arrives, panting, beside her. Stroking his head, she whispers, "I have a little job to do. Check around quietly and bark if you see anything, or anyone snooping on me. Do you understand?" She pats him, "Good dog."

If he understood anything, Mitch translates it to grabbing a branch ten times his length and weight and trying to drag it up a bank.

Juliet creeps forward. The little man, dressed in bright yellows and greens, peers between shoots of ornamental grass, and watches the path.

Juliet gets her mouth close to his pointed ears, and whispers, "Boo!"

The little man shrieks almost above the hearing range of humans. Turning pale green with terror, he spins round, pushes an ox-eye daisy aside to look at the towering and bony, gold-haired woman in torn jeans and para-boots. After a quick glance up to her fierce, pointy features and blue-eyed gaze, he wrings his hands and stares at the ground, while twisting the ball of one foot into the ground.

Juliet says, "Yes, I can see you. Hi, I'm a student at Muffy and doing the pixies, nixies, and brownies module; call me Juliet."

The little man continues to squirm in silence.

"And you're a pixie, I reckon." She waits in vain for an answer. "A shy pixie?" Still no answer. The twisting foot makes a small crater in the soil and is clearly aiming for something of lunar proportions.

"You're a pixie who thought putting that dog turd in a place a man would inevitably tread and therefore make his shoe smell was a really witty naughty and pixyish thing to do?"

At last, Juliet gets a response in the form of a tiny jerked nod.

"May I suggest that that was a teeny bit pathetic?"

The pixie leans forward, arms stiff by its sides, and yells, "Stop it!" Tears, the same size as those humans make, squeeze from tiny eyes. "I'm only a little pixie!"

"Size doesn't matter. What am I going to do with you?"

"You've already told me off. Please don't go on at me."

"I haven't told you off. You haven't done anything worth a telling off."

The pixie covers his eyes, and sobs.

"Hop into my hand, little pixie, and we'll talk this through. Let's go and find a private place."

"What?"

Juliet holds out the palm of one hand and points with the other. "Hand—hop."

He weighs precisely nothing; if Juliet weren't looking, she wouldn't know he's there. She also wouldn't be able to look at his wide eyes and see him chewing his knuckles.

"Cut out the cute, mister, before I decide to clap." She brushes her way between branches of apple blossoms, hops over a fence and sits in a hazel thicket. "Sit there." She points to a stone. "And we'll take a look at your project creation, planning, execution skills, and professional development."

"What?" The pixie hops down and sits, chin on knees.

"What's your name?"

"I haven't got one yet."

"I'll give you one if you work with me."

"A nice one?"

"No."

The pixie grins for the first time. "Thank you."

Juliet scratches mud from the knees of her jeans. "OK, tell me about the man you're picking on."

"He's a man."

"Have you studied him?"

"Should I? I didn't know."

"He's called Brian and is a right smug git. Always turns up at the local fête as if he's God's gift to the village. His wife, Lesley, is lovely though. Wish I had long, curly red hair like her."

The pixie interrupts, "His wife has blond hair. I see it every day."

"I suspected you were colour-blind when I saw your clothes. Anyway, Lesley will be in London working at the moment."

"No she's not."

"What? I smell a rat. He has another woman in there?"

"In a minute. He picks her up from the bus stop every day.

62

About now."

"The total bastard. Right, mister pixie, what are you going to do? He's a first-class target."

The pixie stares at her, wide-eyed, head thrust forward. "What? You're not supposed to encourage me!"

Juliet, eyes narrowed, says, "Pixie, sometimes I can't help myself. OK, what are your specialities?"

"Er … cats. His cat, anyway. Animals and things."

"And?"

"That's about it."

Juliet stands and heads back into the man's garden. "OK, let me think for a bit. Hmm, come with me. Can you round up his cat?" Mitch blunders though the fence. Juliet shouts, "Mitch get out of here; Mitch don't eat him!"

Being swallowed by an over-enthusiastic and under-brained spaniel with a tongue that spatters gloops of steaming slime would be bad enough for a human. For a pixie barely four centimetres tall it could be the cause of a major and emotionally crippling life-event. Juliet suspects she'll be in serious trouble with the college if they have to foot the bill for extensive therapy.

"Mitch, godammit, cough him up or I'll dig him out of you with my bare hands." Mitch disgorges a well-slimed pixie who's wearing an expression of frozen horror that would frighten all the gargoyles in Christendom.

Mitch goes on to send lumps of turf flying from his claws as he runs in circles on the grass and leaps at imaginary flies; Juliet and the pixie dodge behind a low wall to avoid the deluge of whirling saliva blobs.

A car roars along the lane.

The pixie frowns, whistles, and a tom leaps through the cat-flap, jumps to the wall, freezes as it sees Mitch, and grows to twice its size as the fur tries to emulate a small explosion.

Juliet screams, "Mitch… Oh gods, nooooooo!"

~

Midday is the time for all students to lounge in their bed, other people's beds, or hide among rushes by a river. Juliet's chosen the latter. "Pixie, you have been very naughty, very very naughty. This rather spectacular event is bound to get on the front page of the parish paper. I'll have to tell you off and stab you with my ice cream."

"You were naughty too!" The pixie dodges Juliet's lunge and licks her ice cream as it passes his head.

Juliet rolls on her back; the pixie jumps on her face and sits astride her nose.

"Pillock, I can't see you like that—you're too close to focus on."

"Tell me the story that will be on the front page of the paper." The pixie jumps up and down in excitement.

"The story of the banker, the mistress, the car with the open sunroof through which a cat jumped, closely followed by a mad dog in hot pursuit, and what happened to the neighbour's greenhouse and swimming pool?"

"Yes!"

"Why bother? Seeing it for real was far better. How did you choreograph the cat? Is it magic?"

"It's what we do. Do I get a name now?"

64

"Didn't you notice? I already gave you it."

The pixie leaps up and somersaults. "Brilliant! Thanks—the best name ever." His head goes on one side. "Are you going to be in trouble with the college for what we did?"

"Lol, I don't think much would get me into trouble, unless I did it without style."

She raises a hand. "And that was awesome style. High-five, Pillock."

Chapter 7

Juliet, boots and book in her hands and Mitch safely in his gem, walks barefoot across a pasture, warm grass massaging and tickling her feet.

She's pretending to read and study, a skill she'd mastered by the end of primary school. Deep in thought, she's headed home, stopping from time to time, frowning and placing the side of a curled finger over her lips.

She thinks, So … what powers a pixie? How can one direct a cat through the air? Who can tell me or is this another thing I have to work out for myself? I think self-directed learning is a cop-out. Maybe the professors are so crap at actually teaching they feel we're better off without them. I wonder if that means we set our own exams too?

"Juliet!" Cheryl's voice stabs into Juliet's reverie with such force that she jumps, lands, and screams.

"Cheryl, don't do that! How many times do I have to tell you?" Juliet, after years of developing lightning-fast responses to brothers leaping out at her, lives in fear of belting her best friend and having to call an ambulance. As a bonding process she doesn't think it holds much potential. "Ow. You made me tread on a nettle. I'm suing you for unnecessary foot tingle."

Cheryl, dressed as usual in a flowing frock, runs

breathless through her garden gate and across the pasture, her auburn locks working really hard at emulating both pre-Raphaelite and windmill. "Guess what? You'll never guess."

"Er … the Napoleonic wars are not quite over and a French zombie army is even now encircling the M25?"

Cheryl stops running, frowns, and wrinkles her nose. "What? What are you on about? No, Brian Baker crashed his car into a swimming pool. His cat got into the car and panicked. I saw it all!"

"Just a cat?"

"Funny that; I thought I saw a dog too, but no one else did. Poor Audrey is so shaken up that I'm not helping her with her maths today."

"Audrey?"

"His niece. She was in the car and..."

"Niece … right." Juliet mentally slaps herself.

"Yes, his niece. We're doing calculus."

"Isn't that something you remove with vinegar?"

Cheryl frowns and heads into lecture mode but stops as Juliet grabs her elbow, and says, "Let's sit under this tree, chill out, and talk about men, sex and … that'll do."

"Sit?"

"Yes."

"Here—on the grass?"

"Sorry, I quite forgot the chaise-longue. My silly little head, you know. Nothing bad ever happened from sitting on grass." She sits. "See? no one died. Here, I've got a book about plumbing you can plant your dainty little arse on."

Cheryl looks at the ground as if it may act in some way that she won't enjoy. She smiles. "This is like a picnic."

"Yeah, for slimmers. You meet any cute blokes in Cambridge?"

Cheryl sits. "I wasn't really looking."

"Don't let trivial things like university interviews blind you to the more important things in life. Anyway, I'll bet you're still busting to go there. Think of all the new friends you'll make. People with brain obesity, who'll understand some of what you go on about."

Cheryl bites her lip. "I don't know." She sags and wrings her hands in her lap. "I'm not very good at friends."

"Good. All the more of you for me. I couldn't have a better friend than you in my wildest dreams. Juliet lies back, hands behind her head. "Uh … do you believe in fairies and pixies and stuff?"

"What? No, of course not."

"We saw them when we were children."

Cheryl wrinkles her nose. "That was just make-believe."

"But why don't you believe in them now? I mean what if you saw one—and it was real—like you weren't suffering from that beer we made from dodgy wheat?"

Cheryl groans. "You won't give me that again will you?"

"No, I promise, but hey, how was I supposed to know? It was a laugh though. Anyway, would you believe in fairies if you saw a real one?"

"If they were proven to be real I'd have to. Scientists believe in a lot of things they can't actually see. Like black holes. And your beer wasn't a laugh. Watching that film together and then not stopping me phoning the police to say zombies had invaded Sotwell was mean of you."

"Well, everyone was lurching in the street. How was I to

68

know the King's Head had just closed?"

Cheryl frowns. "Not everyone. The police didn't lurch."

"So why did you give Jake some beer? I mean he was on duty and everything."

"I wasn't thinking straight. I really try not to think about what happened."

"What's wrong with arresting the whole village for being strange? I think he was saner at that moment than he's ever been. We're an odd lot even when we're behaving in public. Oh, guess what?" Juliet claps her hands and beams at Cheryl.

"Guess? This isn't something about French zombies again is it?"

"I'll be in Cambridge a lot. I have some work there. We can meet up. There's a museum with squishy things in jars, and a place in the market where we can eat Thai noodles. You'd best go with me in case you get the two mixed up."

"You're so rude." Cheryl pulls up a handful of grass and throws it at Juliet but misses by miles. Juliet doesn't mind. It's the thought that counts.

Cheryl goes on, "Are you really going to be there?"

"For ages—years maybe. You should see the toilets I went to. Handmade lead connections and decorated porcelain bowls. The cisterns were the same hues as willow-pattern plates but all classical Greek patterns. I'll show you. You'll love them."

Cheryl tips her head to one side and in a rare moment of insight says, "Do some people think you're weird at times?"

"Yes, Cheryl. I'm weirder than hairy cutlery and getting weirder."

Victoria, pulling the straggling tops of a garden hedge

aside so she can scan the pasture, shouts across to Juliet, "There you are."

"Am I? I thought so but was beginning to worry. Thanks for the confirmation. Hell's bells, this place is getting busy."

"Hello to you too, Cheryl. Sorry, but I need Juliet. Hurry up, love!"

Juliet rises and slips her boots on. "See you later. Sounds like I need to get into my super-hero plumbing suit and save the universe." Juliet gives Cheryl a wave, and zigzags between thistles. Reaching Victoria, she says, "OK, what's up?"

"Mike has set an appointment for you. He sent it to your manual but I know you didn't take it so I came rushing back. You need to go to college." They race down the narrow lane separating their gardens, and brush head-high cow-parsley aside.

"No day off, huh?

"No, there is no such thing as a day off when you're a Muffy student."

"Hey, tell me why Brian and his niece couldn't see Mitch."

"Work it out. Now, the house may be being watched, so we're going to make it look as though this is a genuine call-out. I've put your college things in the van. Get changed in the back as I drive."

"But we may be—ow, stop flicking twigs back like that—may be followed."

"We have precautions and backup. I'll explain later. Write me a list of what you need in your manual and I'll bring it all along this evening. You may be away for some time."

"What do I call Professor Mike?"

70

"Call him Mike: only that. Run faster!"

~

The dim light of the college entrance hall heightens Juliet's other senses. Students come in a variety of smells. The one right in front of her pongs like a wet rat. Pushing past him, she's unsurprised to see grey whiskers and a quivering shiny nose.

The quickest way to Mike's office is marked in red on her manual's map as is the time for the meeting, which changed from black as the deadline passed, three minutes ago. Not knowing if this is a bad thing or a very bad thing, Juliet sprints into the corridor anyway, raises her spear, and shrieks in what she hopes sounds like a berserking banshee on a genocidal charge.

She sees the little yellow sign on the ground saying, 'Corridor Closed for Cleaning' a fraction of a second before she sees the cleaners scream, trip over buckets, and dive down side entrances. One of them gets to the T-junction at the end of the corridor and hurls himself towards the very office to which Juliet is headed.

The door crashes open and the cleaner shouts, "Professor Robe, save me!"

Juliet, unable to stop due to the foam and soapy slime on the flagstones, skids in, having lost little momentum. Her war-cry turns to a wail of terror as she trips on the edge of the carpet. The cleaner dives over a desk, the professor sitting behind it crashing backwards under his weight. The only other person Juliet can see is a slight woman singing into a

71

suit of armour. Juliet dismisses her as, 'probably not an immediate problem' and thumps, sprawling, on the carpet.

She runs a quick damage check and is glad to find all her limbs present and in the right shape, leaps up and looks around. The circular office is decorated with a mixture of marine fittings, like a man-o'-war, and Edwardian ebony office furniture. There's a ship's wheel behind the desk. It's attached to the wall and to the bookcase via a set of gears, presumably to move bookshelves around without the professor having to get up and walk.

Two hands grip the far edge of the desk. A bald head rises slowly between them. Mike's eyes come into view, wide with terror, and spectacles askew.

Juliet says, "It's only me. Sorry I'm a bit late," turns and yanks her spear, still vibrating, from the suit of armour.

The cleaner half-rises, crouching and ready to fight, wielding a broken chair leg as a club. Juliet bobs her head and gives his pale sweating face her sweetest smile. "Hello."

The cleaner looks at Mike. "Is it safe?"

Mike replies, "Don't be stupid, 'it' is Victoria's daughter. *She's* probably safe; it's the rest of us I'm worried about." After a deep breath he straightens his glasses and stands up.

The cleaner, still staring at Juliet, lifts the chair and lets go of it. The chair topples again. "I'll call maintenance, shall I?"

Mike gathers his wits and sets a deep frown on his brow. "Juliet, everyone in this college, from the cleaners right down to the students, have an obligation not to cause undue terror and dismay. However, that was one hell of an entrance."

The woman by the armour pokes a finger through the hole the spear made. She frowns and sings into the helmet's open visor, frowns again and looks at Juliet. "That's a bit better, but I'm still not sure it'll do."

Juliet decides to completely ignore her, believing there may be more immediate problems to address.

Mike pats the cleaner on the shoulder. "If you're fit to stand, do it. If you're fit to pour everyone a glass of port we can all get to know each other and bring some convivial sanity to the occasion." The woman starts singing again. Mike says, "Electra, can you give it a rest for a moment?"

With no one attacking her and the total lack of either the panic or fury she was expecting, Juliet relaxes and decides to unravel the mystery of the strange woman and her even stranger behaviour. "I'm Juliet, I take it you're Electra, nice to meet you. I hope you don't mind me staring but it's not often I see someone singing into a suit of armour."

Electra, barely three-quarters Juliet's height, were it not for the fact she's standing on a chair, bows, candlelight shining off the silver skin of her bald head.

"I'm trying to replicate the sound of siren song for a forthcoming concert. Mike's helping me."

"You're going to sing and he's going to throw himself in the sea and drown? That's nice, you get a free meal."

Electra blinks. "Er … no. Mike is an expert on speech and sounds. He thought of the suit of armour. You see siren song is not about enticing men to throw themselves into the sea. It's all about the male sirens' total lack of interest in romance or sex."

The cleaner pushes a crystal glass of port into Juliet's hand. Electra must have read Juliet's blank expression, as she goes on, "The poor female sirens have to burden every word, every note, with a degree of seduction beyond the capacity of any other race. Indeed they do it so well that it works across species. If you think human sailors have had a hard time in history, you should see how the whelks have suffered."

Juliet takes a sip of port. "Whelks—yeah—poor bastards."

"The sirens embed subtle resonances by vibrating their ribs as they sing. Excessive stridency is modified by the damping effect of their breasts. My problem is..."

Juliet winces as connections are made in her brain. Sometimes, like now, they connect like colliding bullet-trains. She interrupts, "Solved."

"What?" Electra stares at her, open-mouthed. Even her gums, tongue, and lips are silver. There's absolutely nothing to attract werewolves into a quick snog.

Juliet says, "Go to your screen, type, 'SS Solutions Ltd' and look at sanitary wear. I've got some I could lend you."

Mike interrupts, "Doing it now," and pulls a scroll from the sleeve of his gown. Juliet downs the remaining port in one as Electra, the cleaner, and Mike pore over the information.

Electra's pupils go from pale silver to incandescent yellow. They burn at Juliet. "You want me to sing into a metal toilet?" Her melodious tones have switched to murderous hiss. "Are you taking the piss?"

"You could disguise it, put some flowers in it … I dunno. Think of it as a glorified pan-pipe."

The cleaner laughs. "They're pretty expensive. Hope you're feeling flush. Ha-ha."

Juliet and Mike stare at him. He clears his throat. "Yes … I have cleaning to get on with. See you later." He heads into

74

the corridor. Electra, still glowering at Juliet, follows.

Mike says, "Please close the door and lock it, Juliet. We have much to discuss and I don't want any more explosive appearances."

She turns the heavy brass key and pulls the chair Electra was standing on. "On you go, Mike. Keep it simple. I've been having a day or maybe the day's having me." She slumps in the chair, arms dangling over the armrests.

Mike sits on the desk, steeples his fingers and taps them against his nose. "I'm trapped between the inevitable, irresistible, and the impossible."

"Take the day off."

"Half the academic staff spent most of last night discussing what to do with you."

"That's a conversation I'm so glad to have missed."

"I'm giving you a résumé now. Awakening should take three years at a gently sustained rate. You blasted right into seeing and talking to brownies on your very first day. It's OK for a lecturer to show a brownie to students but only if he or she thinks the audience's sanity won't be compromised. You were dealing with fire and operating at a level few first-years achieve. We need to slow you down or you'll be telling us you can handle brownies and pixies next week."

"I saw a pixie today."

"No you didn't. Your sanity must already be compromised. You were hallucinating. Wishful thinking gone mad."

"I helped him with a little professional development."

Mike closes his eyes and takes a deep breath before staring at her again. "Juliet, that's impossible. It would be

75

easier to convince me you drew a smiley on the moon."

"How was he able to steer a cat through the air and into the sunroof of a car? He even made the cat turn upwind. That's pretty clever."

Mike goes rigid, eyes wide. After a moment, he says, "Is this true? Can you verify this story? Were there any witnesses?"

"Yes. It's all round my village. The evidence is a bent car half in a swimming pool, a newly formed drive-through greenhouse, and some serious embarrassment on my part."

Mike splutters and chokes before saying, "You admitted responsibility?"

"What? Are you kidding? No way. People would think I was mad."

Mike slaps the table. "I'm going to have to take drastic action, go against the whole ethos of the college, and intervene in your studies. You're stopping the awakening process this minute." He lifts a phone. "Zola? It's worse than we thought; could one of your people take Juliet under his or her wing from right now? Who? What? Whatever. Send him over."

He puts the phone down. "I'm giving you a mentor, well, someone to keep an eye on you. A post-grad abominator; a gorgon named, in our language, Daniel. Juliet, you were in terrible danger, dealing with things that can send a person permanently insane."

"And working with a man who has a head covered in snakes is safer?"

Mike sags. "Slightly. Look, don't make any jokes about haircuts or curling tongs: just don't."

76

Chapter 8

I'm bloody exhausted. Give it a rest, will you?

Juliet's sitting in a spare room; a quiet sanctuary of old wooden high-backed chairs polished by thousands of bottoms over hundreds of years. Around her, stone columns, faded tapestries, and stained-glass windows have lured her into studying mode.

Her manual has been busy, growing increasingly grumpy and flippant, and says it needs a break.

While waiting for Daniel to arrive, Juliet has called up and read almost everything the manual can find regarding gorgons, lamias, spectres, and other exotic creatures.

She closes tired eyes and leans her head against the back of the chair. Gorgons, no one knows how they came about. Theories about inventing them to scare children, that some snakes became allergic to the ground, that snake-hair started as a fashion statement but grew a mind of its own, all seem as unlikely as the existence of a creature that has evolved to no longer possess ears and eyes but abdicated those senses, along with speech, to the snakes themselves.

She thinks the manual ran out of real material and started inventing bullshit just to keep her happy.

Not realising she's even fallen asleep, Juliet wakes with a yelp as something licks her cheek. She bats away several blurry objects moving too close to focus on.

Leaping from the chair, she says, "What the Hell?" and sees a humanoid with writhing serpents growing from its head. "Daniel?"

All the snakes talk at once, some of them to her, some to each other.

"Humans taste funny." "Why was she banging our heads with her hands?" "Hello, are you all right? Are you warm enough? Would you like anything?"

Juliet rubs her eyes. "One at a time, please."

"One what?" "What's it saying?"

"Can just one of you speak at a time? I can't follow all of you at once. Sorry if I hurt any of you. You got into my personal space and startled me. Which one of you is Daniel?"

"But that's anybody's space." "I don't think the human likes things close to it." "How does it have sex then?" "Do you do sex by post?"

Juliet stifles a scream. "How do I speak to Daniel?"

"You talk to us and we pass the message on." "Yes, and we say what he thinks back to you." "As an additional service we add recommendations for fruitful further enquiry."

"Say hi to him and ask what we're supposed to be doing."

"He says good morrow and how nice it is to meet you." "Which isn't much, because he resents you being dumped on him." "He likes you a little bit. Not enough to fall in love but that may come." "You probably know this, but just in case, I think all your little snakes are dead." "That's called hair, moron. Humans also have it in weird places that snakes

78

wouldn't want to go." "Why?" "Must be to alert us to the presence of dangerous odours."

Juliet gathers all the screams lining up in her speech-centre and chains them there. "What are we supposed to be doing?"

"He's thinking. Please hold." "Hey, people, I've just worked out that humans can't see behind them." "They could put mirrors on their shoulders. It's amazing they haven't thought of that." "Um, human, how can you tell if you've wiped your bottom properly? Ew..." "Ssh, everyone. Daniel wants the human to follow him. He's going to investigate data on a new abomination in Divine Administration." "Is that an abomination in Divine Admin? or data in Divine Admin that relates to an abomination?" "Who cares?" "Come on, human."

Juliet follows the gorgon into a gloomy corridor, glad that she's no longer bombarded with words but not sure if the synchronised waving of heads and barber-shop style singing that the snakes resort to is any great improvement. She wonders why such a thing as a gorgon actually exists. She thinks, Right, someone imagined gorgons existed, so God made them... Ooer, does everything that was ever imagined exist? I've imagined some pretty scary things that I'd rather not remember let alone sit next to in the canteen. Ah-ha I'm on to something—though I'd probably prefer to be off it. Does God make things that people believe in and feel bad about unmaking them when people stop believing and so let them remain?

A snake interrupts her train of thought, "Excuse me, human."

79

Juliet whirls round to face the voice. The gorgon has gone through a side entrance but she walked straight on.

The snake says, "This way. You need more eyes or you'll get lost. We've decided to have only one of us talk to you, because you seem a bit simple and easily confused. I've elected myself head of snakes."

Juliet follows Daniel and his bad-snake-day through the side entrance and into a huge hall made entirely of living trees. Columns of wood, walls of interwoven branches and roots, give the place a cathedral-like feel. Lances of sunlight cut through the canopy overhead and stab the dusty air.

The snake says, "We have lots of questions. For instance..."

Juliet interrupts, "What's an abomination?"

"Something in the wrong place." Daniel marches to an ivy-covered arch half hidden behind a flutter of blue butterflies.

"Like someone putting sandpaper in a toilet-paper dispenser? Or Earl Grey tea in a truckers' canteen? Come on, do be more specific."

"You could be an abomination and cause outrage or drive people mad..."

"You're mixing me up with my mother at parties."

"...if you were in the wrong place." The snake pauses to snap at butterflies as Daniel enters the arch. "We invented humans in order to scare children and make them behave but we only use humans in stories. If you turned up in our world an abominator would have to sort things out. Some gorgons visited your world once but they were chucked out by abominators, see?"

80

Ducking under the arch, Juliet shields her eyes against searing white light. A tall, glowing figure dressed in a white gown and with white hair hanging almost to the marble flagstones, leaps forward and points a silver trident at her throat. He shouts, "You may not..." and collapses as the pommel of Juliet's spear punches his stomach almost all the way to his backbone.

Juliet snatches the trident from his hands and turns it on him. "Do go on." As her eyes get used to the light, she sees he's thin, frail, looks at least a hundred years old, and is lying on the floor, gasping. As he straightens his halo, Juliet drops both weapons, kneels, and cradles his head. "Oh, you poor thing. I'm so sorry."

She helps the wheezing angel to sit up, and says, "My mum told me it's always better to strike first and sort out problems later."

The angel rubs his stomach. "Better for you because the problems are someone else's?"

"More or less."

He puts an arm round her shoulders. "Help me up, there's a kind lass. I'm Archangel Angus of Achnashellach, semi-retired. Call me Angus; few English people can say Achnashellach without dribbling or losing teeth." He grunts as Juliet hauls him to his feet and straightens his robes.

"I'm Juliet, a student." She lifts the weapons and offers him the trident.

"Yes, Victoria's daughter in your first-year gown. As I was saying, but let me rephrase, it's really not a good idea for a student so junior to come to Divine Administration without a more experienced guide than an abominator. Why are you

81

here, young lady?"

"Not sure. I think I was causing trouble or frightening people in the college and they wanted me out of the way."

Daniel's snakes hiss and splutter. "We don't have time for this."

Angus waves them away. "On you go, pal. I can't let the lassie go with you. I'll take over from here."

"She is with me on the orders of Professors Robe and Zola."

"Change 'is' to 'was' and everyone's delighted. Well, no gorgons called Daniel get sent to Hell One for a week's refreshing break to ponder upon the wisdom of trying to argue with me."

"But..."

"Is not an advisable beginning to a sentence when addressed to an angel with a short temper. You are needed urgently in the Angelic Canteen. Someone delivered Earl Grey tea by accident."

As Daniel heads away, still hissing, Angus winks at Juliet. "Consider yourself rescued."

"You're a hero. I was minutes away from becoming a hairdresser. Earl Grey? You were eavesdropping."

"I have good ears and no desire to waste them. Well, now you're here in Divine Admin, would you like a guided tour?"

Juliet nods. "This may sound like an odd request but..."

"My dear, of course I'll show you the plumbing. We have everything, going right back to neolithic hollow log pipes. We also have some of the very first taps. You may have seen Rotherham brass but we have a..." he looks towards the arch, "Ach, hang on. Here comes another first-year. I'd better stop

82

him before he gets into trouble."

A figure darts under the arch, sprints forward, and stops, shielding his eyes. Angus points the trident at the gangly, ginger-haired man squinting in the fierce light. "Stop right there or die!"

The man sees the trident-heads nearing his throat, squeaks in terror, drops the sabre he is carrying, and collapses in a faint.

Juliet has had men falling at her feet before, usually because they were, 1) stunned, 2) bleeding, and, 3) her brothers. Years of practice has her kneeling, resting the victim's head on her knees and talking him gently back to reality. She pats the man's face. "Errol, you arse, Angus wouldn't hurt you. He's just a bit daft and overzealous."

Errol opens his eyes, tenses, sees Juliet, feels his cheek being stroked, and relaxes. "I can see right up your nose."

"You've been practising chat-up lines? Tell me who your mentor is and I'll kill him for you."

"You know the inside bit of your stud?"

"Intimately."

"It has a bogey on it."

"I'm saving it for lunch. We can share if you like."

Errol sits up, rubbing elbows and knees that connected with the ground too hard, which is all of them it seems. He mutters, "What was I...? Oh yes, a most unfortunate development." He looks at Juliet. "I was looking for you. Ah, complicated story but the upshot is that your mother and my father have gone missing."

"Do you think it's love?"

"Try and say something that isn't a joke but is considered

and actually helpful. Your mother phoned my father and told him she felt her house was being watched. He went over to see how he could help. She phoned him from her van but was cut off during what sounded like a fight. He went to see what was going on. He found your mum's van abandoned. He also found a lot of blood, human hair, and what looks like cat fur. He phoned me and now he's not answering." Errol checks that he's not about to be stabbed by the trident, and stands. "We have to see what's going on."

Angus raises a hand. "Hold hard, laddie. Tell me the whole story."

"That's it."

Juliet stands too. "Actually, it started a little earlier. We had some sort of spy-drone lurking outside our house. The cat, mum's moderator, caught it. We think someone saw me reading my manual in Cambridge and sussed what it was."

Angus frowns. "Interesting news but I'm not about to let two naïve first-years get embroiled in what sounds a highly sensitive and potentially volatile situation that could be disastrous for the college and Divine Administration. This will be dealt with by professionals. I'll find something else for you to do. Follow me." He turns and strides away. "Someone turn the entrance lights down. I'm getting a migraine."

Juliet says, "Angus, that's your halo."

"Oh yes. I never really worked out how to handle halos. I'll throw a bit of gown over it."

Juliet whips out her manual. There it is, a scrawl from her mother.

Juliet of Great Soddingwell

Everything's fine. Harry and I are kicking arse.

Don't get involved or you'll screw up.

Love, Mum.

Juliet shows the message to Errol, who says, "Harry's my dad. She working with him? Poor woman; he's such a prick."

"That might not be a problem."

As Angus's halo dims, their surroundings almost stop her worrying about Victoria's predicament. Juliet's standing on a marble walkway and looking down through thousands of such walkways supported by arches. Gleaming white architecture goes on as far as the horizon and to the centre of the—she wonders if Divine Administration is an entire planet. Shadows, that move apparently at random, dot the otherwise sunlit scenery. Puffy clouds rise, fall, fly in all directions, and pass through each other.

Juliet and Errol stand frozen by the mind-numbing spectacle.

Angus, still walking away, calls back, "I said follow me!" and waves at a passing cloud. "Cooee! These two need a lift, if you'd be so kind." He steps off the walkway and into thin air, screams, disappears from view, and rises again. "Ha-ha —wings, never forget them."

Errol looks at Juliet. "What do we do? Do we trust him?"

"I'm keeping college simple and not trusting anyone."

Chapter 9

A tentacle of vapour reaches from the cloud, lays shadow over the white marble walkways and pinnacles of Divine Administration, wraps both Errol and Juliet in a fierce grip, and lifts them. They're pulled into a cloud-lined room, the walls swirling and revealing glimpses of Divine Administration far below.

Errol covers his eyes. "I feel sick."

Juliet says, "Can you face away from me? You know, just in case."

The floor, if there is one, Juliet's not sure, is almost knee-deep in scrolls. A semi-transparent spectre with several arms, a deep frown, and extra eyes that travel at random over its skin, works with feverish haste. The room is full of almost invisible ghosts that fill the air like drifting smoke. The spectre grabs the nearest one, slaps it awake and demands its name. Scribbling something with a quill he presses the scroll against the ghost, who yelps and vanishes.

As fast as the spectre gets rid of ghosts in this way, so more appear. He says to Errol and Juliet, "Eh up! Nice to meet you. Get weaving, we haven't got all eternity, like. Har-har. That was a joke, like."

Juliet says, "Hi, I'm...

"You talk too much, lass. There's been a baby-boom in

86

Tir-nan-Og."

"That's totally fascinating but..."

"And a whole mountain has been turned to rubble in Hyperborea. It's just a pile of stones now."

"Wonderful. We're supposed to be following the angel Angus of … somewhere."

"No time for that. Take scrolls and assign them. Quick like. Forget Angus; this is your new life." He throws a swan-feather quill at her.

She catches. "I'm sorry to disappoint you but..."

"Every stone needs a soul, not to mention all the babies in Tir-nan-Og. Silly elves. They got religion, banned public entertainment, even maypoles, and now all they can do to pass the time is fornicate. Get on with it; I'm drowning in scrolls here and all these ghosts need a new life."

Errol says, "Excuse me but could you drop us off at a place to which the word 'Sane' could correctly be applied?"

"Only when this panic is over, which is never. Grab a scroll, wake up a ghost and ask its true name, write it on the scroll, put scroll and ghost together to reincarnate it and then do it again and again. You two do the stones; I'll deal with the elves."

Juliet asks, "Stones have souls?"

"By gum, lass, everything has a soul. Hurry!"

Juliet whirls round as a crashing noise startles her. From the room, a long corridor extends, sloping upwards into the distance. It's lined either side with thousands of wooden pigeon-holes, from which fall scrolls that roll in waves towards her. She snatches a few from the floor and reads labels like, 'Elf', 'Stone', and 'Tube of Ceiling-Tile Glue'.

Errol, comes to his senses. "Let's get out of here."

Juliet says, "Errol, brilliant idea. Did you think of that all by yourself?"

The spectral man interrupts, "No one gets out of here except if I open the floor and you fall to your deaths, like. Get weaving or end up a pair of messy splats like hairy strawberry jelly. You have ten seconds to decide. No pressure."

Angus appears, wings a-blur. "Give me my students back, Xalvador of Helmsley!"

"Not on your nelly. I've been asking for help for six centuries and..."

Angus, face red, gnarled fingers clenching his trident, lunges at the spectre. Errol grabs Juliet's arm and pulls her to the corridor. "Let's find a way out."

They ignore the whirling weapons and battle cries, and wade through scrolls. It doesn't take long for Errol and Juliet to decide that the corridor is likely to be little use as a means of escape. Juliet uses her spear to plough a passage through the cascading surge of vellum, papyrus and writing-paper. She gasps out, "Errol, I've got an idea."

"Oh good because I haven't."

"Find the pigeon holes under the letter 'U'." She moves further up the corridor.

Errol asks, "Are you going to tell me your idea?"

Juliet flounders on and says, "Um ... 'UU', 'UT', 'US', nearly there."

"Tell me your idea. If you die in the next couple of seconds, I could use it instead. It would be a shame for it to go to waste."

Juliet snatches up a scroll. "How do you spell Xalvador and Helmsley?"

Errol spells; Juliet writes. "Right!" She wades back into the room, pins the scroll on her spearhead and hurls it at the embattled spectre.

The frenzy of combat subsides; the whirlwind of scrolls settles; Angus, looking confused, stabs his trident at falling paper. "What, where've you gone? Come back and fight."

Juliet says, "He won't be back for a while."

Angus, still half-crouched, peering around with wide eyes and thrusting his trident as if expecting attack at any moment, pauses and turns to Juliet. "What? Where did he go?"

Errol kicks scrolls aside. "Ha! We had this splendid idea."

"What was that?"

"I don't know. Juliet's rubbish at sharing."

Juliet says, "He was ghostlike, therefore dead. So he had a soul but wasn't in an object or body. I found him one and reincarnated him."

Angus relaxes and lowers his trident. "Well done. Very well done indeed. But no doubt the idiot will be back when he dies again. How long is that likely to be?"

"Depends if the plumber doesn't crack the porcelain when installing it like I did. Accident on a job at a service station north of Banbury. Xalvador is the replacement urinal and should be busy for some years."

Errol snorts. "Tell me which one. I can't wait."

Angus raises both arms, first to straighten his white hair, still a tangled halo-like mess from the fight, and then to spread them wide. He shouts, "Begone!" The scrolls, corridor, ghosts and seals disappear. In a quieter voice, he adds, "Ooh, it worked—damn junk mail." He smiles at Juliet and Errol. "Now you have a cloud office of your own. What would you like to do with it?"

"Coffee machine," replies Errol.

Juliet says, "En-suite bathroom and shower—without a soul."

Errol laughs. "Is it safe to use the word 'Shower' when standing in a cloud?"

Angus passes his trident to Errol, and sweeps wrinkles from his gown. "Since you have an office, you may as well get some experience of admin. What sort of jobs would you like to have a go at?"

Juliet shakes her head. "I want to explore."

Angus narrows his eyes. "I suppose I could let you wander around Divine Admin and see what happens here. You would be pretty safe in a cloud. Alright, I'll let you loose but on one condition only." His bushy eyebrows lower to a frown and his gaze hardens. "You will not try to get involved in whatever's happening regarding your parents."

Errol nods. "Of course, we totally promise."

Juliet tries her best shocked innocence expression. "Absolutely. You can rely on us."

Angus does not look impressed. He takes his trident from Errol. "Go to Hell."

Juliet's shocked that an angel would speak that way. "That's not very nice..."

Angus rolls his eyes. "Idiot. I mean go to *Hell*. Start your studies there and work your way back up here. Just keep a very close eye out for any areas currently marked in red in your manuals, in Hell, or here; they're much the same when it comes to danger."

Juliet says, "How do we get to Hell?"

"That's for you to find out." Angus opens his wings and flies part-way through the wall, stops, looks back, winks and smiles. "Or you could just sin."

As he passes from view, Juliet turns to Errol. "Whatever you're thinking, stop now." She picks up her spear, letting the lethal blade swing roughly in his direction.

Errol shrugs. "What I'm thinking is how to control a cloud. What were you thinking?"

"Er … I wasn't thinking anything. Well, actually, I'm thinking what was that all about? One minute he says this place is too dangerous for us to be in without him, the next he lets us loose. There's something going on. Maybe it was an experience; a planned lesson. What did we learn?"

"That depends. We have to work out the secret of the universe or something. I've been struggling to decide if teleology, epistemology, or cosmogony is the best way forward. Frankly I'm stumped. Maybe we need all of them but I'm not sure if any of them are up to it. What's your opinion?"

"The world is flat; the sun and moon go round it, and anything that happens is mainly down to pixies mucking around."

Errol stares at her. "That's really clever. You sound like you talk but don't think first. It's as if making people laugh, or winding them up is all you want to achieve through verbal communication." He sighs. "But somehow you seem to cut through confusion and obfuscation. You have a simplicity of thought quite perspicacious."

"Up yours. I think a lot. You miss the important things I say like, 'What did we learn there?'."

Errol frowns and strokes his goatee. "I reason and analyse but sometimes don't get anywhere. Maybe we should join forces. Are you a synthetic or reductionist thinker?"

"Use shorter words."

"A lumper, or splitter?"

"Use pictures."

Errol fingers his sideburns. "Do you tend to see the universe as one thing or made of individual components?"

"I don't see the universe; it's too big. What did we learn there?"

"We learned that Hell, Tir-nan-Og, and Hyperborea are real. That implies the existence of a whole lot more."

"We learned that everything has a soul, even stones and bathroom fixtures. That's important; I can just feel it."

The wall to Juliet's left grows transparent and opens. A dark-haired woman, stately and graceful, walks into their cloud. She carries a lyre and three scrolls. Her flowing, silvery gown makes a sighing whisper as she moves.

Eyebrows raised, she looks from Errol to Juliet. "What a heavenly couple! How lucky can I be today? I don't believe we've met. I'm Andromeda of Polichnitos. Have I come to the wrong place? I was looking for Xalvador."

Juliet says, "He's gone out for a drink with the lads and won't be back for some time. I'm Juliet of Great Soddingwell, and this is Errol of … uh."

"Toft,"

"Toft?" Juliet splutters.

Andromeda says, "How wonderful to meet youngsters.

92

Your souls are so fresh and new. I could just eat them up. Can you take all your clothes off? I'd love to sculpt the pair of you in the finest white marble but, Juliet, do keep hold of your magnificent spear." She winks at Errol. "No doubt you have something you can hold too."

Errol's instant blush matches his hair. "Actually, we're busy. Another time, perhaps."

"Busy? You lie delightfully. You're students and have probably only just got out of bed."

"We are busy. We're here to learn about Divine Administration and we're not getting far. All we've seen is a less than divine punch-up and Xalvador's utterly chaotic approach to resurrection."

Andromeda laughs and brushes the scrolls over the strings of her lyre. "Then you have already learned much about Divine Administration. Come with me, my department is much more sophisticated and entertaining." She beckons them, turns, and adds, "We like to be beautiful and happy, tra-la-la," and steps back into her cloud.

Errol says, "Ah..."

Juliet nods. "That's what I was thinking. Should we go?"

"Oh right, this is one of those situations where a person asks for someone's decision so they can blame that person if it all goes wrong."

"Correct. And your decision is?"

"We're supposed to be rescuing our parents. Sadly the matter is being dealt with by Angus, which is probably bad news but we know so little about anything. We don't even know how to control this cloud. We're going to be stuck here unable to do anything unless we find out as much as we can

93

about how this place and the college work—or don't work—and then apply what we learned."

Juliet taps the flat of her spear against her forehead. "I think you just tell the cloud what you want it to do but you have a point. Let's find out more. I suppose her department can't be worse than Xalvador's."

"What if I were to say, it's probably going to be more of the same but different?"

"I'd probably scream, so don't."

They step through the opening, Juliet testing the cloudy-floor with her spear to see if she's going to fall through. "How can we walk on a cloud?"

"Carefully. We don't want to do anything to precipitate disaster."

They enter a vast cavern. The interior of this cloud is shaped into tables, desks, pillars, balconies and chaise-longues. Fountains tinkle into pools and the air is filled with delicate laughter and soft music.

A blue-veined marble statue walks towards Andromeda. A desk follows him. Andromeda says to the statue, "Anaxagoras, darling, will you be a sweetie and just take over for a teeny-weeny moment? I want to show this delicious couple around. Take these scrolls and find a resurrector to give them nice souls, there's a dear."

She turns to Errol and Juliet, clasps her hands, and tilts her head to one side. "Well isn't this exquisitely lovely? What would you like to play at today? You can make people fall in love, be angels, devils, hauntings..."

Juliet says, "We'd like to find out about the Knights of Kramer. They might be giving our parents a hard time."

94

Andromeda gasps and wiggles her hips. "Really? The Knights of Kramer? The forbidden fruit? Angus will explode, though if your parents are in trouble I can understand your concern. Give me a moment to find out what's going on; I must go and speak to people. Then yes, let's be awfully naughty together."

Chapter 10

Errol's happy with the fact that the chaise-longue he's lying on is warm and not cold and clammy as you'd expect from something made of vapour. He recognises that, when hot enough, even rocks can vaporise and make clouds. What's he's not at all happy with is the constant undulation from the turbulence within.

He says to Juliet, lying on another chaise-longue, "I don't think it's fair to feel travel-sick when I'm not actually travelling."

Juliet points at bowls of food on the table between them. "More olives? goats' cheese? asparagus? pickled garlic?"

"Stop it. I feel like I'm going to throw up."

"Anchovies?"

"Do you hate me?"

"Most of you and then some. Andromeda is taking way too long. When she gets back, I'm going home to check on mum's van, grab some clothes, and come back here. You?" She giggles. "Look at your face! green and ginger—cool."

Errol groans. "This place gets weirder. We need to hold onto our sanity. I think it's in short supply here. Xalvador indicated he'd been working alone for centuries. Look what it did to him."

"He'll have plenty of company now."

96

"I think Andromeda works alone too. Everyone else here is a statue. They all look classically Greek. Goodness knows what eccentricities she's developed over three thousand years."

Twelve women, looking identical in form, face, and clothing, approach; all their steps and gestures synchronised. They speak together, "We have no eccentricities. We simply like to work in an atmosphere of kindness, joy, and love. We have learned about the predicament of your parents and elected to help rescue them. We go to your fair city of Cambridge. We do this for the pleasure of it, extending our sweet compassion to you two worried young lovers. Fret not and put your tender fears aside. We will return with joyous news."

Juliet chokes on an anchovy. "Errol, do I need glasses or am I drunk?"

"Neither. They are a chorus. It's a Greek thing."

The women go on, "Though we bathe in the cheer your presence brings, we require that you work here to cover for our absence. Your worksheet for the day will arrive imminently. Sadly, though we can supply each of you, for the duration of your stay, with a brownie to assist and keep you safe, we have no budget for your disguises as angels, devils and all the rest that you will require. My lady Andromeda informs me that, in the course of your brief time in college, you've shown more than enough innovation to find ways of presenting yourselves appropriately." The women bow and wave goodbye. "Farewell. Let not your hearts be troubled."

Juliet waits until they're out of earshot. "Errol, I was too busy choking, why didn't you say anything?"

"I didn't want to encourage them. I thought they were going to go on for ever. Saccharine is a Greek word. I can see why they needed it."

"Uh, that's not what I meant—she's never going to fool anyone with that disguise."

"Who? What?"

"That was Andromeda making an arse of herself. She honestly thinks she can walk around Cambridge looking like an escaped cloning disaster?"

Errol snorts, "She'll be fine if she takes a bucket. Everyone will think they're collecting for rag week. How could you tell they're Andromeda? They were plastered in makeup."

"Because I've got eyes and a brain. What's your story?"

Errol shrugs and starts a conversation he hopes won't end in more abuse. "If you're going home. I'll go into town and create some costumes for us."

Juliet narrows her eyes. "Can I trust you with that?"

Errol stands and runs fingers through his bushfire hair. "I won best fancy-dress outfit three times. I'm a champion. Ninja, rock-climber and knight. Well, those were at primary school but it's all relevant experience."

Juliet stands. "Oh whoopee, I'm looking forward to seeing my first green and ginger angel. See you later. She tells her gown to take her back home.

~

Only she's forgotten that she changed in the van while Victoria was driving.

98

Appearing in pouring rain, in a country lane, and just above a puddle, wasn't part of her plan. After the initial scream comes a splash, some swearwords, and the screeching of breaks as a car comes round the bend.

Juliet stands, uses her spear to vault onto the verge, and is hurled down by a surge of water. The car comes to a halt and Cheryl's father leaps out. "Are you? Did I? Juliet?"

"Yes, no, yes." Juliet gets to her feet. "In that order—I think. I'll bring you updates as I get them. Help me out of these thistles."

In the car Juliet shocks herself by learning she can lie faster than tell the truth. She's returning from a fancy dress party, got dropped off at the main road, and very sorry she's making the passenger seat wet.

She learns that Cheryl has been invited back to Cambridge and is already blowing people's minds. Following phone calls from the professor who interviewed her, she's helping him and his research students with her genius.

Juliet's dropped off outside her house, notes the van sits in the drive and seems undamaged, hurls the front door of the house open, and treads on Sheba's tail.

Toby, sitting smug on the shelf, says, "Hello, you look soaking wet. I'd take those clothes off right now if I were you. You could catch your death. I'm to inform you that your mother says, 'hi' and that you're not supposed to be here. Oh, and Sheba got left alone here and is lonely."

Juliet fails to pay attention; she's busy screaming. "Get off me, you bloody moron!" She tries to bat the cat off her leg without having the attention of twenty claws and a mouth full of teeth diverted from it to her hands. But Sheba's hugging

Juliet's calf and currently very happy about where her teeth and claws are.

The jug adds, "You're making a puddle on the mat. Other than that, it's all been pretty dull around here."

"Mitch! Get this maniac off my leg." Mitch does his erupting act and the two animals disappear into the kitchen, from which come the sounds of furniture toppling and the rubbish bin clattering across the floor. Juliet heads upstairs to the bathroom to tend her bleeding leg.

An hour of showering, putting plasters on, washing her gown, evicting Sheba and Mitch from racing around inside the tumble dryer, getting the two manic animals into her pendant, checking her phone for messages, reading the text, 'Don't' from her mother, loading two bikes for use in Cambridge, and Juliet is wrestling the van along sodden lanes.

She passes Brian's house and screeches to a halt, stainless-steel toilets clanging behind her. A car rests in the neighbour's swimming pool. A different car.

Winding the window down, she swears under her breath and roars, "Pillock!" disregarding the chance of Brian hearing and taking it personally, which she doesn't see as much of a problem anyway.

A tiny dot whizzes through the air, the open window, and onto Juliet's nose. Pillock clings there, his head bobbing from side to side and looking into Juliet's eyes in turn. He says, "Hello," to each about twice per second until she shakes him off.

Closing the window she says, "You're coming with me. You need further training."

"Oh, goody—but aren't I an expert yet?"

"You need to do different things and to different people." She accelerates and turns the wipers onto fast.

The pixie's eyes widen beyond belief, as if inflating. "Wow, wow, wow!" He jumps on Juliet's nose again. "I never thought of that. Can I be your best friend?"

"Yes. I really like best friends. But not on my nose, especially when I'm driving. Hop down and do me a favour. I need to know all you can find out about working in the department Andromeda of Polichnitos runs. Can you get my manual to work? It's a bit moody at times."

In between lectures on the various heavens, hells and divine protocols, read out in Pillock's piping voice, Juliet rings Cheryl. "How's it all going, big-brain?"

"Juliet! I'm having a great time. I can tell you all about it at the weekend."

"You can meet me for lunch in the market today and tell me everything over Thai noodles with chilli sauce and stuff. Bring tissues; the sauce stains are a bitch. I'll be there in an hour and a half."

"Oh, I'm really busy today. You remember when Brian's cat got into his car?"

"Uh ... sort of. What about it?"

"Well, the cat turned in mid-air and went upwind. I worked out that was impossible but it happened. I'm on the brink of turning everything upside-down. You see, given that all probability is expressed as a value between zero and..."

"Alternatively we can talk about something else."

"But it's so exciting. It means that the axioms haven't taken something into account. Whereas we believed that nothing could travel faster than light or that minus one degree absolute couldn't be reached in our universe, if the impossible isn't impossible, then the fundamental precepts of..."

"Arrrg! you're killing me. Let's talk about aqueducts."

"I'm having to invent a whole new mathematical … aqueducts?"

Juliet, after years of dealing with Cheryl's explosions of enthusiasm, used the word 'Aqueduct' to derail Cheryl's head and buy the necessary nanosecond to consult her own conscience, metaphorically kick it un-conscience, devise a plan, bite her lip in horror at her lack of any principles whatsoever, convince herself anything is morally justified if it saves the universe, and say, "Take a break and meet me for lunch. I want to introduce you to my boyfriend."

"Boyfriend?"

Juliet grits her teeth. "Boyfriend."

"Ooh, I'd love to!"

"See you later." She cuts the connection. "Pillock, write in the notes section of the manual, 'Errol of Toft, give me your phone number this instant or die'."

Several teeth-gnashing seconds later she speaks into her phone, "Errol..."

"What's so urgent? Is it about our parents?"

"You'll never find out if you interrupt. Shut up."

"As you wish."

"Go to the Thai noodle place in one hour and fifteen minutes. Don't approach me until I'm talking to a woman who will be dressed in a frock so out of date it almost looks cool. Come over, look as if you're really glad to see me, hug me, kiss me..."

"Kiss you?"

"Uh, just my hand. Tell the woman how lovely she looks and take an interest in her."

"What's this about?"

"It's about my friend Cheryl who may be on the very brink of proving the universe can't possibly exist."

"I heard something about that when Hildegarde inducted me but only that there was a possibility of it happening, not that it was happening. I'm confused."

"Confused? get used to it. I reckon Cheryl's the mathematical genius Satan wanted. She needs distracting. If I introduce you to her as my boyfriend, she'll fall in love with you on the spot. It usually lasts about two weeks, then she wails that she's found the wrong man and I'll have to knuckle you into never seeing her again. I call it the, 'Sweet, tears, and blood cycle'. All very intense. You'll love it."

"Can we avoid the knuckle bit?"

"What? That's my favourite."

"So why will she fall in love?"

"She always does. She doesn't trust her judgement in men, only mine."

"Paradoxically, that's one hell of a compliment."

"Paradox is a really good word and should be her middle name—and all the others. Anyway, all her hormones, suppressed by her obsession with study, explode outwards and she's a passion-bomb until she gets exhausted and misses her books. That's when I get pulled in."

"I'm not sure..."

"It'll be the best two weeks of your life. Do this for me and I'll skip the knuckles bit, honest."

"But..."

"Errol, this is an emergency, *really*, OK? You and Cheryl are going to happen and you are currently not bruised and battered. Let's keep it all that way."

"Are you actually threatening me?"

"No, I'm sort of begging with a hint of violence. Alright, just begging with—fine, just begging. Please?"

"You really want me to go out with your friend?"

"I want the universe. Life's going to be pretty dull without it."

"And what will we achieve in those two weeks?"

"You won't achieve anything except distract her from maths. You'll need to sleep in between sessions. I'll have to squeeze three years' education, a masters, and a PhD, oh ... and a Nobel Prize for universe-saving into that time."

"I can't believe I'm actually saying yes to this. What is it about you?"

"Deep down, you respect me, love me, think I'm cool."

"No, must be something else. See you at the market."

Juliet looks down at Pillock sitting on the steering wheel. He's staring at her and looking stunned, hands on his head. He squeaks, "You're a worse pixie than me!"

~

Juliet's a bit tired of this high-octane life and arrives at the market feeling ragged but buoyed up by the prospect of seeing Cheryl.

The noodle-queue is shorter than before, and Juliet's pinching her lip, wondering whether she's going for chicken

104

or prawns, when she spies Cheryl talking to a man in the street. The man points, Cheryl nods and heads into the market.

Juliet shakes her head, giggles, and thinks, only Cheryl could stand next to a market and still need to ask for directions to it. Putting fingers into her mouth, Juliet lets out a shrieking whistle that renders the area silent as people jump, look round, or dive under trestles to shelter from possible falling bombs.

Cheryl runs towards her, Juliet braces for the impact and gasps as she's pulled into a bear-hug and danced round and round.

Cheryl says, "Juliet, it's so good to see you! Everything is so exciting."

"You look fabulous. I've never seen you looking so happy." The market settles as they choose noodles. Errol arrives, sweeps Juliet into another hug, kisses her hand, and says, "Darling, who's your gorgeous friend?" He takes Cheryl's hand and kisses it. "I'm Errol."

Juliet orders food and watches the inevitable play out. Cheryl's pupils are huge and fixed on Errol like she's a starving cat watching a mouse in a microwave. By the time Juliet's given them plastic containers of noodles, they're already on the subject of Kolmogorov's and Cox's theorems, Errol valiantly struggling to keep up with Cheryl's torrent of words and appearing to hang on every one.

Juliet enjoys fifteen minutes of peace, chilli, and no threat of imminent death from tridents. Her manual rustles in its satchel and she pulls it out.

Juliet of Great Soddingwell and Errol of Toft

I have news and a desperate need for your

sweet company. The office seems so empty

without my dear and beautiful new friends.

Please come. I miss you both so much.

Andromeda of Polichnitos

Juliet pretends to check her watch. "My goodness, you two. Errol, we'll be late. Must dash, Cheryl, lovely to see you."

She drags Errol to his feet. He says to Cheryl, "Maybe we can catch up later. I'd love to hear more about all this. It's so fascinating." They swap phone numbers and Juliet leads Errol to her van.

She says, "Tart."

"Pimp."

"Ooh..."

Errol looks at his manual. "I take it our messages from Andromeda amount to an emergency summons?"

"That's what I'm thinking. Uh..."

"Yes?"

"You're amazing. A hero." She drags him into an alley. "Look, can you ride a bike? I brought a couple. I couldn't get the van anywhere near the centre of town. You can hardly squeeze handlebars down some streets. The van's a handy place to get changed into our gowns. I chained the bikes at the entrance of this college." They turn a corner and Juliet gasps. The bikes have not gone as such but fifty to a hundred other bikes have been piled over them and they're all chained to each other. "Oh bugger, let's run instead."

~

They're hardly through the entrance to Divine Administration, when Andromeda's cloud drops and envelops them.

"Darlings! Oh, my darlings." Andromeda glides towards Juliet and Errol. "Your parents may be in the hands of the Knights of Kramer. I'm dealing with the situation personally, along with some of the most powerful people in Divine Administration and the college. I'll keep you informed but you must take over here for me." She places a scroll in Juliet's hands. "This is the worklist and the next job starts in thirteen seconds. Fly, my children! Do what Anaxagoras tells you."

She disappears, revealing the blue-veined marble statue behind. He says to Errol and Juliet, "I need one of you as an angel in Wessex right now. Just follow procedure; your nixies and brownies will take care of the rest. The portal opens!" He thrusts scrolls at Juliet and Errol. "You'll need these." Dark cloud swirls around them, snatching the hems and cuffs of their gowns.

Errol empties his rucksack, slaps something on Juliet's head, says, "Hang onto these two handles and keep these straps round your wrists, and..."

Juliet doesn't hear the rest; she's too busy screaming.

Chapter 11

Crows croak and flap from tall elms as a man, dressed in oiled leather and a surcoat of grey chainmail, pushes towering cow-parsley aside and steps onto a muddy path. Grey eyes, grey beard, and greying hair, he looks slit-eyed at the people gathered.

He throws out a trembling hand. "You, the Alder People…" he points to the figures on one side of the path, "…and you, the Clan of the Oak." He gestures to the others. "I reject allegiance to any warring family. The time has come for the old laws to arch over petty squabbles."

"Fool," growls a man, bearded and clothed in leather armour and iron helm, sweat dripping from heavy jowls. "You reject your own kin, Asclepius." He nods at the group dressed in rust-red cloaks and standing between hazel trees. "You think these animals know what law is?"

Asclepius's hawkish features crease into deeper lines. "Both families, clans, tribes, call them what you will, dwindle in numbers. Our young would do well to find breeding partners other than their half-brothers and sisters. Lord Lealands, you must see the wisdom of this."

Lealands swells at the mention of the title he's recently given himself, tenses muscles under waxed leather armour. "The old laws ruled over whole kingdoms. They do not apply to a few skanky fields."

Asclepius whirls round to face him. "Kingdoms arise from alliances of families!"

Lealand snorts. "And that strumpet fawning over Eadweard amounts to an alliance?" He points to Edith of the Alder people, who stands in the centre of the path with her lover.

Eadweard, his heart overflowing with love to the point he's prepared to disown his kin, throws off his black, oak-dyed cloak. "I love Edith. I eschew the small-minded ways of my folk. I disdain the old enmity. I embrace Edith and the future of our united families."

From among the Alder people a woman strides onto the path. She opens her ruddy cloak and metal sings as she draws a blade. "Enough of these insults. Enough of this abuse of my sister by that," she jerks her chin at Eadweard, "seducer of my kin. I, Brihtgiua, challenge any of the Oak Clan to a fight to the death." She glares at the figures standing in the dappled woodland shadows on the other side of the path. Her last glare lands on the matriarch, Hemlock.

Hemlock snarls, "Oh, big, brave words, my princess of the oink-people. Who are you going to pick for the fight? There's me with one gammy leg; my lord, who can only see things a hand's-breadth from his eyes, Aelfwyn, a five-year-old girl, and Eadweard who's too besotted with your piggy-eyed sister to walk anywhere without bumping into trees and bursting into poetry. Oh, great heroic warrior, who is worthy of your mighty…" she looks at Brihtgiua's weapon. "…little, rusty sword?"

Argument stops as a peal of thunder shudders through the

109

sky. The clouds darken to a threatening yellow-grey. All the people turn to the source of the noise—a towering, twisting column of black air tearing a huge elm tree from the ground.

The sky blazes with lightning, a constant blinding curtain of it fills the tormented wind with the bitter tang of its fury.

The terror passes. Silence falls and figures look up from where they have thrown themselves to the ground. Mud and twigs drop from pale faces. A rain of leaves and stunned sparrows flutters from the sky. Aelfwyn runs, arms uplifted and catches a spinning leaf.

"Ow, get off my fingers, you little brat," snarls Lord Lealand.

Asclepius rises, his chain-mail rattling. "It is a sign. The Lord is furious that you deny His laws."

"Oh shut up, you mad git," calls Hemlock from the ground. "And help me up instead of spouting rubbish."

Even she is silenced by the scream in the sky. All look up. Spinning and swinging from lines under a two-metre-wide sheet of orange fabric, a teenage woman descends. Legs kicking, her frantic struggles, piteous wails, and shining golden hair hold everyone's attention.

With a final screech, the girl plants both feet on the top bar of the gate at the end of the path. The wood smashes under the impact; the girl curses as she's dragged through thistles and nettles until the fabric and lines catch in branches.

"Total bollocks," she shouts, pulling wrist-loops from her arms. Thin, with spiky hair and multiple face-piercings, she brushes off the worst of the foliage caught on her gown.

With a huge snarl of indignation she turns her back on the dumbstruck people gathered by the path, waves her fists at the sky, and screams, "A kite, a bloody kite? Oh har-har, very funny; get stuffed."

She turns back. "What are you lot staring at?" She slashes down nettles with a black and silver spear and walks towards the open-mouthed gathering.

Aelfwyn drops her leaf and runs to Juliet. "You were flying! Are you an angel?"

Juliet's aggression melts in an instant. She kneels in the mud and ignores the way it squelches under her knees. "Hello, sweetpea, I have no idea what my job description is today. I'm on secondment from college. I think I'm supposed to be an angel right now—I didn't actually see the timetable. Call me Juliet. That kite, instead of wings, was my colleague's idea of a joke." She reaches out and ruffles Aelfwyn's hair. "Don't worry, I'll get the bastard."

Aelfwyn goes on, "You are an angel. You've got a halo!"

Juliet's hand flies to her hair and pulls something away. "Two glow-bands held together and stuck to my hair with gaffer tape…?" She leaps up, whirls round and waves a fist at the sky again. "Cheapskate!" Looking back down at Aelfwyn she says, "Here take it."

Aelfwyn gasps. "Can I really have it? It's so beautiful. It shines."

Asclepius kneels before Juliet. "Oh, great angel, I am but a humble sinner. I strive to be priest to these wayward people. Since Saint Bartholomew brought a piece of the true cross from the Holy Land over the sea…"

Juliet silences him by raising a hand. She pulls the manual from her satchel. "Hang on, I'm getting a text." Brushing a snagged holly leaf from her shoulder, she flicks through pages and reads out, "Uh ...'Last judgement scenario...' oh wot?" Her lips purse and brows descend in concentration. "I think Pillock covered that this morning." She shrugs. "Guess I'll just have to wing it."

Asclepius gasps. "The Last Judgement? Has Armageddon come?"

"What? No, yes, sort of..." Juliet shrugs again. "Most of those answers." She scans faces. "Right, you lot. I've got to do this fast. There's a lot to get through."

"How may we assist...?" Asclepius asks but Juliet cuts him off.

"I'll go through your last judgements."

"The Lord has passed judgement on Mankind?"

Juliet rolls her eyes. "Do be quiet. No. Your last judgements on each other."

"I don't understand."

Juliet frowns again. "You haven't read your William Blake? Hang on, what year is this?"

Asclepius replies, "The eight hundred and thirty first year of our..."

Juliet slaps her forehead. "Crap. Right, listen up; I haven't got all day." She waves her hands to maintain silence. "You go to Heaven or Hell depending on what your last judgement was before everything went poof."

"Poof?" Hemlock splutters. "What's poof?"

Juliet groans. "Why did I sign up for this?" The strange visionary experience she first felt in Hildegarde's toilets surges through her mind. She sees the realities of the people around her are largely illusion based on what they hope or expect to see and denying most of what just happened.

"Yup, 'poof'. I think half of you died in a freak tornado thingy. The rest of you have suffered head injuries and are probably hallucinating—or something: I dunno really. Sorry, I think I should have made that clear at the outset." She pauses and frowns. "Was that very clear?"

Hemlock shrieks and runs to Aelfwyn. "My darling, my cherub." She smothers Aelfwyn's face in kisses. "You may be dead and gone: you've hardly had time to live."

Aelfwyn writhes out of Hemlock's passionate embrace and stands, hands on hips, scowl on face. "Do I look dead?"

Juliet shrugs. "It's a bit complicated. Right, you." She points to Brihtgiua. "Yes, we'll start with you."

A nixie leaps from the kite, across the path, and into Brihtgiua, who freezes, still sword-in-hand. Her eyes widen as she stares back in time to the argument. In a monotone, and against her will, she says, "I wanted to fight, prove myself strong and courageous. I want fame and glory, wealth and servants."

Juliet rubs her chin. "In this case judgement was tainted with greed—pretty normal evil behaviour. I'll put you in Hell One. Sadly, it may be a bit of a disappointment, a bit like thinking you've bought tickets for 'Zombie Dusk Meets Alien Predator' and finding you're actually booked into 'Princess Nincess and the Pink Ponies', but hey-ho." She steps forward and touches Brihtgiua's forehead, "Time to go to sleep." Brihtgiua fades, leaving her body in a crumpled heap on the ground.

Juliet turns to Lord Lealand and points. "You: your last judgement."

Lealand freezes too. "I thought I could use the argument

113

to extend my realm and take Brihtgiua as a concubine."

Juliet snorts, "Power and sex: the usual. Fine, Hell One for you too. Say hi to fluffy with the blue eyelashes and hooves for me."

She points to Hemlock. "Your turn."

Hemlock intones, "I wanted the whole thing over and done with. It's time for dinner and I've made venison sausages."

Juliet hisses. "Arg! What sort of a judgement is that?" She bangs her forehead with the heel of a palm. "What am I going to do? I could send you to the reincarnators but the only one I met was a total nutter. Ah, thank God for Buddhism. You can be a deer in your next life. Sorry, but I don't have time to think this through in any depth."

Juliet puts them both to sleep and kneels in front of Aelfwyn again. "You snuffed it big time, kiddo. That elm splattered you thinner that a supermarket economy pizza topping. What was your last judgement?"

Aelfwyn stands, hands clasped behind her back. "All adults are stupid and fuss over nothing. If piggy-face wants Eadweard to snog her, why not let him get on with it? No one else would."

Juliet's eyebrows leap to the top of her forehead. "Hell's hairy nipples. What am I going to do with you?"

"Just don't make me eat mum's sausages."

Juliet takes Aelfwyn's hands. "I could use a level head on my team. Divine Admin is full of prima-donna tosspots." She pokes Aelfwyn in the belly-button and wiggles her finger. "You want to come with me?"

"Do I get to keep my halo?"

"Yes. Come on." Juliet rises and leads Aelfwyn away.

"You got a head for heights? Because this thing scares the tits off me."

Walking to the kite which has been extracted from the branches, untangled, coiled, and neatly folded by its brownie, Juliet says, "Call yourself a brownie of safe-keeping? You nearly had to carry me back in buckets. Get it right this time, or your next incarnation is as a toilet roll."

Chapter 12

Juliet of Brightwell-cum-Sotwell
Next stop Limbo. Someone has been dead for
ages but won't take it lying down.
Errol of Toft.

Aelfwyn has taken to being a ghost like a natural. She whizzes around making loud 'wooo' noises that almost drown out Juliet's screech of terror as the kite opens and hauls her into the air.

They head into a gloomy cloud. Aelfwyn says, "This is fun, being dead, you should try it."

"I promise I will."

"What's that in your hair?"

"Uh … my head?"

"No, a little man with a funny hat. He's asleep."

"That'll be Pillock. He's a pixie." Juliet yelps as her feet thud onto something solid. The scene clears a little. Grey sky and ground, a flat, featureless landscape, the absence of smell, texture, and sound, make this a place of total desolation and gives Juliet the same sensation as having double maths at school on a Monday morning.

"This must be Limbo. We're here to talk someone into

116

dying. Maybe you can be a role-model."

"Why do you have gold hair? Can I have hair like that? I bet I can. What's Lim—the thing you said? Is it that duck?"

"Rule one. One question at a time or I scream. Uh … did you say 'Duck?'."

"Follow me!" Aelfwyn floats ahead. Her hair is gold and she trails a black gown.

Juliet smirks and realises this is the first time in her life that someone's ever tried to dress like her. She runs after Aelfwyn and, in the distance, sees the hazy outline of a duck. Juliet's a bit confused; the duck seems to be further away than she expected. She keeps going until she's eye-to-eye with a man-sized mallard who quacks out, "Go away. You lot have been bugging me for ages. You're wasting your time. I'm not dead."

"Actually you are."

"But still walking and talking? You don't know what you're on about."

"This is a spear." Juliet jabs it into his throat.

The duck leaps backwards, wings flapping and scattering iridescent feathers. "Ow! Bloody hell that hurt."

"It hurt but you're not dead. That proves you're dead."

"Eh, what? Oh right. So what? I'm staying here and that's that."

Juliet shrugs. "Fine, whatever."

The duck's head jerks back. "You mean that? You're not going to send me to Heaven or Hell or reincarnate me?"

"Nah, I won't send you anywhere if you don't want to go, but why not reincarnate? It's pretty boring here."

"Why? Ponds, that's why."

"Uh … you have a problem with ponds?"

"Problems! Would you like the whole list or just the top million entries? I'll start with all the neck-strain. You humans probably think we ducks have our heads underwater half the time because we want to nibble food but it's really about sheer terror. Do you realise how chronically scary it is to know that at any moment you could have your tender parts bitten off by a pike? Next, the smell; ponds pong. If you're in a pond you pong too—and what have you got to wash in? Ooh, that's a hard one. Do you need a clue? it starts with 'P'. So many animals live in ponds and none of them can use a toilet so guess what they do? Would you want your feet in an un-flushed bog all day and night? Then there's..."

"OK, OK. What do you want to be?"

"There's a choice? Really? Doesn't that break rules?"

"I'm beginning to think that there aren't any rules in my new life, only egos. Now, what do you want to be?"

"Um … something less stressful and more interesting. A human. Yes human. I want romance, tragedy, triumph, suspense, humour, kings and queens, storms, battles, tears and laughter, sex, drugs and rock and roll. I want..."

"You do like your lists. You want all that in one life? Fine, I'll make you human but that'll mean changing your identity. What's your real name currently?" Juliet extracts her quill and a scroll from her satchel, and writes, 'Human Male'. "Be careful what you say at this point, these scrolls contain powerful but easily confused brownies."

Aelfwyn giggles and says, "I bet he's called Bill."

The duck glares at her. "Shut up. Bill of Portland Bill. Laugh and your head comes off." He lunges at the giggling

Aelfwyn but flinches away as Juliet's spear flashes between them. He says, "Don't you shake that spear at me."

Juliet points it at him. "Nice duck or duck on a stick?"

"Nice duck."

"OK, let's finish this." Her quill spatters ink over the scroll. "So it's 'Bill of...' Where do you want to come from?"

"Somewhere with good food, you know, things that don't try to swim away or wriggle when you swallow them."

Juliet taps the quill against her nose. "Hmm, they do a good burger at that place we plumbed in a big kitchen. Uh … right. 'Stratford-on-Avon'. Sex, drugs and rock and roll, huh? 'Born 1964'. All done, there you go." She tosses the scroll to Bill. "Catch."

Duck and scroll touch and vanish. Juliet says to Aelfwyn, "I think I'm getting the hang of this job. Just not the hanging from the kite bit. I reckon Errol should be the angel from now on. I'll stick to wearing horns, except he probably bought plastic reindeer antlers, knowing him."

Juliet of Brightwell-cum-Sotwell

OMG!!!!! What have you just done? You total maniac. Get back here before you ruin the whole of creation.

Errol of Toft.

Aelfwyn peers over Juliet's shoulder. "That's writing. Can you read it? What does it say?"

"I think it says I can take early retirement. Let's go."

119

~

Errol's thumping a chaise-longue and shouting at it, "Stop wiggling!"

Juliet arrives, throws the wrist-straps down and roars, "Kite? Kite? You'll pay for that, buster."

Errol whirls round. "Do you realise what you just did?"

"I don't have a head for heights."

"Bill Spears... Bill Spears was born in Putney in 1964, not in Stratford in 1564."

"1564? Crap, it's these stupid quills. When they're not squirting ink about like juice from a squashed cockroach, they're drying up and missing bits of letters."

"You've just re-written history. Bill Spears was my hero. Poor man, they didn't even have computers in 1564, let alone pens. I doubt he'll be bothered with quills. You've just doomed the best animator in human history to oblivion. All that genius gone to waste."

"I was talking about kites."

Errol shrugs. "Guess how many shops in Cambridge sell angel wings? Go on, guess—or can't you count up to zero?"

Aelfwyn says, "Are you two married?"

Juliet splutters. "Do we sound that bad? No, not married, just practising."

Errol frowns. "Who are you speaking to?"

Aelfwyn glides over to him."Woo." Errol doesn't respond.

Juliet lays on a chaise-longue and lets it massage her shoulders and back. "I'm talking to my friend Aelfwyn who died a few minutes ago. She's a ghost and having the time of

120

her life. Looks like you can't see or hear her. Anyway, I'm not doing any more flying. Give me the reindeer antlers and I'll do devils."

"How did you know...?"

"Cheryl is a super-intelligent person too. As a species you're as resourceful as beached jellyfish. While you're being all angelic, I'll go and find something for me to wear."

"Are you absolutely sure you want the jobs that don't include the kite?"

"Yes. I hope that answer is easy enough for you to understand."

Errol winks. "Oh good. The next job is for a fiend and happening any minute now. It's weird and keeps starting and stopping." He waves a scroll. "You'll need to read whatever appears on this and say your responses out loud. Looks like some sort of conversation. My manual says it's a scroll of summoning."

"You total bastard. You want me to do the next job too?"

"It was your decision, so who is the bastard?"

Feet thunder into the cloud-office and a strident voice yells, "Juliet of Great Soddingwell. You're under arrest."

Juliet fails to jump, get up, or indeed respond in any way. To the chaise-longue she says, "Down a bit, yes, left a bit—ooh yes."

A gaggle of college guards dodge between statues, pillars and furniture. Errol says to Juliet, "I think you need to worry about these people."

"Deal with them, Errol."

"I doubt intellect will help. This is a brute force and ignorance situation."

The voice calls again, "You're under arrest."

Juliet snarls, "No I'm not. I'm having one. Oh, sod it. Right, Errol—teamwork. I'll supply the brute force; you do the ignorance bit. Oh, and lie flat on the floor." She leaps up and readies her spear.

The guards surround them and the four-armed female Juliet hit before steps forward. "I, Zoongaash..."

Juliet's arms blur as she holds the pommel of her spear and makes the head whirl in unpredictable figures-of-eight; the point hissing millimetres from guards' faces. They jump back as one. She stops at looks at each of them. "Ooh, I love a good loosen-up before I kill. Who wants it first?"

"I, Zoongaash, lieutenant of the Vigilante Guild, declare your attack on myself and my colleague to be illegal. Put down your weapon and come quietly."

"No. Now what are you going to do?"

From the floor, Errol says, "Ignore their orders, Juliet. You do what you want. The Vigilante Guild is just a bunch of self-appointed thugs that like to dress up and boss people around."

Zoongaash hisses, "We are our own authority. We make the rules. Do as we say or suffer." She looks down at Errol. "And you'd better shut up if you know what's good for you."

Errol raises his right eyebrow. "You made the rules? Then logically there are none. You see, given that you have taken the right upon yourself to make them, I employ equal right to make a rule that is more in keeping with the ethos of the college. From now on meritocracy will replace tyranny. Go away and study some books—not the sort you colour in."

Zoongaash rolls her eyes. "There are eight of us and we're

all armed. There are only," she looks from him to Juliet, "one of you."

Juliet says, "I've heard that all before. You're nothing but school bullies who failed to grow out of the playground. Do you know what I do to bullies? I can show you their bloodstains in my secondary school bicycle sheds if you like. I even signed some of them."

Zoongaash nods to another guard. "Deploy the nixies."

As the guard upends the sack, Juliet shouts, "Mitch! Sheba! Kill!" Pillock leaps from Juliet's hair and dives at Zoongaash.

The air fills with panicking nixies, the overexcited yelps of Mitch, the terrifying howl of a cat out to massacre little animals, screams from the guards in general, and Zoongaash in particular. Pillock has invaded one of Zoongaash's spears. It wrenches itself from her grasp and bashes her about the arms and head.

Like the other guards she turns tail and flees, only to fall flat on her face as the spear tangles her legs.

In a few seconds all is quiet again, apart from a yelp of surprise from Mitch who wasn't expecting the statue he's urinating on to walk away.

Errol flops back onto the chaise-longue. "Peace at last. I hate interruptions."

Juliet shakes her head. "No, not interruptions. I think I'm getting it, how this place works. I reckon everything is planned. We all get the same treatment or tailor-made lessons. It's how we deal with stuff that is what this place is about."

Errol's eyebrows rise. "Interesting idea." He opens his manual and asks, "Is Juliet's hypothesis correct?" He looks at

Juliet again. "Very clever you. How did you work that out?"

"A sort of wild guess, a feeling. Because, uh … people we've never met knowing so much about us. Angus knew I liked plumbing. Andromeda said we were capable of innovation. They must be discussing and organising stuff. It's too weird otherwise."

"Oh yes. Weird is the order of the day, the side order, and we'll probably get a little bowl of weirds to suck when we get the bill. I'll tell you what's amazingly weird and interesting. You went back in time, several hundred years. Time travel actually exists."

He asks his manual, "How is it possible to go back in time?" He frowns and falls silent.

"What?" asks Juliet.

Errol looks up. "It says it doesn't know about time travel."

Juliet asks her manual, "When I went back in time..."

You can give up on that sentence now. You're not making any sense.

Juliet snaps the manual closed. "My mum said make sure I ask the right questions, only she forgot to tell me what they were."

"Maybe we're looking at this the wrong way. What we need is a paradigm shift."

"What we need is not what you just said. We need food." Juliet grabs the summoning scroll. "Anyway, who decided I had to do all that angel stuff and not you?"

"We only had seconds to choose. I held an emergency discussion with myself and reached a unanimous agreement."

"Let's go to the canteen and do this summoning thing there. All this unhealthy Mediterranean gunk is no replacement for black pudding."

"You want black pudding? I'm not sure it's very healthy."

"I like it dead—not healthy."

The summoning scroll writhes and opens. On it appear the words, "We summon the great fiend of madness, Perverted Demoness Anna of Phylaxis the Depraved. We need guidance on destruction and genocide."

Errol reads too. "Ah, definitely your job."

Chapter 13

In a dense forest of mixed trees, under a dazzling blue sky and surrounding a huge flat rock, stand several trees, deep in concentration.

Alderman scans the gnarly faces of the figures gathered around the great stone of summoning. His burr of a mouth cracks open and he says, "Elma, get your roots off the table."

"It's not as if we're eating off it, dearie." Elma continues to paint the ends of her roots.

"Where's Ashley?"

Several of the council glance at each other from behind their fringes of leaves; one tree sniggers.

Alderman scowls them into silence. "Where is she?"

A towering conifer with a mane of emerald-green needles, says, "There's a rumour that she has squirrels."

Alderman stretches out two of his branches, unrolls an ancient sheet of vellum, places it on the table, and writes. The others watch in silence as brown pitch, exuding from his finger-like twig, forms the runes of divination. "There are no squirrels," he says in a voice moaning like branches in a storm. "We saw to them. We are masters of the planet. MASTERS!"

Elma whines, "Only the land. In the sea..."

Alderman crashes a branch on the stone. "Silence! We do

126

not mention the slimy aberrations found elsewhere." His eyeballs creak as they turn to another tree. "Hazel, a nut."

The smaller tree trembles. "I have so few."

"That is the problem we're here to resolve."

Hazel offers a wizened, brown nut. Alderman takes it, puts it in the centre of the ring of symbols, and carefully places the tip of his index twig upon it. "Everyone extend a twig and place it on the nut."

Linden, a tall proud sinuous tree with shiny bark, hesitates. "I think this is all a bit spooky. I'm not sure..."

"Put one of your twigs on the nut," Alderman roars, "We are in desperate times." As all twigs meet at the centre, he booms out, "We summon the great fiend of madness, Perverted Demoness Anna of Phylaxis the Depraved. We need guidance on destruction and genocide."

The nut begins to move, slowly at first but with increasing speed and touches letter after letter.

Alderman reads out, "Anna of Phylaxis here, wossup?"

Hazel says, "We are in desperate times..." She reads the next words as the nut moves, "You need an emergency plumber? They don't exist. Pillock, stop mucking around with my spear. Ow, you maniac. Errol, do something before he kills someone. Oh wot? Your fault, you should have grabbed the other end, and stop whingeing; it doesn't look that bad."

Alderman growls, "Careful everyone. Someone must be pushing the nut; this is not making sense. Let the demoness move it." In a more diffident voice he says, "Most accursed Demoness, since we wiped out the plague that was the animal kingdom, the Earth has turned against its own inhabitants in a genocidal frenzy. We need your divine guidance. I, Alderman of Aquitaine, beg your advice. Our air is thin and unhealthy; the planet freezes."

Hazel adds, "It's wretched, we can hardly breathe and there's ice-caps everywhere; you look round and there's another one popped up."

Aldreman shouts, "Quiet!" He reads from the letters spelled by the moving nut, "My colleague in demonosity—shut up, Errol, demonosity is fine—Errol of the bleeding hand, says you're probably lacking carbon dioxide."

Alderman replies, "This is true. The last humans died out and seem to have taken it with them."

The next words he reads are, 'Humans died out?'

"Yes. There were very useful to make vellum and we probably peeled too many of them."

"Vellum?"

"To write on."

"Uh, right. Get some more humans."

"We no longer tolerate the existence of animals except birds and bees. We are the masters." Alderman lets out a manic, thundering laugh of triumph.

"The humans made carbon dioxide for you, plonker. You're snookered."

"We'll die without them?"

"Yup, and when you get some don't peel turn them into writing materials."

"Demoness, we require a solution that doesn't involve those scum! I demand to speak to Satan himself."

"Uh … sorry, we don't actually work for Satan, our company only represents Hell. I have no authority to contact him."

128

Alderman screams, "I wanted Hades, not some imbecile in a call-centre. Study the small-print on the scroll. This summoning requires that I am to be satisfied or Beelzebub himself will fry you."

"Ooer, I didn't read all that stuff at the bottom. Errol, any ideas?" There's a pause, the trees wait in tense silence. As the nut moves again, Alderman reads, "Light a really big fire, one that covers the whole continent."

"Ridiculous. That's suicide, not a..."

"Actually it's a brilliant idea. Other continents won't burn but their trees will get all that carbon dioxide you release. Errol says this solution fulfils the clauses on this scrolly thing. Think about it; all that self-sacrifice to save other trees will count in your favour when I come to pass judgement on you and send you to Hell for killing all the humans. Is there anything else I can help you with today? No? Fantastic to talk to you. Have an amazing day."

~

Juliet rips the scroll in half and throws it on the table. The silence in the canteen changes to a low hubbub as people stop staring at her and return to their conversations. She lifts her food and says to Aelfwyn, "This is a black-pudding burger with fried onions, mustard and horseradish. This is food. The stuff Errol's got is called salad and is what cows eat." Aelfwyn drifts away and attempts to spook those first-years in the canteen who can see her.

Errol winces as he moves his injured hand. Juliet's wrapped it in a napkin and offered to pour salt into the cut to

129

sterilise it. He's not keen. He says to her, "The spear that attacked Zoongaash moved all by itself and now you claim to be speaking to a ghost."

"Yup, life is a right lark, innit? You need to learn to see things like that. Do it quick. I reckon we don't have much time, which brings me to my next question. What's your plan with Cheryl? Have you got condoms? You'll need about fifty."

"We're merely going to discuss maths for a few hours."

"That's why you'll only need fifty."

"I don't have a plan."

"I'll give you one then. Look into her eyes a lot—all the time but not to the point you trip over; she'll be doing enough of that. Let her do all the talking and when you don't understand something, smile and stroke her face and neck."

"Is that what you do?"

"No, I'd wear my fingers out. I throw things at her and scream until she shuts up."

Errol studies a lettuce leaf as if checking it for slugs. "And what's your plan, back to admin?"

"Nah, that's nuts, that is. I've got some thinking to do."

Errol checks the other side of the leaf. "Thinking?"

"How did I change time? How can that even be done? What was that Vigilante Guild lark all about? How come you can't see Aelfwyn and Pillock? Will you learn to see them? Tons of stuff."

Errol puts the lettuce leaf down. "Let's deal with one at a time. You changed time perhaps twice. You were in your present when you went into the past but also into someone else's present. You did something there, passed judgements on

130

people and simultaneously affected their futures and the history of your universe. You returned, and..." His eyes widen. "Oh my goodness! Bill Spears and William Shakespeare are the same person but in two incarnations. History is stable. You only appeared to do something. We've been carrying copies of Hamlet around; it's not as if they popped into existence after you reincarnated Bill. Maybe everything has already happened and we're just watching reality; you know, like watching a film." He groans. "But that means we have no freewill, choice over what we do or say, and that goes against what God intended, doesn't it?" He slaps his hands on the sides of his head. "Ow! Juliet, I'm so confused. How am I to deal with all this?"

"Easy. The plumbers' way."

"Go on."

"Don't do anything. Say you can do it tomorrow, leave it two weeks and then turn up. The client has either sorted it themselves or drowned: end of problem. Let's move on to the next point if even you can't work out time travel."

"About me not seeing things and or the vigilante guards turning up? Can't remember the order; your choice."

"You think that spear moved by itself and the nixies from the sack ran away with nothing chasing them."

"That's what my eyes tell me. What nixies? Nothing came out of that sack that I could see."

"Get glasses. Pillock is a pixie; he can get into things and do stuff, just like our manuals have a brownie and..."

"A what?"

"You don't think your manual writes all by itself, do you? You think it's magic or something?" Juliet's heart breaks as

131

Errol's face crumples into despair.

He slumps back in his seat, and whispers, "I don't know what to think. Maybe we are learning different things, creating our awakening in different ways. I'm just assuming that I'll see these pixies and so on eventually but I don't know."

She leans forward and squeezes his hand but takes hers away as he tries to hold it. She says, "Is that lettuce leaf safe to eat? I make a point of trying a bit every year in case they invent a decent flavour." Errol nods; Juliet goes on. "Brownies generally like to hide in objects and do simple tasks. Nixies aren't so shy and will do jobs outside objects, like tumble out of sacks and tie people up. Pixies don't do what they're told. They like to wind people up and watch what happens. Pixies, nixies, and brownies are all the same species." Errol continues to look miserable, so Juliet changes the subject. "Let's move onto the guards."

Errol rallies and sits back up. He selects a piece of cucumber to study. "I don't think there's anything more to say about them; they're, as you said, a bunch of bullies. I think they may be students who feel they're failing and at least want to pick up some sort of minimum pass and get jobs sealing off dangerous passages and so on."

"Why does the college put up with their bullying behaviour?"

Errol looks at Juliet in surprise. "At last I can really answer one of your questions! Yes, I've been studying the political structure and culture of this place."

He smiles and Juliet relaxes for an unguarded nanosecond, tenses again and says, "Keep it simple. None of your long words. I'm going to eat all of this bit of lettuce. I have to talk my body into swallowing every nibble, so you've got all afternoon."

Errol leans forward. "There is a culture here but … Juliet, concentrate; forget the lettuce. Besides, that leaf is probably feeling equally nervous and revolted as you look. Listen, here in this college, Divine Administration, whatever, there are no rules, no laws, nothing."

Juliet frowns. "No way! Everywhere has laws. You can't be serious. You mean I could take what I wanted, kill who I liked? Uh … disliked, you know what I mean."

Errol shrugs. "Yes and no. People would react individually but there's no authority that would deal with it, no judiciary, and no police. Everything is done on agreements and oaths."

"But that's mad. People would all steal from each other, kill each..." She looks round the canteen, at the people chatting, arguing, sharing food, and stealing each others' chips. "Ooer … uh … why do we have so many rules in real life?"

"I've been thinking about that. I suspect it's down to bankers and politicians. Without rules they would look very silly indeed. The bankers wouldn't be rich and the politicians would be powerless. They'd be like normal people and would have to deal with the emotional reality of that. It would kill them. I put it all down to their insecurity, being bullied at school, and bad potty-training."

Juliet closes her eyes, braces herself, and almost touches the lettuce with her teeth. "Oh, and another thing..."

"What?"

"Complicated." Juliet scowls in concentration. "The

people that were killed by that tornado and tree..." She pauses, frowning. "Half of them were dead but didn't know it. The others were alive but didn't know the stiffs were dead. They all were carrying on as normal. You know, even walking through the fallen tree as if it wasn't there."

Errol groans. "Are you saying what they believed was real —to them? My father says the incredible human power of self-deception is the strongest attribute of our species and has caused most wars and nearly all marriages. Our ability to deceive each other probably accounts for the rest."

Juliet's manual rustles in its satchel. She pulls it out and flicks to the notes section. "Now what?"

Lecture on magic. Nine minutes. Lecture room 777.

"Hey, Errol, there's a lecture on magic. Magic? No chance. Pixies, yes; magic, no."

Errol looks into his manual. "I've not been informed of any lecture on magic." He asks his manual, "Why not?" looks at Juliet and says, "Apparently it's invitation only. That supports your hypothesis that our education is tailored. Hmm, Angus said we needed to go to Hell. Maybe that's important."

Juliet pushes her seat back. "Bye-bye, lettuce, another year perhaps." Her manual writhes out of her hand and flops open on the table.

Bring replacement clothes. No cameras allowed.

Chapter 14

Juliet follows the directions from the manual. An orange-highlighted corridor is the shortest route to lecture theatre 777. Juliet reckons if red means the corridor is being cleaned, orange means the cleaners are standing about and debating the merits of cleaning but actually drinking tea.

Walking under the arch and brushing aside cobwebs and scuttling spiders, she wonders why the corridor twists like the rifling in a gun barrel. Walking along it is not difficult as she doesn't mind being sideways and upside-down from time to time. To her, Cambridgeshire is hopelessly flat and fails to induce vertigo. She thinks this will make a nice change.

Spear at the ready, Juliet marches nearly to the other arch, but stops, as anyone would, when a squashed ladybird, albeit rather large and about the size of an elephant, drops from a portal above.

Crushed beyond any possibility it could be alive, the ladybird nevertheless extends a broken limb to her, and says, "Juliet of Brightwell-cum-Sotwell, you total bastard. I'm going to have my revenge. Do you know how heavy you are? I've made myself heavier. You'll be sorry."

It's clear to Juliet, from the rising fury in its voice and the trembling extended limb, that this is not a very happy dead ladybird.

135

She thinks the colour-coding system for corridor danger may need to be overhauled. Stepping aside, she waves the mangled, dripping form past. "Feel free to go and get your revenge. Don't let me stand in your way."

"Revenge on you, you murderer."

"Funny, I thought you were going to say something like that."

"Death by bottom."

Juliet ponders this statement. "When people say something weird to me, I usually ask them to make it clearer. I think I'll skip that this time. Can you let me past?"

"No."

"Why is it that I couldn't have placed a bet on your answer?"

"You sat on me in that field."

Juliet thinks about this and can't find a response that isn't likely to antagonise the ladybird further. She smiles, says, "Oops," and wishes she hadn't. She adds, "Sorry."

The ladybird gnashes its broken jaws and spatters the corridor with yellow slime. "Sorry, oh yes. There's going to be a lot of sorry in a moment. Screaming sorry in sticky messes all over the place. But first I must fulfil my contract."

"Oh good. While you do that, I'll just wander past you and go to my lecture. See you later."

Another limb extends to block her way. The ladybird says, "I've been given permission to exact revenge upon you provided I follow the riddle protocol."

Juliet points back the way she came. "Riddle protocol? It went that way. I saw it scurrying off looking all mischievous. You follow it first; I'll be right behind."

The ladybird doesn't move. "I am going to have such fun killing you."

Juliet thinks that trying to take on a dead ladybird, that looks as if it weighs thousands of kilos, is going to be a little on the bad side of utterly suicidal. 'Dead' appears to be a sadly less than terminal problem in her new life.

The ladybird goes on, "I have to make up and set you three riddles. You have to give the right answers. One wrong answer and you die by bottom. My bottom, well, what you've left of it. I'm going to squelch you to death. The first riddle is … er..."

"The answer is no."

"You can't refuse."

"I'm not refusing. That's the answer to the first riddle."

"But I haven't made it up yet and anyway that could be the wrong answer."

"It's the correct answer. You just need to make up the right riddle. Think it up and move on."

The ladybird crosses its already wonky eyes. "That's not fair." It shudders in profound concentration for a while, looks at her again, and says, "I don't know. These protocols are all confusing. I think you just cheated. The next riddle is..."

"I can tell you the answer now. 'Henry the Eighth's scrotum'."

The ladybird scans the protocol scroll. "Is it? I just made up the riddle. I … ooh … how does that fit with the answer 'colander'?"

"Sweat-glands, jousting, and steel armour on a hot day."

"I think you're being mean. Right, I've got the third riddle all ready." This time the ladybird doesn't give Juliet time to

137

sabotage it:

> "Groping in the dark. Saying things we can't explain.
> It's the study of the quark and means we can get money
> from gullible cabinet ministers."

He adds, "Sorry, I'm not good at rhymes."

Juliet knows when she's out of her depth. "Uh, did you just say, 'Quark'?" The word is familiar to her. It's the sort of word that signalled the need to throw books at Cheryl.

"Oh yes. From your tone, I deduce that you don't know what one is. Ah-ha, you're dead."

"Quark..." Juliet flounders. "Isn't that something a posh duck would say? You know, one on a pond beside Windsor Castle?"

The ladybird frowns. "I … what?" It starts to heave with laugher, fractured chitin graunching and squirting ladybird juice around. "God, you're so thick." It curls up and rolls from side to side. "I can't believe you're so..."

But Juliet has already darted past and sprinted through the arch.

She belts down the next two corridors and crashes into Hildegarde. They cannon off each other and grab opposite walls for support. Hildegarde says, "Slow down, young lady. Breaking professors is frowned on—if only by professors."

"Sorry, I've narrowly avoided being sat to death and I'm late for a lecture on magic."

Hildegarde pushes herself from the wall and straightens her pearls. "Magic indeed. Interesting."

"Is it?"

"It's about to be."

"I hate it when that happens. I say something to someone and they say something back that makes me think everything is about to go wrong and I'm going to wish I'd never been born."

Hildegarde smiles, draws a pointed stick from a sleeve, and a revolver from her handbag. "How very perceptive of you." She points the gun at Juliet and pulls the trigger. Nothing happens, apart from Juliet moving very quickly. The butt of her spear hums through the air and bats the revolver from Hildegarde's grasp.

The professor shrieks, waves her hand and sucks stinging fingers. "Calm yourself, idiot! That really hurt. No need to get excited. You were never in any danger." She nods at the gun still spinning on the ground. "Pick it up and shoot me with it."

Juliet narrows her eyes and, keeping them on Hildegarde, puts the tip of her spear through the trigger-guard and lifts the revolver.

Hildegarde says, "Do it. Shoot me. It's a real gun and loaded with real bullets."

Juliet takes the gun, aims it down the corridor and pulls the trigger. The trigger doesn't move. Hildegarde says, "Now, isn't that interesting? I want you to tell me why it doesn't work but why this wand does." She sweeps the stick through the air and Juliet's gown rises from the bottom hem, up over her body, yanks her arms over her head, and flies across the corridor.

Juliet shrieks, spear and satchel falling to the floor. "Stop that! It's not magic; your wand just has a..." The wand moves

139

again and Juliet's knee-length para-boots untie their laces and try to pull themselves off. Unfortunately for Juliet, that means she's hopping round the corridor and screaming as she's jerked around.

She thinks, Two can play at this game. "Pillock! Where are you!"

"In your spear." Juliet's bra unfastens itself and the cups cover her eyes.

"Right, Pillock, all her clothes to the entrance hall."

Hildegarde screams. Juliet wins the fight with her bra and sees Pillock trying to remove Hildegarde's twinset and accidentally strangling her with the string of pearls. Juliet gags at Hildegarde's magic knickers and bulging thighs. "Pillock, OK, stop now. I don't think I can stand seeing any more of her."

Hildegarde, red-faced and breathless, slides to the ground and leans against the wall. "Well done You have a pixie on your side! Well done I say. Now, get dressed. We need to talk."

Juliet pulls the gown over her head quickly, so she can keep Hildegarde in clear view. "OK, wot? I'm late for my lecture."

"No you aren't. That was it." Hildegarde smooths her skirt. "Magic—people believe in it but you've already worked out the truth. I want you to pretend you're a witch." She tosses the wand to Juliet. "The brownie's name is Hengist."

"I'm supposed to be learning about whatever I'm supposed to be learning about, running Andromeda's department, saving my mother from people who want to put

140

her on an underwater naughty stool, and stopping the end of the universe. Sorry, but you'll have to speak to my appointments secretary and I haven't got one."

"This is more important than anything else."

"If I could get five minutes' peace for every predictable sentence I've heard today, I could get enough of it to become a Buddhist monk … nun … thing … and spend years looking at cherry blossom and stuff."

Hildegarde stands. "This is about rescuing Prof—your mother."

"Ah, so she is a professor?"

"Among other things."

"I reckon my mum doesn't need saving from anything; this is just another college game but do go on. How do I supposedly save her?"

"By being the bait. It seems the knights do know about you."

"Cool. I'm up for that. Tell me all about it."

"You need to go home and have people start a rumour that you are a witch. Waving the wand around and doing the odd weird thing will help."

"Won't that be an abomination?"

"Oh my goodness! What were you thinking of doing? We don't want dancing dinosaurs invading Oxfordshire. You should do something far more subtle. Something that will distract some of the Knights of Kramer to your village in order to deplete their numbers here. Then you may have to go into Cambridge and walk around, apparently reading Hamlet."

"Won't that bring them all running back?"

141

"Do you think we are idiots?"

"I've met Andromeda."

Hildegarde flinches. "Point taken but none of the knights that go to Brightwell will make it back."

Juliet groans. "Mike wanted me out of the way. Angus of … uh, somewhere that sounds like Mitch sneezing, told me not to stick my oar in. Now you want me to get involved. I take it you've reached plan 'Z plus 10'?"

"There's someone I want you to meet who will help you. Give me the gun. I need it for a lecture."

"Students a bit rowdy?"

"I have a plan. It's all set up and starts with you driving your van back home, drawing knights away and starting rumours." Hildegarde takes the pistol from Juliet. "While you're driving you can work out why this gun isn't able to function."

"Question one: did it work outside the college? You know, before you fiddled with it."

Hildegarde beckons and marches along the corridor. "The answer to your question is, 'ja'."

They pass under arches. Juliet's mind whirls until she says, "The wand worked because it has a brownie in it. You've taken it or them out of the gun."

They enter a room of typical pillars and arches; what's unique to this room strikes Juliet immediately. On either side are tall, arched windows. Sunlight pours through them from both sides, angling down symmetrically to meet in the centre of the floor. There's a peace and tranquillity that absorbs all Juliet's tension. She stops and frowns. There's something else odd. On her right the windows are clear. On her left some are

142

stained glass. The first shows a picture of her in the pool of awakening. The second is herself and Victoria bathing in the bubble world. The third is a car in a swimming pool. Juliet runs forward, passing window after window until she sees a picture of this room. In it, she's standing with Hildegarde and another figure, short oddly-shaped and carrying plastic shopping bags.

Juliet frowns. "Um … who is she?"

"An angel," says a familiar voice.

Juliet whirls round. "Aileen! I thought you were…" The woman has a twisted spine, warty face and an angelic smile that radiates joy. As if the smile were not enough there's a gleaming halo over her head to make everything quite clear. "Oh my God—you're an angel!" Juliet's mind blanks with the implications and questions overloading it but her heart almost bursts with happiness. She throws her arms round the woman. "Aileen!"

Chapter 15

Hand-in-hand mother and son step between piles of collapsed masonry and outcrops of nettles. A gentle breeze twitches the tops of trees. Twigs scrape against the crumbling roofless walls of one of the few abandoned buildings in Brightwell-cum-Sotwell.

"Ow!" says the mother. "I shouldn't have worn sandals." She looks down at her son. "James, keep your elbows in and you won't get stung by nettles."

"Why are we going this way, mum? Did you dream it too?"

The mother freezes, squats down and steadies herself by clutching ancient mortar. Dust and fragments hiss and clatter; a beetle tumbles and scurries into shade.

"Ah! now I've made my jeans dusty." She stares at James. "What did you say?"

James falters at the intensity of her gaze, thinking he's said something wrong. "Nothing."

The mother jerks her son's hand a little. "James love, this is important. What did you dream?"

He looks away and taps the toe of his trainer against a stone. "It was like a dream but I was awake. I dreamt the witch-woman told me to come here."

"The who?"

"You know, the old lady that died. She always smelled and people said she was a witch."

"That was very rude of people." Mum shakes her head, not sure what to ask next. "Um … James, what did Miss Alnwick say in the dream?"

"She told me to come here." He glances up. "I don't play here, not since you told me not to."

"Good for you, James. This old creamery is falling down and there's all sorts of danger. She wobbles his chin with the tip of her finger. "You're precious to me and I don't want you getting hurt."

"Did you dream about her too?"

"I ... well … can you keep a secret?"

James nods.

"I had a vision just like yours. I've never had anything like it. She told me to come here with you. I tried to ignore it but…"

Footsteps crackling on corrugated iron interrupt her. Crashing aside the dried sticks of last year's wild raspberries, a man bursts into view and wipes twigs and old leaves from his face. Eyebrows shoot up on his sun-reddened brow.

"Meg, little Jim, what you doin' here?"

Meg clutches James's hand tighter. "Hi Chuck. I … we … we're out looking for beetles—and you?"

A variety of expressions flicker over Chuck's features. He rubs the side of his nose and looks away. "I, er…" He looks behind and calls, "Linnie, come on, I've made a way through the weeds for you." A six-year-old girl, wearing wellingtons and holding Chuck's jacket over her head to stop leaves tangling in her hair, emerges from the shadows.

145

She smiles at James. "Hi. Did you have the dream too?"

James, locked into a pact of secrecy with his mother, looks to her for guidance.

Linnie goes on, "About Miss Alnwick who shouted a lot and had fits. I dreamed about her: daddy did too."

An almost transparent spaniel, trailing nettles and goose-grass, romps through the weeds. Loops of saliva fly as Mitch tries to say hello to everyone at once.

The two adults grab the children and stare at what appears to be a phantom dog.

Juliet, hiding behind a blackthorn bush and watching everything, decides it's time for action. Stamping down tangled brambles she shouts, "Mitch, you total maniac, I've only half-done you. Come here so I can make you visible. You'll freak people out like that." She rounds a holly tree, pulls the hem of her T-shirt from thorns, and stops in her tracks. "Oops. Hello, people." She looks from face to face. "It's a bit crowded here."

Meg says, "Juliet?" She puts James down. "Invisible dog?"

Juliet nods. "Yeah. Sorry, didn't mean to scare you. He's magic. Uh ... you've been having visions, haven't you?" Getting no verbal response but grinning at people's averted gazes and awkward movements she claps her hands. "You have; it's alright, I know. Old Aileen Alnwick's been sending you visions; she just told me. Aileen, the smelly old woman who shouted abuse in the middle of the night, scared the tits off everyone and went ape-shit when she forgot to take her medication." She laughs. "Well bugger me, are you in for a surprise."

Meg says, "Juliet, mind your language, there are children here. What are you on about, anyway? Aileen died last year."

Juliet ignores her, kneels down in front of James, and says, "What do you remember of old Aileen?" She glances up at Meg and back to James. "Mum won't mind you being honest." She takes his free hand and one of Linnie's. "Come on, kids. It's important."

James looks up at his mother who nods. He says, "She was scary. People said she was a witch."

Eyes closed and head back, Juliet laughs, the music of it contrasting with the desolate surroundings. "No, I'm a witch, well, sort of; it's complicated. Aileen was something much more special." She looks up at Chuck and Meg, tilts her head as if in question and looks back at the children. "Aileen was not very intelligent and she was always sick and different and ugly. She scared people but she was a truly lovely person. The tragedy is that she liked people but they didn't like her. She was the loneliest person ever." She squeezes the children's hands. "She died but I've just been talking to her. She blew my mind when I learned just what her mission on Earth was. I also cried a bit." She studies the children's stricken faces. "Hey, you two, she didn't have a nice life but you, James, always said hello to her any time you met her. Linnie…" she looks at the girl, "you always smiled at her." Juliet looks at Meg and Chuck in turn. "Meg, you used to give her flowers from your garden. Chuck…" She stands and pokes him in the chest. "You drove off a bunch of kids that were laughing at her after she'd had a fit in Bakers Lane. You helped her home and waited until the doctor came."

Juliet reaches down and picks up a stick. Throwing it into

147

the scrub, she shouts, "Mitch, you smell-bomb, whatever you're doing in there—stop!" She turns back to the others. "Don't look at me all dumbstruck. Aileen told me this and you know it's all true; you did those things for her."

She ducks down and takes the children's hands again. "Aileen was an angel. A real angel from Heaven."

Linnie shakes her head. "But angels are beautiful."

"No, Linnie, angels like Aileen are there to show us how beautiful or ugly we are. Other little children ran away from her but your smile lit up her day. You've no idea how something as tiny as that can mean so much to someone who's lonely."

"If she was an angel, will she bless us for being good?"

Juliet shakes her head. "Nope, not at all. This may be a bit complicated for little children but you blessed yourselves when you did things for her. I'm just working out how amazingly important stuff like that is."

Chuck runs thick fingers through his wiry unkempt hair. "That explains the vision then. It was weird—and sort of real. A bit scary."

Juliet releases the children's hands and gives Chuck a playful punch on the chest. "Don't be scared. Aileen says you are a good dad and what else is there to care about?"

She stretches and looks from face to face. "Any questions?"

James puts his hand up.

Juliet kneels in front of him again. "You don't need to put your hand up with me, James my man. I'm a friendly witch-thingy, not a scary teacher. You just speak up."

"If angels aren't beautiful, how will we know if we meet

another?"

Juliet rolls her eyes. "If you meet one? *If?* Actually, James, good question. We're well supplied; there're always angels in our lives, more than you can possibly imagine." She turns. "Gotta go. Witching won't wait." She strides through head-high nettles, stops, and turns. "Meg and Chuck, Aileen also said that you're nice people and both a bit lonely. Maybe you should meet up more often. Oh, and she says hugs to you all." Turning away she disappears behind greenery. "Mitch, you miserable git, get your moronic arse in gear or I'll never take you walkies again."

Mitch, tail wagging in circles, thunders after her through the undergrowth. Juliet taps him with the wand as he passes. "Ha, got you. And behave yourself; people can see you clearly now."

Juliet wanders through sun-dappled woodland and wonders what she needs to do next.

Pulling her phone out she calls Errol. "Stop shagging and talk to me."

Errol replies. "What? I'm on my way to see Cheryl. I thought it was for a chat but it's some sort of formal college dinner. I had to buy clothes. Last time I wore a tie was to a wedding, and my mother tied it for me."

"Errol, I need your head. I think something is about to explode. I don't want to ruin your day but we're in the centre of it all. Hildegarde wants people in my village to think I'm a witch and actually do things that will convince them. That's blurring the boundaries between the real world and college. I reckon it's incredibly dangerous. It's also utterly pointless. If the knights are after me anyway, why bother with this witch

149

act? I reckon there's something else going on. She also gave me a problem that I can't get my head around. She gave me a wand with a brownie in it. Brownies do stuff that looks like magic, yeah? Can brownies really do magic? Does it even exist? I mean really? I'm so confused. She also gave me a pistol but it didn't work because it didn't have brownies in it. Does everything work because it has a brownie in it?"

"Did the gun have a safety?"

"Safety? What are you on about? Guns are supposed to be dangerous, moron. You'll be telling me they come with first-aid kits next. I pulled the trigger-thingy and nothing happened."

"I thought you said you didn't want to ruin my day? First I have to deal with Cheryl, then you dump time and volition paradoxes on me like a trailer-full of manure; now you're telling me that the principle of cause and effect is an illusion. For someone that thinks she's a nice person you could try a bit harder."

Juliet heads for home and tries to ignore the scream of a man somewhere deep in the woods. She hopes it's not something she should deal with but a knight suddenly wishing he weren't in the vicinity. "I saw a room full of windows. The first were stained-glass, all pictures of me since I came to college. The rest were all clear on that side. The other side is all blank too."

"Is that how many days we have until your predicted explosion?"

"They weren't days, just events. The last one was me meeting an angel."

"Not another Angus I hope."

150

"No, a total inspiration. One that gives people the chance to do good. I reckon good and bad are important. I mean really important. She told me we're surrounded by angels. That would be a lot of effort for something that doesn't matter."

"Stop talking. Every time you speak my pile of manure gets deeper. I'm going to have to buy a snorkel. Think instead. I love the way you think. It's so far out of the box I'm pretty certain you've never been in it. Right, why are good and bad important?"

"Maybe so we can send people to Heaven and Hell? Trouble is we don't know how to get to either of them to find out."

"Angus gave us a clue."

"Not one I'm happy with. If all the lying and scheming I've done lately doesn't amount to sin, I hate to think what does. Besides, don't you have to die? No chance; my diary hasn't got enough space." Juliet dodges round a bank of bramble, and screams as a sheet of brown water rises and scatters among the surrounding foliage. She's too slow to avoid a face-full of high velocity mud, fur, and dog that throws her flat on the ground.

Wiping and opening her eyes, she sees Mitch leap up and snap the end of a vibrating crossbow bolt from a tree.

Errol's voice, tinny and burbling through a layer of mud, says, "Juliet, talk to me! Are you alright?"

Juliet rolls, scoops the phone up and dodges along a deer trail leading through the ash-thicket by her garden. "Gotta go. I'm going to get my spear and do a cardinal sin on someone's throat."

"You screamed. What happened? Keep yourself safe, for God's sake."

Juliet races to her back door, mud and twigs flying from her clothes.

Zoongaash, down to two arms, leaps from a woodpile and squints behind a gleaming metal longbow held horizontally. Into the woods behind Juliet she launches an arrow made of grinning nixies that all shout, "Wheee!"

Zoongaash sprints to Juliet, and says. "Get yourself back to college quick. The situation is under control here but there are hundreds of the idiots. They followed you from Cambridge. Time for you to get out."

Juliet crashes through her back door. "Are we on the same side now?"

"We always were. Wake up quick. As you are now, things are never what they seem."

"Oh bloody really?"

"Nothing is what you think it is, not the college, not what's happening around us, not me, and not you: especially not you."

Chapter 16

J uliet's wiping a long night's sleep from her eyes, standing in the college entrance hall, and waiting for Errol. She's nervous; so nervous she could only finish a single steak and onion baguette for breakfast. She's beginning to worry that she's dumped too much on him and asked him to do something she'd never do for anyone, ever. On the bright side, Cheryl should be distracted and happy for a while.

She's also worried about Aelfwyn, who's disappeared and may be lost or lonely. She tells her manual.

Find a ghost? Get knotted, lady. Do you know just how many there are? There're all the dead ones, all those that are still to be born...

"I mean Aelfwyn, you moron, and she's awake."

Oh, right, awake? I'll scan everyone's texts to each other. Someone may have seen her.

"Isn't that immoral?"

Totally, but you grasp rules like other people grasp wet soap. Here we go. Yes, it's all over the city. Poltergeist activity, weird screeches, animals going mental. She's fine.

Errol looms from the shadows of the college entrance arch and stares down at Juliet. He's not looking happy but she's glad he doesn't appear exhausted. "How did last night go?"

He ignores that. "Thank God you're alright. I was seriously worried about you until I heard you had returned to the college. Come with me. I've found a way to go to Hell."

"You OK?"

"Follow me." There's a hardness in his voice Juliet hasn't experienced before. It's assertive with a hint of desperation. To her astonishment she finds it sexy.

She shakes her head. "We can't go to Hell. There's no time. I'm supposed to be bait for the Knights of Kramer."

"Listen, we go to Hell."

"Listen, we don't." Her response surprises her. She's trying to encourage assertion in him but doesn't know if it's for his benefit or hers.

He sighs. "Please follow me. While we walk I've a load of ideas to bounce off you." They enter a gloomy corridor.

"Where are we going?"

"I can't tell you."

"Because I'd refuse to go?"

Errol's voice turns to a snarl, "Will you just...?" He falls silent. "Sorry—let's lighten up and start this all again." He closes his eyes, takes a deep breath, and says, "Good morning, Juliet, nice to see you. You're looking radiant."

"Nice try but I hate empty flattery."

"Radiant—think Chernobyl. I said 'Good morning'."

Juliet tries to join in the humour. "Good morning? Is this going to be one of those conversations in which I get swamped by your long words, have to be dumbed down to, and end up feeling miserably inadequate?"

"I only said, 'good morning'."

"I don't trust you, where's it leading?"

He points to the left. "Not down that corridor certainly."

"But I need to go that way. I've got to see Hildegarde."

He whispers, "Go down that corridor and you run right into the arms of demonators."

"What are they? What do they do? What's the problem? They can't be weirder than anybody else here."

"Weird? They're weirder than a bottle of geologists. Apparently they change their appearance to look like demons. Some of them never change back. I'm about to take your arm and guide you in another direction. I'd like to warn you that, given the low light levels, my hand may connect with something not entirely your arm. This will be quite accidental and should not be interpreted as anything else."

"Keep your bloody hands to yourself. Why should I be scared of demonators anyway?"

"Nobody wants to go into demonaics but the universe needs demonators. The college has to press-gang or trick people into taking the module."

"But they can't..."

He interrupts, "They can do whatever they like. Let's go

155

through the catacombs to avoid them."

"Are you utterly insane?"

"I've been using the catacombs as a shortcut. There's nothing to worry about."

"So 'yes' to insane then. But how...? Oh, don't tell me. You've got the catacombs sussed when the rest of the world is terrified of getting lost in there."

"It's clever. You know that moment when you go into a room and think, 'Why did I come in here?' The catacombs are like that but worse. Unless you stay absolutely focussed, you have no idea why you're there, where you came from, or where you're going."

"You've summed up my whole life. Oh my God..."

"What?"

"You have just summed up my life. I wonder if awakening is … something to do with that?"

"Stop it, you're boiling my brain. Follow me."

Juliet thinks she could trust Errol to navigate blindfolded through Hell using only a thermometer. But then thinks, No, wait, how would he see what the temperature was?

He says, "We're just about to enter the catacombs. This is your arm?"

"It's called assault."

"The other one is a pepper?"

He leads her into almost pitch darkness. Tall, ginger, suffering from post-adolescent limb-gangle and in possession of what seems to be an unnatural amount of elbows and knees, Juliet thinks he's OK motionless but when he moves it's like standing too close to fairground machinery.

Everything is damp, the stone so rotten it hisses to the

ground when their gowns brush the surface. The floor is almost sand and crunches underfoot. Some of the cobwebs glow which makes navigation a bit easier but strikes Juliet as a little over the top.

She thinks, Something's wrong—Errol's let go. Sweet though he is in almost all other respects, he wouldn't voluntarily miss an opportunity to have a hand on me somewhere. "Errol, where are you?" she calls into the dark, but gets no response.

A door opens and she's blinded by the light of a multicoloured flashing electric chandelier. She thinks, Neon? Who in the world would want a neon chandelier?

The diminutive man silhouetted in the doorway says, "Ah, I've seen that face before, only not as flustered. Juliet, Victoria's daughter, yes?"

"I've seen you about. Who are you?"

"Professor Frank Blood; a desperate man begging that you take over my clinic for a moment."

"I'm going to see Hildegarde."

He snorts. "In the catacombs? Rubbish. No, I'll let her know you're being appropriated for a short time."

"Appropriated? Get stuffed."

"My next client is a bit of a pain. Tell him I'm away, sick, anything. Just get rid of him for ever. Do this and I'll owe you one."

Juliet's mind works lightning-fast. "Agreements and oaths first."

He sighs. "Why is there no trust in young people these days?"

"You didn't trust professors when you were a student."

157

"What makes you say that?"

"Because I'm not talking to something in a jar."

"Fair enough; what do you want?"

She hopes he's really desperate. "Information on my awakening and reality. Freedom to ask anything and get truthful and complete answers."

"No."

"Yes."

He taps his lips. "If you can't wake yourself up why are you here?"

"I thought I'd applied to do an apprenticeship in plumbing. I got confused. Could happen to anyone."

Something thuds against a door in the professor's room. He whimpers. "Oh no! he's here." Holding a hand up he says, "Oath, first-class. I'll answer your questions completely and truthfully for the rest of the day."

"The entire year." Juliet's in luck and timed it perfectly, the next thud occurs as she finishes speaking.

"For the year then. Now get in there." She's yanked into the room. The professor dodges out. The door slams and, to Juliet's dismay, disappears.

She thinks, Arg! I'm trapped. Why is there no trust these days? Now what the hell am I supposed to do? What sort of clinic is this? On the good side, I'll get broadband information from the weird guy.

The desk is stainless steel—but stained. The chair behind it is plastic, pink, and covered in pictures of blue bunnies. A mixture of tacky romantic and mildly pornographic titles fill the bookshelves. The carpet is a hotchpotch of furs and hides sewn together. Anime animal posters cover the walls. Juliet's

158

left with the opinion that the neon chandelier is the high point of the professor's taste in décor.

Another thud on the remaining door has her sitting and calling, "Come in."

A muffled sob precedes, "I don't want to come in. I want to get out."

"How do you think I feel? Open the sodding door."

More sobs precede, "Why, what's the point?"

"The point is that I've started charging you already. The longer you hang around out there the more you pay."

The door opens and a tearful zombie puts its head round. Only the head—hanging from the hand clutching its hair. The head says, "Who are you?"

"Juliet."

"Where's Frankie?"

"I killed and ate him."

"You look too young to be a professor."

"Sadly, I'll just have to put up with youth and good looks for a few years but I'm sure things will deteriorate nicely. Are you coming in or would you just like me to bring your head in and stick it on a spike or what?"

"You don't sound very compassionate."

"This is me on a good day; don't waste it."

The zombie shuffles in, catching the things oozing from the bottom of its neck, pushing them back in, and replacing its head. He looks behind him and says, "Come in, lie down and don't chew the carpet." Closing the door, he sits on the chair opposite Juliet.

She notes that nothing else, apparently, entered the room. She asks, "You have an invisible friend?"

"A dog, yes."

"Let me guess, a lurcher."

The zombie shrugs. "How would I know? It's invisible."

"So … tell me why you're here."

"I have issues. I don't like being a zombie. I don't fit in with the lads."

"Then fit in with the lasses instead."

"No—the lads. the Life After Death Society, they're all talk and no action."

"And it's action that you want?" Somewhere in the back of her mind she wonders if that was the safest choice of words.

His eyes widen. Juliet hopes they don't roll out. He says, "Sort of. You see I'm not attracted to other zombies. You're tasty though. Do you do sex therapy?"

"I'd prefer to die."

"Oh..." his shoulders slump. "I wouldn't fancy you then."

"Have you considered a career change? You know, werewolf, vampire, that sort of thing?"

He groans. "Transbeastites are shunned."

"You could build a great career in comedy and burlesque."

"And I glow in the dark."

"What?" Every time Juliet gets her mental composure back, it's whipped away. She wonders if there's something going on here.

The zombie leans forward. "One scary night the ground underneath me glowed, grass, stones... After that I glowed too."

"I read about divine events. People make a promise, usually a heroic or slushy one, and when they fulfil it soppy

160

angels bless the area. Don't worry, it'll pass."

"And I have a worm phobia."

Juliet wonders if this is going to go on all day. She says, "Of course, you're a dead body so that's just common sense."

"And I have constant, anthemic heavy-metal music going through my head. It makes me want to kill, maim, and slaughter. I spend all day running up and down the River Cam screaming; it's exhausting and upsets people out punting."

Juliet wonders if she's being played with—distracted from what's really happening in this conversation. Not that she cares a lot. All she wants to do is get rid of the zombie and interrogate the professor. She says, "I suggest a lifestyle change. Knit a pair of socks everyday: it's relaxing. Study and compile a list of your top ten favourite shipping weather forecasts..."

"And I speak in tongues." He opens his mouth wide. "See? I collected lots of them. Anyway, you're babbling."

Juliet decides that there's nothing wrong with him and he's just playing with her.

She thinks, What does this conversation feel like? It's all too familiar, like someone's always three steps ahead. Oh, bloody hell.

"Errol, you tosser, what are you up to?"

The zombie illusion fades and there sits Errol, shaking with laughter. "Top ... ten ... shipping ... forecasts... That was brilliant." He beats the sides of the chair.

The door Juliet was dragged through reappears and the professor walks in, "One minute and forty-one seconds. Not bad, well, borderline, exceptionally average and marginal but

161

she'll do, I suppose."

Juliet slaps the desk with both hands and wishes there were paperweights and monitors to throw around. "Errol, I'm going to kill you. What's this about? If it's..."

The professor interrupts, "Errol sussed my disguise in only twenty-three seconds, a fraction of the time you took to see through his. It's the skill of knowing something is not as it appears that is core to achieving your personal awakening. You know, seeing through smokescreens, assumptions and questioning the obvious. Incidentally, welcome to the demonaics module."

Juliet wants to howl and tear their faces off. She says to the professor, "So that's why you promised me answers so easily." She turns to Errol. "You bastard; why me?"

He smirks. "I got caught this morning and tested the same way. Frank said I had to find a partner to balance my skills."

"How did you do that disguise?"

"Pretty good wasn't it? It's something Frank just showed me. The rules are different here in college; you can change and make things at will. A skill they employ in Hell to scare the tormented. I'll show you in a bit."

The professor says, "Few demonators can work alone. I told him to find someone less intellectual, who went on gut instinct, emotions; you know, someone more primitive."

Juliet's fuming but recognises there is a beauty to it all. To her, being totally outmanoeuvred is as good as doing it to someone else. She's also flabbergasted. "Errol, how the hell did you get caught? I mean, no way—*you?*"

He looks down, pushes his hands into his pockets, and blushes. The professor smirks. "The test is baited. For you

162

the temptation was the information you so hunger for. Errol took a short cut through the catacombs this morning. He found what he thought was you, lost, afraid, and oh-so-sweetly vulnerable."

Juliet snorts. "Afraid? Vulnerable? Sweet!" She's almost screeching. She leaps up and rounds on Errol. "You total wanker. It took you twenty three seconds to realise that wasn't me?"

Errol rolls his eyes. "Twenty three seconds of you talking to me and I didn't get earache. It was too good to be true."

Juliet turns to Frank Blood. "Right. Sod you, professor, I want answers. Starting with Heaven and Hell, where they are, and why good and evil are important."

The professor tugs at his tie and looks at the ceiling. "I can answer all that but I have my oath with Errol to execute first."

"What oath was that?"

The walls fade. Giant monsters of all colours, smells, and terror-inducing forms, surround them. The professor bows. "Welcome to Hell."

Chapter 17

"**P**iss off, don't touch me—NEEARG!" Juliet's whipped off her feet, dangled upside-down by the claws of a gigantic lobster-shaped demon, and hung among other horrendous creatures. A thousand new body-odours assault her senses. Growls, squawks, and hisses fill the air. Her spear is snatched away.

A demon roars, "Take their clothes off."

Juliet swears, twists her back towards Errol, and screams. As she's jerked around, several demons discuss her, "Look at her face, that won't do. It's pathetic." "Nice eyes, though, scary with the gown. She should have another eye, above, no, between the others and they should blink at different times." "Those bits of metal in her face—right. I'm going to make her face all gold. A face of exquisite beauty—but frightening. How can we do that?" "You do the mask thing, I'm going to project faces of the tormented onto it." "Her hair—what can I …? Er, I know, spiders' legs, all white with brown blotches and flicking around."

Juliet tries to hold her face together; something she's never been trained to do. "Get your hands off me, you bastards. Leave me—aaah!"

Errol's not doing too well either.

Voices around him say, "That red hair should be boiling

164

flesh and give off the smell of burning. I'll see to that." "He needs better feet; how about like an eagle?" "No, moron, use your imagination. Do slugs or something." "I'll do his penis." "You always do them." "I've got this great idea, you know, make it like a huge writhing tentacle, oozing green goo, all hairy and warty. Oooh yes! I've had an even scarier idea."

Errol, naked and inverted, howls, falls to the ground, and clutches his groin. "Juliet, don't turn round. You don't want to see this—these."

The professor says, "Don't mind the demonators. They want to make you look demoniacal and convincing. Have fun, I'll see you later. Oh my … Juliet. Have you seen what they've done to your nipples? Very striking." He disappears.

Juliet ignores him; she's busy having a really bad time.

A demonator made entirely of eyeballs, with a single huge pupil represented by a hundred black irises, says, "Ah, we've done it again. Beautiful job. Take a look at yourselves, students."

Juliet says, "Piss off, wankers," and tries to cover her eyes

The demonator goes on, "If they don't want to look, they can still feel. Drop that one on top of the other."

"Don't you bloody—aaak! Sorry, Errol, ew..." Disentangling herself, Juliet tries not to look but her three eyes, opening and closing at different times, reveal too much of Errol. The lower half of his face is skeletal. The curved fangs extending from his upper jaw are so long that an unexpected sneeze could take his kneecaps off. A yellow brain, glowing a deep red inside, pulses above his forehead and ears. She struggles to look away before morbid fascination makes her see anything more—but doesn't quite succeed.

Errol growls, an earth-shaking roar from his vastly over-swollen chest, "What have you done to us? What is this all about? Change us back at once!"

A humanoid demonator, made from a mass of seething maggots, thrusts its face into Errol's. "Hell is about hu-mil-i-a-shurrn."

Another howls, "And despair."

Others cry, "Torment." "Powerlessness." "Torture."

Juliet, now eye-to-eye with what had been a towering demonator ten times her size, screams back, "And which of them needs armour-piercing nipples and a fire-breathing belly-button? Turn us back to our normal shapes and give us our clothes."

A pale female demonator, with skin that peels into hideous wounds so deep you can see through them but which heal spontaneously only to be replaced by more, says, "Is that really what you want? I mean this is all part of the fun. You shouldn't take this module too seriously or it would be hell." The air crashes with assorted laughter. Juliet tries to cover her ears but can't find them. The demonator continues, "We have body-part-swapping parties too. You get to play 'Guess the owner'. It leads to all sorts of jolly antics and hilarity."

"Do it!"

The demonator says, "If you insist. There you go. Best I can do."

Juliet's body returns to its normal shape.

The demonator opens her hand and holds it out to Juliet. "Here're your clothes." Juliet grabs the scrap of black material. It's her gown but would barely cover a hand. The

166

demonator sniggers. "Oops."

"Change me back to my normal size, moron."

"No can do. Soz and all that but no one is afraid of teeny-weeny demons."

Errol says, "So we're demons, demonators, for the moment?"

A seething ball of fur and claws replies, "That you are, lad. You'll be making custom-made hells before you know it."

"And, as demonators, like you, we can change things. So I'll just return to my usual shape and size and get dressed." A moment later he sniggers and says, "Juliet?"

"What?" she hisses through clenched teeth.

"From down here your bum looks enormous."

~

Struggling to work out how Errol made himself shrink, Juliet says, "I really don't think there's any need to make us appear more scary. Despair and the other things you said come from power not presentation." She looks at the demonators surrounding her. "OK, let's get on with this. What do we do?"

Straining with all her might to imagine herself returning to normal size, she notices the demonators appear to be growing larger and realises this could be them—just growing larger to wind her up more. She looks down. Yes, the standard-issue Divine Administration white marble floor is getting closer. She gives herself a mental pat on the back but, as she's shrinking, it goes over her head.

A towering humanoid, formed from a swarm of anopheles mosquitoes, says to the other demonators, "They look a bit

167

small and ordinary now."

Another adds, "The smaller one sounds a bit common too. Does that make her the lowest common demonator?"

Errol and Juliet cover their ears at the laughter. When the cacophony dies, Errol shouts, "If their humour doesn't kill us, their laughter will. It's like a hurricane crashing into an earthquake, bouncing off a migraine during a..."

The mosquito demonator shrinks to their size, and interrupts, "I'll show you the ropes. Let's get you a couple of victims before our shift stands down. Pleased to meet you. I'm Arnold of Drunken Bottom, demonator first-class."

Errol nods at Juliet as she shrinks to the point she can attempt to scramble into her clothes. She's not quite there yet and it reminds him of the time his auntie, at the age of fifty, tried to get into her wedding dress from thirty years earlier and ended up the shape of piled doughnuts. He says to the demonator, "And she thought 'Toft' was a silly name. What's the process here?"

Arnold says, "Easy, you meet evil people, make a little hell for them and bob's your uncle. The administrator that sent them will have rated the person's last judgement and you have to take that into account."

Juliet, small enough to jerk her clothes straight, picks up the spear, whirls round, waves the point at Errol, and says, "If you were watching me get dressed this goes from your arse to your tonsils via your lungs."

Errol grins and raises his hands. "At least I'll die happy."

"Perv—that does it."

Arnold shouts, "Stop right there." He steps between an incandescent Juliet and a nervous Errol, who's wondering just

168

how fast he can sprint in a college gown.

The swarm of mosquitoes inside Arnold rages loud enough to stop Juliet trying to walk through him. He holds Errol and Juliet apart. "People looking at each other is not perverted. Looking without permission is."

Juliet hisses, "That's exactly what he did."

"And you feel that merits a death sentence?"

"That's for me to decide."

Arnold claps his hands, an odd thing to do, as around a hundred stunned mosquitoes fall to the ground. "Absolutely. If you had looked at him in the same way, would you merit a similar sentence?"

"No. A straitjacket, therapy, and strong medication." Juliet yelps as mosquitoes leave Arnold, fly into her head, and return to him.

He says, "Interesting."

"What? What did you just do there?"

"I studied your memories as you will be studying the memories of the damned before you sentence them. You did look at him."

"No sodding way." Juliet cringes as Arnold employs his powers as a demonator and forces her to remember. She yelps and covers her eyes which isn't the most logical or successful way of trying not to see a mental image. "That was … that was an unconscious action. I wasn't deliberately ogling."

Arnold nods. "Interesting. You did try to resist, just not very hard, perhaps just hard enough to convince yourself that you could forgive yourself—but still get in a little ogle. Welcome to Hell. Now, do you want to carry on with unbalanced judgements and take revenge on Errol or are you going to damn or forgive the pair of you? This is a simple module. It only takes as long as you let it but I'm not releasing you back to the college until you pass."

Errol says, "Excuse me, Arnold, did I understand you correctly? We judge people, make hells, and choose punishments?"

Arnold says, "That's exactly what you do."

Juliet says, "No way! Isn't there a saint, um … thingy that does it?"

Arnold's mosquitoes spin as he rolls his eyes. One of them is travel-sick. "We're extremely short of demonators called 'saint um-thingy' here; a terrible problem that God has continually overlooked. Thanks for reminding me. I'll bring it up next time I see him. Now, are you ready to learn or do you want to ask endless stupid questions?"

Errol says, "I have a question. If one accepts that all people, and therefore all demonators, have a different set of moral values, where's the consistent, objective approach? We could all make different hells and punishments for the same sins."

Arnold turns, or to put it more correctly, the mosquitoes reform as if Arnold is facing Errol. "It's more about knowing that you too may face a demonator one day. A demonator who will see right through you and punish you for being over or under-zealous during your time here."

"But they'll be making a subjective judgement too! Surely it should be God judging?"

"Saints … gods … take a look around for them. No rush, you have eternity." Arnold taps a buzzing finger against Errol's chest. "Your judgements are in there. You'll learn

170

more about yourselves than you'll ever learn about those you damn or absolve."

He pauses and regards each of them in turn. "As people die their lives flash before their eyes or whatever. This is the soul parcelling itself up for us demonators to study. Some of the more exotic of God's creations don't have eyes, and the parcel can be freaky. Jellyfish really do my head in; slime moulds have me in therapy for weeks. I find gin helps." He snatches a passing ghost from the air. "Let me see … this one's been labelled 'Hell level one'. Nine-year-old boy … er, take a look."

Juliet and Errol get a flash of the boy's moral history. Juliet's surprised by a mental footnote that says, 'No outstanding previous damnations'.

Arnold waves a hand and creates a room. Another sweep of the hand writes a sign over the door.

All the spiders you pulled the legs off

He wakes the ghost by slapping it, waits until the boy has read the sign and screamed, then pushes the struggling soul through the door. Turning back to Juliet and Errol, Arnold says, "I've reversed the relative proportions a bit. The spiders in there are about three times his height. In about ten minutes, he'll have had enough, decided to leave spiders alone in future, and rise upstairs to Divine Admin for reincarnation."

Errol says, "Will he be an arachnophobe in his next life?"

"Next life? Nah, I'd say from about three seconds ago. Right, you two, get weaving. Grab a passing ghost."

Juliet snatches a sleeping spirit from the air. It's tagged,

'Hell level 7'. Arnold says, "Ooer, interesting, we don't get many of those. Slap it awake."

Juliet is more than happy to do so. She decides damned souls feel like giant slugs floating in snot, and doesn't want to hold it any longer than necessary. As the ghost wakes, she's hit by a blast of its memories and makes her divine assessment there and then. "Oh wot? We've got a right tosser here. He got a fifty-million bonus for ruining a bank and bankrupting hundreds of family businesses. Arms-dealing, drugs...? My God, the list is endless."

The ghost materialises into a tall, impeccably dressed, manicured, and barbered elderly man, his knobbly hand resting on a ruby-topped walking stick. He has more gold in a single cuff-link than Juliet has in her whole face. He looks her up and down, grimaces, and says, "What on earth are you?"

"I'm your personal demon. I'm sure we're going to get along plumbingly."

"No."

"Wot?"

The man stares down at her. "Remove your repulsive self from my presence immediately, cretin, and get me someone more senior, more educated, better presented, of equal social class and polish—not scum—and not female. I will not deal with someone inferior to me in any way. You are wanting in every respect. It horrifies me that something as revolting as you can even exist."

Juliet gulps and whispers, "I love this job already. Oh boy, am I gonna have fun with you."

Arnold, watching Errol, points to a ghost, and says, "Errol of Toft. Stop faffing around. Grab that one!"

Errol looks at the ghost indicated, flinches, and says, "You mean that ball of fury spitting sparks and tagged, 'WTF'?" He grabs it and pats it like he's gently waking a sweet, tender child.

Arnold tries to roll his eyes but they've gone on non-rolling-strike pending a health and safety investigation. "Slap it!"

Errol winces. "I don't really like hurting things." He remembers where he is, what module he's on, and taps a little harder.

Arnold reaches over Errol's shoulder and gives the ghost a slap that would have a sweet, tender child bouncing off walls.

The ghost changes to a small woman with a scowl that would send vampires, werewolves, even starving carnivorous dinosaurs running for safety. Through a visible haze of gut-knotting body odour she screeches, "About crapping time! Get me Satan now!" She scans her surroundings. "Call this shit-hole Hell? There are going to be some changes round here, let me tell you. Move. Get that fucker Satan here and tell him it's time he started pissing himself."

Errol winces, holding his nose. "I … er … Satan is unavailable. How may I be of service?"

The woman's voice changes to a growling whisper that would have the aforesaid vampires, et al, leaving smelly trails as they ran, "I haven't studied demonology into its blackest depths and immersed myself in every possible aspect of sin and depravity for a whole lifetime only to speak to a wet streak of piss like you. Hell is going to be upgraded and I'm the..."

Standing with hands over her ears, Juliet winks at Errol,

173

who nods. With a sweep of her arm Juliet creates a black sphere around the elderly man. Errol pushes the woman in, and Juliet seals the entrance.

She says, "Pox. We should have stuck a camera in with them. They'll get on like a house on fire."

A quick high-five with Errol and they turn to Arnold.

Errol raises his left eyebrow. "Satisfied?"

Chapter 18

Errol stirs his coffee in a figure of eight or a sign of infinity or the shape of a bicycle-wheel after an unfortunate day on the streets of Cambridge—he's not sure which and really doesn't care: he's exhausted.

Sounds fill the air; he absorbs the muted snorts, grunts, voices in spectral tones, and languages that move through emotions and other ethereal media. They drift through the college canteen along with scents that both fascinate and repel. He says to Juliet, "Time... Time is very weird."

Juliet's leaning forward, her forehead using a giant burger as a warm pillow. She mumbles something.

"Pardon?"

Juliet lifts her head, flour and sesame seeds trickling either side of her nose. "I said, 'Poetry about custard is weird'. I think I said, 'Fuck, I'm knackered' too but I wasn't really listening."

"I mean time here."

"Here is weird. Years ago I thought people who wanted fountains coming through a concrete-cherub's penis were strange. Now I order a jumbo burger and I'm scared to look inside unless I'll see a slice of elephant's bum."

"You said, 'Years'. We've only been here four days."

"You know what I meant ... do you know what I meant?

How can you know it if I'm not sure myself? If you do, tell me about what I do and or don't mean—where was I? Who cares? Can you take a peek into this burger? Wait, I'll get my spear ready."

Errol drops his teaspoon clattering on the table. "Juliet, you've done it again."

"I would make a clever joke about incontinence pads but I can't be arsed."

"We have three years to awaken. You said, 'Years' and you've hit the bullseye. I think college time has raced ahead, well the learning part. We've packed years of learning into days. Goodness, this is complicated." He leans forward to take her hand; she pulls it away; he makes it look as if he was only going to check her burger. He lifts the squashed bread. "If that's an elephant's anal sphincter, scrotum, eyeballs, or even minced kittens and puppies, I can't recognise anything. Therefore I pass it as a genuine burger. You can eat, grow fat, and not suffer any guilt about how you got there." He drops the bread. "We've been here years, haven't we? There's a parallel chronological phenomenon going on here."

Juliet rests her head in both hands. "You mean time is all fucked up? I reckon. Look at you. In another couple of years you'll need to shave."

"I could do you while I'm at it."

Juliet snorts. "In your dreams."

"In which case you can thank me already."

"Too late; I can do myself. There are many ways to use a spear. Did I say that? Tell me to shut up... Oh bollocks, I can't eat this." She picks a crumb of bread. "Yeah, OK, years. We're due our final exams? Oh right..."

Errol frowns. "What is 'right'?"

"You know, I reckon we're supposed to set our own finals, and some people here set themselves low standards."

"Like who?"

"Anyone in Hell, Divine Admin, the entire college … is there anyone else to slag off?"

"Only you and me, and you've done me on an hourly basis since we met."

"I don't want to end up like all the nutters in this place. My mum managed to stay sane," she thinks for a moment, "well—ish." She lifts her plate and sets it on the floor. Pulling out her pendant, she calls, "Mitch and Sheba, kill that burger."

Errol opens his manual at the notes section and asks it, "Is time created by perception and not a universal constant?" He looks at Juliet. "Bullseye." Picking up a teaspoon and tapping it against one of his sideburns, he muses. "So … time … years can pass within days, even if the days are passing normally." He looks at his antique fob-watch. "What's the point of a watch then?"

Juliet ignores the yowls, whuffles, and flying saliva at her feet. "To remind you to go and see Cheryl this evening."

Errol's eyebrows shoot up faster than a supermarket's petrol prices when all the other local suppliers have been squeezed out of business. "Grief! I'm going to be late." His bench screeches back over the rough stone floor; coffee spatters over the table. "I have to go. See you later."

Juliet stays, resting her elbows on the table, face in her palms. She thinks, What the hell is going on? Where am I with all this? Why do mere humans have to decide what is

177

good or evil? How come there isn't a saint what's-his-name to sort it out? and where the hell is God? You don't plumb a bathroom and just look at it. You don't make a dolls' house and not play with it. Why make a universe at all?

She lowers her hands and sees a ghostly figure sitting cross-legged on the table and staring at her. "Aelfwyn! How's it going, sweetpea? I was missing you. I was worried too. Maybe I can get you a ghost of a manual so we can chat when you're away. I hear you've been having fun."

Aelfwyn grins, puts her hands on her hips, and wiggles from side to side. "I've got a job. It's special. I work for profoffs—important people."

"Anything profoffs do is not necessarily important in any way—except to them. Putting a fancy gown on is their way of trying to cover up the fact that they, and the things they do, make no sense. They are masters of deluding themselves, believing in whatever they fancy the most … uh … it's pretty much the same for the rest of us too, I suppose. What's the job?"

"I'm a spy, that's a person that snoops. I found out that a..." her face crumples into dimples as she concentrates, "Um … a … a sin is coming to get you; a long one. The profoffs are coming to tell you about it."

Juliet's gaze flicks to Zoongaash, who's weaving among the tables, her weapons strapped to her back and, unusually, not held. She's wearing a sleeveless gown that covers her arms but doesn't hide the wave she gives Juliet. Nor does it hide the way the wave goes wrong and she hits her own head. Arriving at the table, she kicks a bench into place and sits. "Ello, I've been sent for. I think I'm supposed to be working

178

with you. Can you order me a cool mint tea with a long straw?"

"Uh? yeah." Juliet waves her spear to get the attention of the drinks waiter. "Why a straw?"

"Yesterday I was in your world and so had to go down to two arms. Today I'm evening things up, so I have six. Trouble is, I don't have enough coordination."

"And you have to hide your arms under that gown?"

"No, idiot. Have you ever tried to put on a six-sleeved gown? Without coordination I could beat myself to death while suffocating."

Juliet orders cool mint tea. Aelfwyn drifts off to the spectral foods counters. Professors Mike and Frank enter the canteen and head for Juliet.

Zoongaash says, "What's going on?"

Juliet sighs. "Oh that's easy. Everything in my life and in my head is pants and someone's turning them inside-out."

"Exciting! Wonderful! I'm so happy for you."

Juliet's brain seizes at this reply but she doesn't have time to sort it out as Mike and Frank join them.

Juliet says to Mike, "Any news of mum?"

"Our informant tells us that the knights have despatched an assassin, or assassins, to kill you and Errol. Neither of you should leave the college. Zoongaash will keep you safe."

"Can I put you right on a few things?"

Mike frowns. "What?"

"First, this is not news; speak to Hildegarde. I've already been saved from a crossbow bolt by Mitch. The knights have sent assassins to kill Errol and to only try to kill me. Errol has already left the college and right now Zoongaash is useless for anything but swatting flies. Why does someone want us dead anyway?"

Mike shrugs. "We can only guess. They do suspect you to be associated with the college and have seen you with Errol in Cambridge. My hypothesis is that they want to capture and question you, learn about the college, and have an entertaining barbecue. None of us can think why they would want to kill you until they've learned all they can about the college."

Juliet rises, takes her spear, and heads away, saying, "I'm off to protect Errol, not that he deserves it; I just feel like killing something."

"Wait!" shouts Mike. "You can't go into town wearing your gown. The place is swarming with knights and you could be arrested for carrying a spear, let alone using one."

"Everything's under control," replies Juliet, wishing it were true. She leaves the canteen and fails to come up with a plan.

Stepping through the pitch-blackness of the college entrance arch, she bangs her head on the van roof. Two minutes later she's in overalls, wearing a belt of plumbing tools round her waist to add to her disguise, and carrying her spear hidden in two metres of soil-pipe.

The noise from the building-site beside her is too loud, so she decides to call Errol from somewhere where people are not pouring a million tons of concrete foundation. She wonders if the builders have dug right through to the college canteen and are trying to fossilise the occupants.

Marching towards the centre of Cambridge, she flicks through her phone menu and stops walking to let a group of school children pass. Errol fails to answer; Cheryl fails to answer; Juliet fails to avoid swearing in public. "Bollocks, stop doing whatever you're doing and answer, wankers!"

The teacher says, "Excuse me. Please don't swear in front of the children."

Juliet glares at her. "Sorry, how thoughtless of me. I'll swear behind them instead." She rests against a sun-warmed wall and sees a man dressed in a grey suit and walking his poodle.

She looks at the people up and down the street, and thinks, Oh dear, mister grey-suit, how convenient. You've had the van watched and now you're going to lead me into an ambush. I'll bet there're some buggers coming up behind me. She looks round again and decides, Nope, all very un-assassin-like. Unless I'm going to be set on by little girls and boys. If I can't find Cheryl and Errol, arg! one of them is going to have to change their name, being led into an ambush will at least divert the assassins from him.

The school-group moves away and Juliet writes into her manual:

Errol of Toft

Get back to the college now! And while you're at it work out why God made the universe in the first place. Both urgent :O

Hugging her soil-pipe, Juliet wanders after the man and poodle. Hearing footsteps approaching from behind, she whirls round and sees a girl in school uniform. Juliet decides to look harder: the girl's hair is clearly a plastic wig and no one that young should have breasts that big or be wearing quite so much makeup.

The girl smiles. "Hello. I've been looking for you all over."

"What are you going to do, satchel me to death?"

"Do you like my disguise, good, isn't it?"

"No, it's rubbish. Are you really going to try and kill me in a public place?"

"Kill you? No, I want to sing!"

Juliet's brain asks if it can go and live in another person's head, someone living a normal life. Out of the corner of her eye, she sees the grey-suited man walk through a group of students. They're in pirate fancy-dress, carrying charity buckets, and pulling a huge model of a ship's cannon.

The girl says, "Can I use your toilet?"

Right, Juliet thinks, this woman/girl is here to scramble my mind and distract me from the fact that thirty-odd men, all of them pretending to be students but looking too old, all dressed as pirates and carrying cutlasses, are walking towards me. Clever. They have cloaks and could easily surround a victim to hide the fact that they are binding and gagging—or killing—her and stuffing her into that cannon. Pox. Time to run back to the van and get out of here.

The girl/woman tugs Juliet's arm. "Please? It's urgent."

Juliet prepares to leg it but her brain puts its hand up and points out a connection between singing and toilets. "Hey, you're the person that sings into armour."

"Electra, yes."

"Come with me!" Juliet dashes back to the van. The pirates start to run. Throwing the back doors open, Juliet says to Electra, "Get in and start singing!" Electra begins to speak but Juliet lifts her, throws her into the van, and slams the doors. Running to the driver's door, she screams as she sees the wheel-clamp on the front tyre. Throwing the plastic tube aside, she rams her spear between the clamp and wheel, and discovers that thirty-odd bloodthirsty assassins can provide superhuman motivation.

With an ear-numbing lack of harmony, both Juliet and the steel of the clamp screech loud enough to be heard over the rumble of construction work. Metal explodes. Juliet leaps into the van and guns the engine. "Electra, bloody sing or we're dead!"

Tyres smoking, Juliet hurls the van the wrong way up a one-way street, through a no-entry sign, crashes plastic barriers aside and hurtles to the other side of the building-site. Killing the engine, she throws herself into the back of the van, opens the doors, rescues Electra from among plumbing equipment and rolling stainless-steel toilets, sits her up, and yells, *"Sing!"*

She lifts a toilet, gives it to Electra, and prays. Electra, half-blinded by her dislodged wig, sings a single note into the U-bend. Workers stop working, tools clatter to the ground, and Juliet's rewarded by the sight of pirates helplessly running straight towards the van but falling into acres of chest-deep cement.

With a heavy-duty ballcock Juliet bats aside a passionately aroused construction worker. She slams the doors and launches herself back to the driver's seat. "Stop bloody singing!"

Chapter 19

Juliet switches the van's engine off and rests her head back. She's squeezed the van into a cramped but very private car park Electra knows about, well out of sight of prying knights, pirates, or police.

She yelps as her phone vibrates—a message from Errol. She also notices five missed calls from Cheryl, all made within seconds of each other.

She thinks, Oh shit, she must be desperate if she's actually tried to remember which way up to hold a phone. That can only mean she wants to break up with Errol already and wants my help. Errol, you git, call yourself a man?

Electra slides over the back of the seat, fights with her wig and the double-sided carpet-tape she used to keep it on, and says, "Problems? I mean other than modifying most of Cambridge's lampposts and your front bumper?"

"Oh yes. I think Errol must have been using novelty faux-fur condoms or something. Wait a sec." Juliet scans the text, 'Cheryl has a problem. See you in Fitzbillies.' Juliet looks at Electra and says, "Nice meeting you again but I've gotta go. Oh, go and see a demonator about disguises." She slides her spear into pipe-lagging, leaves the van, vaults a crumbling wall, and heads for the café.

~

Cambridge city was built in the Middle-Ages by a town-planning committee with a typically unclear vision of the future. Unwittingly they created a city that confuses tourists, terrifies car-drivers and has pre-adapted humans to develop the spatial awareness of bats in order that bus-drivers can negotiate through streets designed for a single very thin horse.

It's getting quite dark and it's no surprise that Juliet's a bit lost—if two hours of wandering in circles can be considered a bit. She's standing in a gloomy alley and dithering. She can hear traffic, even the screams of terrified passengers and pedestrians that the bus-drivers use for echo-location, but hasn't seen a main road for thirty minutes. Her phone would help, if she'd remembered to charge it sometime since starting college.

The tiniest sound makes her slide the spear free of its disguise. It's a very quiet but sustained sound made by something or someone not wanting to be heard. The sort of sound an assassin would make when drawing a sword from a velvet-muffled scabbard.

A figure, black-clad with only eyes showing, flows over a high wall and drops silently, half-crouched before her.

Juliet sees the sabre in each hand, mentally maps every fence, wall and wheelie-bin in the area, and notes the ease with which the figure moves, especially as it launches itself at her.

A spear in a cramped alley—Juliet's limited to vertical slashes and stabs: no quarterstaff-style swipes. She's calm, focussed, and really pissed off.

The first sabre-attacks come faster than bullets leaving a machine-gun, hissing and screeching against her spear as she deflects them. She has the longer reach but the assassin pushes forwards, denying her that advantage.

Someone shouts from behind a garden wall, "Not again. bloody cats, shut up!"

Juliet thinks, Move sideways, never back...

The trouble is she's running out of sideways faster than a spinning bobsleigh in its run. Her attacker surges forward in a double flèche attack and Juliet has only backwards or... She leaps onto a wheelie-bin and, holding the spear near the head, sends the butt humming towards the attacker's back.

And misses, but with height on her side she only has to jump to avoid the counter-attack aimed at her ankles. The bin topples towards her assailant. Juliet gives it an almighty kick to help it on its way and swings her spear, point-first, in a rising arc deep into the shadow. She's rewarded by the sight of a sabre spinning through the air.

Someone shouts, "Cats, here I come!" The silhouetted head and shoulders of a man, partially obscured by a super-soaker the size of a bazooka, rise over the wall to her left. He screams and falls back as the attacker's remaining sabre slashes the pressurised water-tank, exploding it in the man's face.

Juliet, scoops up her pipe-lagging and runs, giggling, down the alley with her assailant. "Fitzbillies, get me there quick."

Victoria pants and gasps out, "How did you know it was me?"

"Only you would have the insanity to do a flèche attack

from behind a wheelie-bin. What were you thinking of?"

"Rubbish, I nearly had you and you know it. Anyway, Fitzbillies is closed now. If you want Cheryl, she's with Errol and going to an oyster-bar." She opens a bin, dumps her sword in, unwinds the scarf from around her head, shouts, "Follow me," sprints to a panel-fence, and vaults over.

~

Juliet decides the only thing wrong with an oyster-bar is the oysters, and this limits her choices from the menu. She wonders why, no matter how much garlic is added, anyone would want to eat something that looks as if it's been coughed up by a smoker.

Victoria has no such problem, takes Juliet's untouched plate and says, "I failed to educate you regarding food. No matter, I'm loving it. We'll get you a pizza later."

"Why did you attack me?"

"For a laugh. Um … well, to keep you on your toes. Harry has infiltrated the knights and they want Errol observed and you captured. The head of the order is the same professor Cheryl's working with. He knows Cheryl's on to something for which he'll get a bucket of kudos and he knows you're one of the enemy the knights have been looking for— for five hundred years. He must be all of a twitch, getting no sleep, off his food; poor little thing."

"And what have you been up to?"

"Oh, this and that, here and there..."

"In the college."

"Maybe."

"Sticking your nose into my course?"

"As if I would." Victoria nods in the direction of Errol and Cheryl sitting together at a table for two and illuminated by a single candle. "When they actually notice us, we'll find out what Cheryl's problem is."

"Don't disturb them yet. Errol's performing a vital function. He's distracting her while I work out what the hell I have to do." She stares at them. "He's holding her fingertips."

Victoria's eyebrows zoom up. "You're jealous? … you are jealous! You fancy hooking up with Harry's son, really?"

Juliet sighs. "There's a doom-laden inevitability about it. He's a total moron but we sort of fit together." She pauses, flicking her finger through the candle-flame. "I thought I'd end up with someone more… Um, there was this man … a plumber … dreamy."

"Ooh, you never told me about him."

"About a hundred years ago. Long blond greasy hair, blue eyes, intense expression... He worked in the uni."

Victoria chokes an oyster clear across the next table. "Reginald? Oh God no … tell me you didn't!"

"You know him?"

"Know him? I knew him alright. He was your father."

"My father?" Juliet leaps up and shouts so loud the restaurant falls silent, all eyes, including those of Errol and Cheryl, on her.

Victoria, gets up and pulls Juliet back into her chair. "Stop jumping around; you're causing a scene. I was only joking. "Probably your father … it was a big party … lots of men … busy night..." She laughs at Juliet's stunned expression. "Stop taking me so seriously. Yes, alright, he was you father.

It happened during my stint as an angel in Divine Admin. I never took that module seriously but didn't expect to be quite so laid back."

"Mum, shut up."

Cheryl darts between tables, her chintz frock flapping. "Juliet … I'm so sorry … again."

Juliet stands and pulls her into a hug. "Don't worry. I'll get over it. I may need to kill you first but I'm sure you'll cope. Come and join us and tell me all your news." She sits and the over-stressed bamboo of her chair groans as she leans back and drags another from the next table.

Cheryl watches, biting her lips and wringing hands. "Juliet, I've done something terrible."

"With Errol? Oh good, was it outrageously kinky too? Tell me everything. Do you have photos?"

Cheryl begins to sit, clutching for the chair. Juliet says, "Cheryl, the chair's here." She pats it.

Cheryl looks behind her and then to the chair. "Yes it is, isn't it?" Sitting down, she adds, "Really terrible. I've made an equation."

"Anyone who does equations should be shot. I mean, you lot don't even put numbers in them, just letters that don't make any sense. Call that maths? looks more like bad spelling to me."

With wide frightened eyes, Cheryl stares at Juliet. "It's perfect but it doesn't balance."

"You mean it'll fall over and all the little letters will get hurt? What do you want me to do, call an ambulance? Lighten up, it's not the end of the … oh shit. What've you done?"

Errol pulls a chair over, sits, and puts down a plate of oysters. Juliet briefly wonders if adults liking seafood is the outcome of eating snot when they were children. Errol says, "The equation, the abstract and all the background work are on the uni network in a file Professor Smith-Dinger has access to. He could see it at any time. He may share it with colleagues around the world."

Cheryl tenses, squeaks, and says, "He's bound to send it to everyone. The problem is it proves that the universe doesn't exist."

Juliet's blood temperature hits absolute zero. Painful but it does turn her brain into a superconductor.

She shakes her head. "No. It proves the universe doesn't exist in the way people think it does. It's working alright. Well, apart from the lack of edible food right now, I don't have any great complaints."

Cheryl, Victoria and Errol go to speak but Juliet waves them quiet. "Oh my God." she buries her face in her hands. "Shut up, let me think this through." Her brain makes a connection it started working on days ago. "Right! uh … if you've been created, you believe you exist even if no one else does." She looks at Cheryl. "You don't believe your own equation, do you?"

"No."

"Why not?"

"I understand it; there's something missing. Einstein's equation only balances because he built in a … a fudge factor. That's what I need."

"Who else understands your equation?"

"no one."

191

"But it looks convincing?"

"Yes … to someone who doesn't understand … and..." Cheryl peters out, looking down at her hands and wriggling.

"And?"

"And I think some people may have read it, you know, in the faculty."

"Why do you think this?"

"Because they all left, which is odd. I think they found it upsetting or something."

With wide eyes, Juliet stares between her fingers. "Cheryl, they didn't leave: they ceased to exist."

Chapter 20

Errol, oyster hanging from a fork halfway to his mouth, says, "So we lose a few mathematicians. Is anybody even going to notice?"

Juliet barks, "You know sodding well this was set up by Satan. You think it's going to stop with just them?"

Errol briefly smirks and raises his right eyebrow. "It would have to stop somewhere. OK, we lose the intelligentsia, maybe people of average intelligence too. Oh dear, that would leave only bankers and politicians. It would serve them right. It would be like a world of vampires and werewolves with nothing for them to feed on."

"Errol be serious."

Cheryl looks from Errol to Juliet. "What are you talking about? Satan...?"

Juliet slaps the table. "Cheryl, you genius! There's your fudge-thingy."

"Satan?"

Errol says, "No, Cheryl, Juliet's talking about God. It really annoys me when she of minimal intelligence gets there first. It's just not fair. If and when I meet God, I'm going to ask a few serious questions."

Cheryl says, "God?"

Juliet flushes bright red and glares at Errol. "I am

193

intelligent—just different to you."

Errol raises the left eyebrow this time; he likes to keep his exercise regime balanced. "Put it this way. If I were asked to work out how to stop a ball in mid-air, I'd have to know its dimensions, speed, mass, trajectory, wind resistance, direction, and calculate how much energy would stop it and exactly the right direction to apply that energy: you'd reach out and catch it."

Juliet splutters, incoherent with rage. She thinks he's absolutely right but feels being understood that well is an invasion of her privacy. A nanosecond later she realises that the one thing she hates is someone understanding her better than she does. The next thought admits this indicates Errol is more intelligent than she is. She slaps herself.

Errol says, "Are you alright? Why did you do that?"

"I deserved it. You deserve worse. I need time to think of something unspeakably horrible to do to you; give me a sec, there's so much to choose from."

Victoria butts in, "Ladies and gentlemen, you may not have much time. Not only that, the restaurant is closing. What are you going to do next? Plan while I go and pay."

As Victoria walks away, Juliet says, "Why isn't she doing anything? Why isn't anyone doing anything, except us?"

Errol shrugs. "Because the rest of the college doesn't have our teamwork, isn't able to help, is relying on us?"

"That would be true of anyone but mum. She's up to something. Fine, what do we do now?"

Cheryl frowns. "Did you say college? Here in Cambridge? Are you at uni too?"

Juliet nods. "Sort of."

Errol adds, "We have some problems to work through, Cheryl. Why time is a perception, why..."

Juliet interrupts, "Time … Errol, give me your watch." She thrusts her hand out to him, palm up. "Now."

Errol pulls it from a pocket and passes the watch over. The chain rattles on the wood of the table and clinks on plates. Juliet presses a catch on the side and the back flips open. Inside, wheels grind slowly, others appear static, some whirl almost as fast as the eye can see, one sways back and forth. Frowning, and with narrowed eyes, Juliet stares in. "OK, stop mucking about." One of the wheels falters and Juliet sees through the disguise. Brownies, dancing in frock-coats and crinolines, power the wheels and watch-hands. One by one they notice her looking at them and the couples stop turning.

A watch-brownie taps another on the shoulder. "Oy, you can stop whirling for a bit. She can see us."

Another gives Juliet a tentative wave. "Hello."

Juliet holds the watch up so Errol and Cheryl can see the hands. She says to the brownies, "Don't tell me, that was Chopin's Minute Waltz. How about some rock?"

A brownie squeaks, "Go, baby!" and the brownies start head-banging.

Cheryl gasps, "What? it's gone wonky just because you spoke to it? That's freaky."

Errol says, "Juliet, much as I think watch-hands jerking about in different directions is an altogether fascinating concept and probably explains things like British train timetables, could you set my watch back to normal?"

Juliet winks at him and passes it back. "You do it." To

Cheryl she says, "What can you see?"

Cheryl looks into the watch. "A watch, cogs going round. What's going on? Is this a joke or something?"

Juliet's heart melts. She puts a hand over Cheryl's. "No, it's not."

Juliet's mind whirls like timekeeping brownies, she thinks, There're so many things Cheryl can't grasp. She lives in a world where everything appears to be explained, where everything works predictably, like clockwork … or not like real clockwork—oh bollocks. Brain, will you think things through? You're just confusing me. What do we do here? Oh right, start waking Cheryl up so she can see there's more to reality than she thought? But she could go mad! No, not Cheryl. She's never really been in touch with reality. She said if fairies were real she'd believe in them. Hey, she's halfway there already; she saw fairies when we were young, saw Mitch when others didn't. Shit, Cheryl should be in Muffy, not doing useless maths.

Victoria taps Juliet's shoulder, waits until she looks at her, and nods at the watch. "That was very, very clever. You've come further than I thought."

Juliet snaps, "How much further do I need to go? No, wait, I don't want any answers like, 'As far as you think you have to', or, 'You'll know when you get there', or other crap coming out of your mouth."

"Then I won't answer the question as I don't have toilet paper handy." She looks at them all in turn. "Your plans? I mean other than leaving this restaurant so the staff can get a life?"

Errol stares into the back of his watch, and says, "I can

see brownies! I really can. Yes, Victoria, we're going as soon as I can stop these pests doing the Monster Mash."

Victoria heads for the door. "Then get off your bums and let's go." Chairs creak and grate. Errol snaps his watch shut, and they all rise, apart from Juliet who's still sitting, face scrunched in fierce concentration. Elbows on the table, she's staring at the tip of her right index finger and turning it in a small circle. That's what Cheryl thinks she sees. Victoria sees a tiny black sphere form. Errol recognises it as a miniature copy of the one Juliet made in Hell.

Juliet thinks, Errol, you were wrong. The rules have to be the same everywhere. My manual works in college and outside it. If I can make a sphere in Hell, I can make one here.

Errol says, "Come on. I've a scary idea. I think I may have a plan." Juliet, growls, shakes her head, slaps both palms on the table, and rises.

Victoria holds the door open for her. "How're you doing?"

Juliet snarls, unable to keep fear and anger from her voice, "It's like knowing I'm about to fall into the deep-end: like I'm going mad."

Victoria runs her fingers through Juliet's spiky hair. "Good. Fall. Go mad."

Juliet stares at her. "At last. At bloody last. You've said something useful."

They join Errol and Cheryl standing in the middle of St Andrews Street, amid the ancient stone buildings bathed in street-light and moonbeams. Errol's looking up at the moon and saying, "It looks huge, doesn't it?" He points his phone at it and shows the photo to Cheryl, "But it looks so small to a camera."

Cheryl says, "That's because our visual cortex..."

Errol interrupts, "While that's undeniably true from one perspective, it's utterly wrong from another."

Cheryl frowns. "What do you mean?"

"Regrettably, I haven't the faintest idea. Like Juliet, sometimes I see the answer and have to work out why it's right."

Cheryl claps. "I do that too! That's how about ninety-one-point-three of my physics works."

Juliet dodges a couple of cyclists, and thinks, Errol's the key to this—he can speak to me and talk Cheryl's language. She says, "Plan?"

"Yes, plan. Do you reckon Cheryl could cope with...? Um, you know."

"I've had the same idea. She'll cope if we're there."

Cheryl looks from Errol to Juliet. "What? What are you going to do to me?"

"Ah, problem..." says Victoria.

Errol shakes his head. "I know, I know, people have to awaken when they're ready, in their own time but time is..."

Victoria points up and down the street. "Or should I say, 'Problems'?" Advancing from either end are groups of men, still in pirate costume but mostly covered in hardening concrete. There's no jocular, 'I'm a happy student, albeit looking a bit old' air about them. Cutlasses out and only metres away, there's murder plastered all over their faces— the bits Juliet can see. She considers options; run—no; fight —too many—dive back into—she glances at the restaurant owner locking the doors—no; sod it, when do I get a yes? It's

198

a long time coming. Right, make a staircase like Hildegarde did. How can I make one? Because I can. What about Cheryl? Will she even see it? Blindfold? Shit, no time. "Errol, kiss Cheryl right now!"

Chapter 21

Juliet's rather proud of her staircase, steep, infinite and made of shining gold. The fact that Cheryl is kicking and writhing, despite Errol and Victoria trying to carry and restrain her as they descend, is a distraction—as are her screams of, "Help me, help me! Police!"

Victoria, ducking her head under Cheryl's flailing arms, says, "What's the plan?"

Errol replies, "Hildegarde's office. Cheryl needs to go into a pool of awakening."

Juliet says, "No, Aquaria will be off-duty and possibly hungry. Let's go straight to the Garden of Eden. There's a pool there. I don't think you really need one though; it was the shock of actually talking to a sparrow and Satan that made me start waking up."

Errol, arms tight round Cheryl's legs, says, "Satan! Is that entirely wise?"

"No, but he's the best we've got right now." She slaps Cheryl's head. "Shut up. You're safe. We're rescuing you."

Cheryl stops struggling for a moment. "What? Where am I?" She looks down the infinite staircase, wails, and starts writhing again.

Victoria says, "Take over from me. I've had an idea, see you in a minute."

200

Juliet puts her arms round Cheryl's top half and pulls her tight with the spear as Victoria races up a short distance and pushes open the panel that leads to Hildegarde's office. Errol and Juliet thunder down a few steps, push open another panel, dodge among trees and vines, and stumble to a halt by the pool in the Garden of Eden.

Juliet hadn't expected to gatecrash a party, especially one with goblins, mermaids, gorgons, and other exotic creatures dancing round the pool while naiads cavort in the centre.

Aquaria shouts, "A sleeper! Whoopee! Dinner's arrived."

Errol drops Cheryl's legs, and says, "Oh dear."

Juliet drops Cheryl's top half. "Bollocks," readies her spear, and tries to point it at around two dozen forms advancing on Cheryl.

A mermaid erupts from the pool, grabs Cheryl's ankles and starts to drag her under the water. Errol grabs Cheryl's wrists and tries to pull her to safety.

Victoria, dressed in her gold and black gown, races towards them and waves a student's gown. "I got this for— holy crap." She dips the gown in the pool, whirls it into a tight twist, and snaps it into the face of a drooling zombie, who leaps back, hissing in pain and terror. Victoria drops the gown and draws her sai. "Stop, or you'll..." She's interrupted by war cries from behind. A partially concreted Knight of Kramer, slashing vines down, crashes through the undergrowth. Victoria shouts, "Juliet, you left the staircase open!"

"No I bloody didn't."

Errol yells at the mermaid, "Let go. She's one of us."

The mermaid hisses back, "Mine, all mine."

201

Satan, slithering from branches above, puts his head millimetres from the mermaid's. *"She's mine."*

Juliet, deafened by the cacophony of chaotic combat, prepares to down the advancing knight, only to see him smile. He shouts, "Ooh-arr, me hearties. Splice the mainbrace, chocks away, cast off fore and aft!"

Errol calls to him, "Dad! What are you doing here?"

The knight says, "Not missing this for the world," and slashes his cutlass in the direction of a cockatrice.

Victoria slaps a harpy across the buttocks. Juliet lunges at an advancing minotaur.

Cheryl, released by the mermaid, leaps up and clutches Juliet's arm. "Where are we? What's happening?"

"Let go. I'm busy." Juliet, not wanting to actually kill anything, decides that the only way to dissuade the minotaur from eating Cheryl is to vault up, using her spear, and deliver a two-footed kick to his football-sized testicles. She's rewarded with a roar of agony that shakes branches and fills the air with whirling leaves.

In the moment of respite that follows, she says to Cheryl, "We're in the Garden of Eden and you're about to start waking up." Juliet attempts to down a naiad, which doesn't work, the butt of her spear passing through its watery body and not appearing to do any damage.

Satan, tired of shouting for silence, sucks up the pool and blasts everyone flat with a savage jet of water, naiads, lilies, and mermaids. When branches have stopped spinning away and crashing among trees in the distance, he says, "Will you all desist? I'm getting a headache. Leave Cheryl of Brightwell-cum-Sotwell alone. She's my special guest."

Juliet, shaking water from her hair, drags Cheryl from the mud she's been blown into, and points to the various creatures, naming them in an attempt to awaken her. "That woman made of water is a naiad, they're generally harmless, but don't like being drunk; the hairy guy on the ground holding his nuts is a minotaur..."

She's interrupted by a head squeezing from the tip of her spear. "And I'm Pillock, a pixie." He pops out, grins, blows a raspberry at Cheryl, and drops onto a tree root.

Juliet points to another creature. "That's a gorgon, they're totally weird..."

Cheryl looks around. "Is this a dream? Are we all dreaming this together?"

Errol says, "Cheryl ... amazing ... you've given me an idea."

"What?"

"Er, a collective dream? Wow ... give me a minute. I need to connect ideas ... pixies in guns... Right!" He grabs Juliet's head and turns it towards Pillock. "Juliet, look. Look hard, like you did with my watch. Break the disguise. Let's go deeper into this."

Pillock's talking to the root he's sitting on. Juliet sees the tree is a pixie too; in fact the tree is made of several— hundreds—trillions of pixies, one for each leaf, one for each cell, for each molecule, each atom...

Errol says, "So many pixies, everything is a pixie, all of us ... you ... me... everything." He gasps.

Juliet wrenches her mind from the infinity of pixies surrounding her. "We're going the wrong way."

"I agree, reductionists can't see the whole..."

Juliet gasps, "That's it! Everything is one big ... no wait ... God created pixies but what power did he give them to do things?"

Errol tugs at his sideburns. "Juliet, he didn't. He ... must ... have ... *imagined* them doing things ... and that was all that was needed for them to be done. In a dream things seem to happen for real but you're only imagining them."

Juliet grips the sides of her head. "Nyeearg! You bastard. You've been hiding in clear sight all the time!"

Cheryl squeaks. "Who? what? who are you talking to?"

The sun rises and steam curls up from sodden clothes. Bars and needles of golden light cut between branches and twigs. From everyone and everything present, including Satan, trees, and the air, ghosts appear. They merge until a man forms in front of Juliet. A man wearing a Manchester United T-shirt, baggy shorts and sandals. He's mixed race, but Juliet thinks that's only to be expected. He's also average height. She works out that's because he has both Masai and Pygmy in his genes along with every other type of human. She growls, "Hello, God."

God winks and shakes her hand. "Well done, Juliet and Errol, really well done. Consider yourselves a credit to your parents. You're awake in record time." He slips his hands into the pockets of his cargo-shorts, and nods at Juliet. "By the tone of your, 'Hello, God', I think you've worked out that I'm just an ordinary person."

Errol slaps his forehead. "Got it. So that's why we have to judge good and evil, why time is a perception—we're all you. If I may say so, that's very sneaky."

God goes on, "Some people go through life never seeing

me. Some realise that there's nothing that isn't me."

Cheryl squeaks, "God?" and blushes crimson.

"Hi, Cheryl. You're coping remarkably well for someone with virtually no preparation." Cheryl wriggles, biting her lip and staring at him.

God holds out a hand and shakes Errol's. "Errol of Toft. You had questions for me but you're not asking them?"

Errol sighs. "What's the point? If I don't know the answer, how can you?"

God laughs. "You picked that up quick, cool. And you, Juliet? Have you answered your question about why good and evil are so important to me, why there are so many angels?"

Juliet shrugs. "Uh … easy I suppose, um … because they're important to me."

"Nice one."

Cheryl looks from face to face. "What's going on? Is he God?"

Juliet hugs her. "Sorry, but we had to wake you up, and you must be awake, because you can see him. That's what awake is, I reckon."

"And he came out of us all … I still don't really know … ooh … ooh, I see. Ooh, it's so simple!"

"Yes, 'ooh-ooh', we all do chimpanzee talk when faced with surprises, drop things on our feet, or during sex. What's so bloody simple?"

Cheryl, wide-eyed, goes on, "You said everything is one big pixie. So God is everything; he's all there is." She squirms out of Juliet's embrace, reaches out and takes God's hands. "But where did you come from?"

He shrugs. "I don't know."

"Oh, let me work this out … ah … you … can't know where you came from. How can anyone know what they were before they came into existence unless there's someone to tell them? And you didn't have anyone because you're everything. Oh, it must have been really lonely for you..." She plucks at loose threads in his shirt—even though there aren't any. "You imagined a world, split yourself up into lots of people … and forced yourself to forget what you'd done." She tails off, staring into God's eyes. "You were so alone … that must have been horrible."

God nods. "You've no idea. An eternity of just me, bleh. There is no me now, not really. We, everyone and everything is me. Incidentally, Cheryl, you've just achieved the fastest awakening in the history of creation. I'm god-smacked." He looks down and shrugs. "Sorry about that. I'm hopeless at jokes. Yes, I used my imagination to make everything and used ignorance and belief to make my creation seem real. I imagined this garden, imagined myself human, smelled flowers, felt rain, had people to talk to... Yes, this universe is a dream, a psychosis, but it beats the absolute tits off reality. So there you have it. Now you know everything there is to know. The problem is, there's so little to know."

He nods in the direction of the staircase. "The universe imagined by sleepers, however, is fascinating. It's a bit of a pain when they point a telescope and we have to imagine a trillion more galaxies, and the blasted Higgs boson took us thirty years to get our heads round and actually *make*, but..." He lapses into silence.

Errol's watch chimes. He pulls it from his pocket, flips the cover open, and tries to finish God's sentence, "The fiction

206

we call reality is much more fun. Full of surprises, volcanoes, Santa Claus, Yorkshire pudding … how would my watch-brownies ever have learned to dance without...?" He frowns, "I think the brownies in the second-hand are doing the Funky Gibbon; the hour-hand is definitely Gangnam style … the minute-hand people have gone off to buy drinks. Juliet has knackered my watch but at least it's happy." He snaps the cover closed.

Cheryl hugs herself. "But what happens now we're awake?"

Errol shrugs. "Nothing. We go back to our world and fret about parking tickets, body odour and dodgy condoms. Knowing everything changes nothing, well, except cheating at cards—you'd only be cheating yourself."

God puts an arm round Cheryl. "What does this do to your equation? I'd really like to know."

Cheryl sighs, rests her forehead on his shoulder, and says, "It boiled down to: $E = 0$ but now … if creation is 'E' for 'Everything' then it must equal 'Belief in reality', plus 'Ignorance of the truth', over God. You smell nice."

Errol writes the equation into his manual...

$$E = \frac{B + I}{G}$$

… and holds it up for everyone to see. "Right, Cheryl, we get this onto the uni network tonight."

Juliet says, "An equation that I can read! Right, creation is BIG. Works for me."

Cheryl skips in a circle and claps her hands. "Everything balances now! God is the perfect fudge factor." She dances back to God, "Where will you go now? I mean … you won't disappear or anything will you?" She abandons the pretence of clutching at threads and clutches him instead. "I … um … I mean..." She trails off, blushing again.

God shrugs. "What do you want me to do, Cheryl of the totally brilliant mind and general gorgeousness? Have you something dry to put on? That wet dress clings … and … no, just stay as you are."

Cheryl releases him, looks down and twists her fingers. "I … I..."

Juliet snorts. "Oh, dear God, she fancies you! Bloody hell, I don't believe it. Cheryl, I'm so proud of you. You've actually found your own man for once. Interesting choice; I wonder if he's really in your league. God, don't you dare go anywhere at least for two weeks or you're in deep shit and answer to my knuckles. Actually, after two weeks her boyfriends are usually in deep shit anyway. Up to you."

Errol whispers into Juliet's ear, "Tragedy! I've just been dumped. Should I challenge God to a duel to preserve my honour?"

Victoria picks up the gown she acquired for Cheryl. "OK, Juliet, Errol, Cheryl. Congratulations, you're all graduates. Party tonight! Gowns inside-out with all the nice gold showing." She tosses the gown to Cheryl who calculates its velocity … and fumbles. God snatches it out of the air before it drops into mud.

Victoria blows a kiss to Harry. "See you later." She marches towards Juliet. "Come on, young lady, I want a quiet

208

word with you and to do a little bit of proud maternal gloating. She waves at a passing cloud. "Yoo-hoo, can we hitch a ride?"

~

Hand-in-hand Victoria and Juliet lie on the cloud, drift through the Heavens, and gaze at the Fields of Elysium below. Victoria says, "How're you doing?"

"I'm bloody hungry. You lot all ate oysters. Can we go to the canteen?"

Victoria nods. "OK, cloud, college canteen, please." They change direction. Victoria chuckles as she gazes at Juliet. "This party tonight—it's all about you. You want me to behave?"

"No, I get it now. I want you to have fun. If you don't make a complete arse of yourself, I'll feel insulted. Maybe you can teach me and Errol some of that pole-dancing stuff." Juliet thinks for a while. "Mum, what is it you actually do? No wait..." She snorts and laughs. "I don't think you do anything, do you? You just do plumbing!"

"Yup. Oh, I surreptitiously evict the odd gremlin from computers and phones if I like the client, and I help out at the college from time to time—but nothing else. I like plumbing."

"How do you evict gremlins? I read that was amazingly hard."

Victoria sniggers. "I serve them eviction orders. I'm proud of those; they're really effective."

"How do they work?"

"They don't. The trick is not to tell the gremlins."

"So I can come back and work with you? Pleasy-weasy?"

"You'd bloody better. Those stainless-steel toilets are long overdue and I'm not letting Electra have any—she's way too dangerous armed with one."

Juliet rolls on her back. "Stainless-steel toilets, Electra, Zoongash, Pillock, Mike, Meg and Chuck … the knights..."

"If you don't finish that sentence I'll throw you off this cloud."

"Everything was set up. You're all part of the college and planned every last detail." She rolls back and puffs straggles of cloud into Victoria's face.

Victoria waves them aside. "Everything but the toilets—that was your genius. My daughter's a toilet genius."

"Your fault."

Victoria ruffles Juliet's hair. "You up for helping students too? The rest of your year are way behind you."

"Of course. Can I work with Zoongaash? She's a laugh. Hey, you blew Harry a kiss. Are you...?"

Victoria smirks. "On and off—quite a lot of on and off."

"Tart."

"Mmm..."

A solitary ghost drifts towards them. As it draws close, Juliet recognises Aelfwyn, and says, "Hello, sweetpea. How's everything?"

Aelfwyn joins them and sits cross-legged on the vapour. "I'm bored of being a ghost. I don't like it anymore. Can you give me a body?"

Juliet nods, "That's easy, I can put you to sleep and reincarnate you. You'll have to be born again. What do you want to be?"

"I want to be like you... Oh, you won't make me leave you, will you?"

"Oh dear, Aelfwyn … I don't know how to..."

Victoria interrupts. "Easily sorted. You become her mother."

Aelfwyn leaps up, clapping her hands and jumping up and down. The gloom on her face turning to pure joy. "Yes! Yes! Will you be my mummy? Please be my mummy!"

"I … oh, Aelfwyn, you'd make a perfect daughter. I can't wait..."

"Wow! Will you still call me Aelfwyn?"

"If you like. It's a beautiful name."

Victoria touches Aelfwyn's forehead. "OK, Aelfwyn, if you're tired of being a ghost, I'll put you to sleep, my darling granddaughter. See you soon. I'll look after you until it's time to pop you into Juliet's, er, mummy's tummy." She winks at Juliet. "I think I'd better make myself scarce. See you at the party." Carrying Aelfwyn's smiling and sleeping form Victoria slips onto another cloud.

As Juliet pulls her manual from its satchel, her cloud says, "Will you be needing me much longer? I have to water sheep."

"Uh? Why?"

"Sheep are baby clouds. They don't become adult until they die. We like to keep them watered so their souls are all puffy like mine."

"I won't keep you long. Just don't watch. I need your name. Do you have one?"

"No. Can you think up a nice one for me?"

"Oh boy yes." Pulling the quill from the manual's spine,

211

Juliet writes into the notes section:

Errol of Toft
Join me on Cloud Nine
It's your lucky day

About the authors

Hello from Gary and Christian Bonn. We live in Scotland, UK and collaborate on writing projects. We're both contributors to WriterLot—writerlot.net

Gary has two books published by Firedance Books: The Evil and the Fear, and Expect Civilian Casualties, both aimed at young adults.

Together Gary and Christian have created a series of science fiction books, the first, Hive Mind, is to be published by Firedance at the end of 2014.

Muffy College, Cambridge is the first of another collaboration of humorous fantasy action adventures. Two more will follow in 2015. We're getting very good at working together and don't throw monitors at each other very much at all.

We'd be very grateful for an honest review of Muffy. You can post reviews on the Muffy College Cambridge page on Amazon (the page you can buy it). There are many other review sites and we'd appreciate your comments. You help shape what we write.

If you enjoyed Muffy—please tell your friends!

Acknowledgements

Thanks to the author Patrick LeClerk (Out of Nowhere, Every Clime and Place) for his support and editorial input. Ditto, Anne Martin, Ren Warom and my sister Sue.

Proof

Made in the USA
Charleston, SC
19 November 2014